Published in 2020 by DCS International

Copyright © 2020 DCS International LLC and Caleb Jones

9450 SW Gemini Dr #43281

Beaverton, Oregon 97008-7105 US

USA

All rights reserved.

Don't distribute copies of this book in any way, digitally or otherwise. This book is licensed to the original purchaser only. Electronic or print duplication is a violation of international copyright law. No part of this publication may be reproduced, stored in a retrieval system, or transmitted in any form or by any means, including but not limited to electronic, mechanical, photocopying, recording, scanning, or otherwise, except as expressly permitted by law, without prior written permission of the Publisher.

This publication is designed to provide accurate and authoritative information in regard to the subject matter covered. It is sold with the understanding that the publisher is not engaged in rendering professional services.

ISBN: 978-0-9995133-3-0

Printed in the United States of America

First Printing May 2020

Disclaimer

Some of the topics in this book have distinct legal ramifications.

Every country in the world and every state or province within those countries have completely different laws regarding sex, marriage, cohabitation, property, children, child support/custody, and divorce. It is impossible for me to cover all of those legal differences in this book.

In addition, I am not a lawyer; thus, I cannot and will not give legal advice, nor am I qualified to do so, nor should anything in this book be viewed as such.

Therefore, please consult with a qualified family attorney in your city before attempting anything discussed in this book

Contents

Section One
The OLTR Marriage

Chapter 1
Overview — 2

Chapter 2
Marriage Types and Definitions — 8

Chapter 3
The OLTR Marriage — 20

Chapter 4
The Three Most Important Aspects of an OLTR Marriage — 26

Chapter 5
Maintaining Attraction — 44

Chapter 6
Managing the Day-To-Day — 58

Chapter 7
Managing the Day-To-Day — 76

Chapter 8
Quality Communication — 90

Chapter 9
Drama Management — 110

Chapter 10
How to Handle Drama — 118

Chapter 11
How to Minimize Drama — 130

Chapter 12
The Six Negative Behaviors and Their Cures — 144

Chapter 13
Ground Rules — 154

Section Two
Sexual Aspects

Chapter 14
Managing the Open Aspect with Your Wife — **166**

Chapter 15
Sex with Your Wife — **172**

Chapter 16
Oneitis Management — **180**

Chapter 17
Jealousy Management — **186**

Section Three
Legal and Financial Protection

Chapters 18
OLTR Marital Legal Structures — **194**

Chapter 19
Prenuptial Details — **208**

Chapter 20
How Finances Tie into The Rest of The Marriage — **216**

Section Four
Family Matters

Chapter 21
Raising Children in A Non-Monogamous Marriage — **226**

Chapter 22
Dealing with Family and Friends — **232**

Section Five
Side Women

Chapter 23
Managing Your Side Women — **238**

Chapter 24
Getting New Side Women   **252**

Chapter 25
Where to Have Sex with Side Women   **264**

Chapter 26
Other Sexual Logistics   **276**

Section Six
Converting from A Monogamous Marriage to An Open One

Chapter 27
The Conversion Process   **282**

Chapter 28
How to Convince Your Wife   **288**

Chapter 29
Other Conversion Methods   **306**

Chapter 30
Troubleshooting   **314**

Chapter 31
The All-Important First Three Weeks   **320**

Other Resources and Bibliography   **324**

Glossary of Terms   **326**

THE ULTIMATE OPEN MARRIAGE MANUAL

FOR MEN - HOW TO CREATE, CONVERT, AND MANAGE YOUR OPEN MARRIAGE

Section One
The OLTR Marriage

Chapter 1
OVERVIEW

I still vividly remember that day despite it being over 20 years ago.

I was a young man, several years into my first marriage. I sat on the edge of my bed, staring at the wall, my eyes squinting in a psychological agony that was so real it seemed to seep into my muscles.

"What have I done?" I asked myself, "What have I agreed to? Why did I agree to it?"

I pressed my hands into my face.

I had realized that several years prior, during the excitement of the courtship, engagement, and wedding, I had agreed to an impossible, almost Faustian arrangement. I had agreed to never have any sexual contact with any other woman, besides my wife, for the rest of my life.

It made perfect sense at the time. We were having plenty of sex back then, so I didn't need anyone else. But now, here I was, several years into the typical marriage, and just like most typical husbands, my typical wife was saying no to sex more often than she said yes.

What options did I have? I couldn't have sex with any other women, and I couldn't have sex with my wife because she was saying no. I had… no options other than to suffer.

Oh my God. What have I done?

"No options" wasn't exactly true. I did have one option – I could cheat. I could hook up with some other woman and hope the wife never found out.

That led to the second part of the impossible arrangement I had agreed to. By getting legally, traditionally married, I had agreed to combine all of my finances with hers and enter into a three-way contract with her and the government. That meant that if I got divorced, this woman would take my house, my kids, at least half of my retirement savings I had worked so hard for, and even possibly half ownership in the company I built from scratch without any of her help. This was on top of the massive legal costs I would incur.

So if I wanted to have sex when I needed it, my only option was to cheat. If I got caught (and almost all cheating husbands eventually get caught), I risked financial devastation on a mass scale unheard of in my entire life. Not to mention the damage it would cause with my children. None of this was their fault.

Why on Earth did I agree to this? What the hell was I thinking?

I twisted my torso in an effort to shake the pain. The more I thought about it, the more I realized that this impossible arrangement, called "traditional marriage," benefited my wife far more than it benefited me. As a matter of fact, it almost seemed like whoever invented this crazy system purposely went out of their way to make it as shitty a deal for the man as they possibly could.

Imagine a girlfriend going to her boyfriend and saying, "Hey, sign this legal government contract that says you'll never have sex with anyone else but me, and you won't have any sex at all if I say no, and if we break up for any reason, you'll pay me thousands upon thousands of dollars, and if you don't pay me, you'll go to prison."

Then worse, imagine the boyfriend saying, "Sure! Sounds like a great deal!" and then signing it with glee.

You don't have to imagine it. It happens literally thousands of times a day all over the world.

I loved my wife. I loved my kids. I enjoyed having a family. I enjoyed being married, for the most part. None of that was the problem. I just wanted something fair. I just wanted to have sex on a regular basis and not have my entire financial life teetering on a precipice. Was that too much to ask?

I guess it was.

Why the hell did I agree to this?

I had agreed to it so many years ago because no one informed me of any of these downsides. Back when I was a young man, engaged to be married under this model, not one man in my life sat me down and explained any of this to me – not my dad, not my buddies, not my brothers, not my co-workers, not even any of my business mentors. They all just gave me plastic smiles and congratulated me when I told them I was getting married. This was despite the fact that many of them faced these exact same problems (or worse), and a decent number of them had already gone through horrible divorces.

And so the cycle of pain for modern men continues.

Unsurprisingly, I eventually got divorced. Once that crisis was over, I set out on my Mission to create a life of maximum freedom and long-term masculine happiness. A few years later, I called this lifestyle model Alpha Male 2.0. Over the past decade, I have lived a life greater than my wildest fantasies. I have written several books and online courses and maintain several blogs and coaching programs teaching men how to do the same thing.

In my main book, *The Unchained Man**, I describe the journey I went through in my dating life after my divorce to create multiple long-term non-monogamous relationships with women. After many years of living this wonderful life, I decided to settle down again. Only this time, I would do it in a way that made sense. I would do it in a way that wasn't unsustainable or unfair. I was a man in his forties who wanted to share the rest of his life with one special woman but do so in a way where I could still maintain my sexual freedom and not have my finances at risk.

This was all several years ago. Today, I'm a married man again. My wife, Pink Firefly, is a pretty amazing woman. More importantly, though, my marriage today looks quite different than my old traditional marriage from so long ago.

My marriage today is sexually open. This means I can have sex with any woman I want, whenever I want, without having to get any permission from my wife. As of this writing, I have sex with two or three other women on a regular basis, usually once a week.

That doesn't mean my wife and I don't have sex. We do, several times a week, often at her initiation, even though we've been together for almost six years. Unlike in traditional, normal marriages, my wife's attraction for me hasn't decreased an ounce. In many ways, it has actually increased over time.

*http://www.alphamalebook.com/

We also have completely separate finances. This means we never need to argue about money. Marriage experts and therapists tell us that money is one of the greatest causes for arguments and strife in marriage (as well as divorce), but Pink Firefly and I don't have that problem and never will. She spends her money 100% independently from me and I from her. No arguments needed on that front, ever.

I have multiple legal, financial, logistical, and international barriers between my assets and hers. If there is ever a divorce, and I honestly hope there isn't – I love my wife very much – I don't lose a single penny of my money. Worst case, I will have to pay about $150 in court filing fees, and that's it. My sex life will continue like nothing happened, and my financial life will remain unharmed.

I have designed the marriage to have minimum drama and arguments from the ground up. I have identified those things most married couples argue about and have either eliminated them completely or drastically reduced them. Instead of a typical marriage where the couple argues about stupid shit all the time, we have a marriage where we are extremely happy the vast majority of the time, and real arguments are rare.

When we do have a disagreement, instead of just screaming at each other for an hour like normal married people do, we have a specific, proactive system that we follow that ensures we get to a rapid solution with minimal upset.

No marriage is perfect, but I think ours is the best marriage that I think can be had in the Western world and in the modern era. Mutual friends and acquaintances, when they see how happy PF and I are together, tell us how jealous they are of our relationship, and how they wished they had something like it.

Fortunately, you can. In this book, I'm going to lay out specific, step-by-step systems so you can build a marriage like this yourself. A marriage based on freedom, happiness, love, and sex, rather than the typical marriage based on conformity, slavery, arguing, and financial expense.

Everything I have done can be replicated by any man willing to put in the work. It's not that hard, and the rewards are well worth it. Unlike most other men on the planet, I have truly the best of both worlds: a woman who I love deeply and want to share my life with, as well as massive sexual and financial freedom, all at the same time.

More importantly, I'm not the only one. Millions of men all over the Western world, yes, *millions* have non-monogamous marriages just like this, or very close to this, or a variation of this. I've communicated with hundreds of them over the past decade. People don't realize how common these marriages are because people in marriages like this keep them very quiet and pretend to be normal for fear of social ostracization.

Fortunately for you, as an outcome-independent Alpha Male 2.0, I don't have that problem, and I don't give a shit what people think about my marriage. I'm here to tell you exactly what I and others have done to create marriages like this so you can have one yourself.

Read on.

Chapter 2
MARRIAGE TYPES AND DEFINITIONS

The term "open marriage" or "open relationship" isn't very specific. It's also somewhat dangerous. Often, when you say "open marriage," people envision their lovers engaged in wild swingers' parties, having sex with 14 other people, getting STDs, and then falling in love with someone else and leaving.

Literally none of that occurs with properly managed non-monogamous marriages. Every time I have seen the (rare) instances where an open marriage fails like that, it was because the people in the marriage were not following the relationship structures detailed in this book.

If you follow the models this book outlines, your odds of success are very high. I'd like to say that your odds of success with properly managed OLTR marriage (I'll define that term in a minute) are actually higher than typical monogamous marriages, but I can't since we don't have the scientific data on that yet. Regardless, it's clear from my own data of talking to hundreds of men and women over the past decade who have marriages like this that the indications are quite strong. I just don't see as many non-monogamous marriage participants getting divorced (as a percentage) as much as I do normal married people.

The first step in structuring a marriage like this is to determine what kind of marriage you want. There are many different types.

First, I need to define the word "marriage" and "married" as I use them in this book. When I say someone is "married," that means they live full-time with another person in a romantic and loving context. That's it. It doesn't matter if they're monogamous or not. It doesn't matter what paperwork they've signed or not signed. In my book, they're married.

This is because, when you live with your girlfriend, you are living the lifestyle of a married man. You're not living the lifestyle of a single guy, nor are you living the lifestyle of a man with a girlfriend. No, you're living the lifestyle of a man with a wife.

You could protest by saying you're not legally married or that you have sex with other women all the time. Fine. You're still "married" because that's the type of lifestyle you live.

So when I say "married" in this book, that means you live with the woman you love in the same home. That's it. Everything else is a detail (though important details to be sure, and we'll get to those soon.)

Now that we've established you're married (and for the rest of this book I will assume you are already living with your special lady), we now need to determine what kind of marriage you have or want.

Non-Monogamous Relationship Types

First, we need to quickly cover the non-monogamous relationship types for those men who are not living with a woman. You will need this data as you create relationships with your women on the side (or "side women" as they are called in this book). In my book, The Ultimate Open Relationships Manual, which I consider a precursor to this book, I describe the non-monogamous relationship categories in great detail, including how to create them and maintain them. I will quickly summarize them here.

FB

Friend with Benefits or Fuck Buddy. This is a woman you consider a friend and one you enjoy having sex with. She's your friend only, and you have sex. That's it. No dating, just hanging out and having sex. You can see an FB regularly or infrequently. You even can have more than one at a time. It is very likely you will have an FB or two in your open marriage (I always have several), so this category of woman is very important.

MLTR

Multiple Long-Term Relationship. This is a woman you actually have romantic feelings for and see on a regular basis. You're doing things like actually taking her out on dates, having long phone conversations, and cuddling after sex. However, she's not your girlfriend, and you're not exclusive. You can date other women as MLTRs in addition to her (and she can date other men if she wishes). An MLTR can be "upgraded" to an OLTR later if things work out and it's something you both want. They can also be "downgraded" to an FB if the emotions fade or her behavior becomes problematic.

OLTR

Open Long-Term Relationship. This woman is your girlfriend. You love her and are emotionally committed to just her. The only difference between an OLTR and a traditional girlfriend is that you can have sex with other women… as long as they're only FBs or one-night stands. These side women cannot be MLTRs since that would be a violation of the emotional exclusivity the OLTR provides. (If you actually have a woman "on the side" who is an MLTR, then your OLTR really isn't an OLTR at all; she's just another MLTR.)

A woman can only be an OLTR after she's been an MLTR for at least six months with almost zero problems and she's gone through The Talk and The OLTR Talk and passed with flying colors. I describe how to execute these two talks in The Ultimate Open Relationships Manual.

The point of having an OLTR is that you don't want to date other women. You just want to date and have romantic feelings for just one woman while having sex with "just friends" women on the side. If you wanted to date multiple women, you forego an OLTR and just stick with multiple MLTRs and FBs instead. I did this for many years, and it was very enjoyable.

To make it easy, just remember the following list:
- You can have as many FBs as you like.
- You can have as many MLTRs as you like.
- You can only have one OLTR.
- OLTR and FBs can co-exist.
- OLTR and MLTRs cannot co-exist.

Open Marriage Types

You must be very clear as to what kind of marriage you want. The OTLR Marriage is the type of marriage that I discuss in this book and what I recommend to most men for reasons that will become very clear as you read onward. Regardless, I still need to be fair and objective and lay out the other types of open or non-monogamous marriages men sometimes have.

It's your job to read through the following list and choose which type of marriage you want. If you are at all wishy-washy about the exact type of open marriage you want with your wife, none of this is going to work. Your actions and goals must be 100% congruent with what you truly want.

We'll start with the type of marriage this book focuses on

OLTR Marriage

An OLTR Marriage, like an OLTR, is an emotionally exclusive but sexually open marriage. Both you and she are allowed to have sex with people on the side, provided those people are only FBs or one-night stands. No "dating" or romantic relationships outside of the marriage are allowed (and shouldn't even be desired by either of you; otherwise, you need to get divorced immediately, since you're in the wrong type of relationship). That said, long-term trusted FBs who become close friends are acceptable, especially when the FBs are friends with both you and your wife. We'll discuss how to manage all of this in great detail in this book.

An OLTR Marriage also has an Iron Curtain-like Financial Barrier between her money and your money. This is in place for the following reasons:

1. To minimize arguments and other conflicts regarding the topic of money.

2. To protect you from any irresponsible things your wife does with her money during the marriage (and vice versa).

3. To protect your assets (and hers) in case of a divorce or breakup.

There are right ways and wrong ways to maintain this Financial Barrier. We will be discussing the correct ways in upcoming chapters.

Of all the non-monogamous marriage types described in this chapter, the OLTR Marriage is safest and easiest to maintain and configure. It is the type of marriage I have and the one I recommend most strongly to men. It's also the most conducive to the freedom and happiness-based Alpha Male 2.0 that I endorse. Regardless, if you choose one of the other types, you may do so, though you may have to modify some of the advice given in this book.

Traditional Monogamous Marriage (TMM)

I include this just for illustration and contrast. The traditional monogamous marriage, or TMM, is what normal people do. It's when a man and a woman promise and expect sexual monogamy forever to and from the other, which, of course, is almost never possible.

They completely combine their entire finances and get a legal procedure done where the government will tell them how to divvy up their money and their children when they get divorced. Violation of this results in going to jail.

I say "when" they get divorced instead of "if" they get divorced because the real divorce rate for TMM, among people who actually get legally married, is now over approximately 76% across the board in the Western world; in many regions, it's even higher than this. Moreover, this divorce rate is rising. In ten years, that 76% figure will be much higher.

Even people in TMMs who don't get divorced usually experience cheating in the marriage (around 70-80% of long-term marriages) since human beings are pair-bonding creatures but were never designed to be long-term sexually monogamous creatures. Pair-bonding is something humans enjoy, but sexual monogamy is something men and women like to do for a while, not forever.

Needless to say, TMM is a terrible idea in the modern era. It's only for people who are either very ignorant and naive or for those who don't mind chaos and drama as long as it happens "later." It's not for you.

Swinger Marriage

In a swinger marriage, you and your wife have sex with other couples as a couple. Usually through things like swinger groups and swinger clubs, you and your wife have sex with another couple, usually simultaneously.

Unlike in an OLTR Marriage, in a swinger marriage, you are not allowed to have sex with women independently from your wife. She must always be involved in some way. If she's not, any sex outside of the marriage is considered cheating and creates all the usual catastrophes.

The finances in a swinger marriage are combined just like in a TMM.

Swinger marriages are not something I would enjoy, nor are they Alpha Male 2.0 compatible since you need your wife's permission all the time and your finances are at risk. The other problem is that as soon as your wife decides she doesn't want to swing anymore (which is bound to happen at some point when she gets older), then congratulations, you're now in a TMM just like everyone else.

Regardless, I personally know many men and women with swinger marriages who are extremely happy with them. My advice is to only go for a swinger marriage if you have a lower sex drive and to ensure you install a Financial Barrier like one would in an OLTR Marriage.

Threesome Marriage

A threesome marriage is as close to monogamy you can possibly get within the open marriage framework. It means you can have sex with other women but only as a threesome with your wife. A threesome marriage is not a swinger marriage since you are not having sex with other couples. Instead, you are (usually) bringing just one person (usually a woman) to your bed along with your wife.

A threesome marriage barely qualifies for a true open marriage, and if you have a threesome marriage, you will encounter pretty much all the negative downsides you would in a TMM. Moreover, every threesome marriage I've ever seen ended up as a TMM, since the wife eventually decided she "didn't want to do threesomes anymore."

I do not recommend a threesome marriage under any conditions. It's just a slightly less dreary form of TMM.

Polyamorous Marriage

Oh boy. These are complicated. A polyamorous or poly marriage is when you and your wife are carrying on full, romantic relationships with several other people. These people can be in poly marriages themselves or living on their own.

Polyamory is one thing; that's more or less when you have multiple MLTRs as I did for many years. But having a polyamorous marriage is something else entirely. Introducing real feelings and romance for other people outside of your marriage creates multiple layers of complexity and a propensity for problems even if you both know what you're doing.

For this reason, I don't recommend poly marriages to anyone unless both you and your wife have a very long history of polyamory and are very well versed in all of its nuances. Otherwise, stick with an OLTR Marriage or similar instead.

Polygamy

Polygamy is where one man is married to multiple wives. The husband is allowed to have sex with all of his wives and no one else (at least in theory), and the wives can only have sex with the husband. It's a "one-way" open relationship. The man is open, but the wives are not.

As I've written about in my other books and blogs, a polygamous "I can fuck other people but you can't" model is men's biological default and a fantasy for many men all over the world. The problem is reality. Very few women in the modern era and in the Western world are ever going to agree to a relationship where you can sleep with other women, but she's not allowed to sleep with other guys. Even if you somehow get a Western woman to agree to this, in short order, she will either dump you or go have sex with some other guy in an effort to make things more "even." I've seen it happen many times. Indeed, I have never seen a polygamous marriage or relationship in the Western world last more than nine months until the woman does this.

Even if you are part of some kind of Mormon cult and are somehow able to pull off a marriage like this, polygamous marriages are full of near non-stop drama and jealousy. Wives constantly bitch and complain to the husband about why he spent more time with so-and-so last weekend. It's brutal (unless you enjoy drama).

Unless you live in certain parts of Africa or the Middle East where polygamous marriage arrangements are a little more normal, please forget about having any kind of polygamy in your life. It's just not sustainable in the real world. Unfortunately, if you want the right to have sex with other women, she must have the right to do so with other men (even if she doesn't actually exercise that right, and she likely won't or won't eventually; we'll talk about that later).

Mediterranean Marriage

The Mediterranean style of marriage is very common in Southern Europe and South America but also exists in parts of Eastern Europe, Russia, and Asia as well. I'm bewildered that so many people put up with a marriage like this, but it's quite popular outside of the USA (though it's practiced inside the USA as well, particularly with much of the Hispanic population).

A Mediterranean marriage is a highly dysfunctional open marriage. It's where the man marries a woman under a monogamous agreement and then promptly cheats on her, often with full-on girlfriends on the side. The wife finds out but doesn't divorce the man. Instead, she puts up with him and spends the rest of the marriage screaming at him and throwing frying pans at his head. He puts up with the constant drama for whatever justifications he has (sometimes cultural, sometimes religious, sometimes financial, sometimes due to neediness, etc.) and keeps having sex with women on the side while constantly battling his forever-furious and distrustful wife.

Mediterranean marriages are dreadful. They are the opposite of the consistent long-term happiness I espouse for the Alpha Male 2.0. The wife is constantly screaming at the guy to stop sleeping around. The girlfriend or other side girls are constantly screaming at the guy to leave his wife. The man puts up with non-stop drama from pretty much everyone. I'm honestly amazed men and women in countries that practice Mediterranean marriages tolerate it.

Unless you're the kind of guy who enjoys non-stop drama, it's no surprise to say that I don't recommend Mediterranean marriages for any reason. I'd honestly rather you be divorced and single than go through that kind of constant conflict. There are much easier ways to have sex with multiple women.

Polyfidelitous or Polyexclusive Marriage

In an OLTR Marriage, you can have sex with pretty much whomever you want on the side as long as she's an FB or one-night stand. There might be a few women you're not allowed to have sex with (like your wife's sister, best friend, mother, etc.), but beyond those unusual exceptions, it's wide open.

The polyfidelitous or polyexclusive marriage (both terms mean the same thing) changes this around. It's an OLTR Marriage where the husband (and the wife if she's having sex with side-people also) is only allowed to have sex with certain, pre-selected individuals. These individuals have also promised to only have sex with him, or him plus one or two other specific individuals. They're all "exclusive" to a very small group of people instead of to one person, thus the term "polyexclusivity."

This is often done to minimize jealousy, reduce STD risks, and build or maintain trust.

There is nothing wrong with a polyexclusive marriage provided you build in some solid safeguards. If you promise your wife that you'll only have sex with her and your FB Jennifer, that's all well and good until eight months later when Jennifer gets a serious boyfriend and stops seeing you. Now you're monogamous. Uh-oh.

Therefore, if you agree to a marriage like this, your wife needs to fully understand and agree that the instant you lose one of your designated FBs, you can (and will!) run right out and quickly replace her with someone new. This must be allowed, or else no deal.

I myself may consider a polyexclusive marriage with my wife down the road someday, but if I do, you can guarantee I'll have at least two designated FBs on the side (so I don't have to suddenly freak out if the one I have leaves) and the "replacement rule" will be solidly in place.

Another variant of the polyexclusive marriage concept I've seen some men use is one where they are allowed to have sex with other women, but all the women on the side must be hookers, one-night stands, or similar. In other words, no ongoing relationships are allowed, even with FBs. Again, this is fine as long as you are happy with the reality that you'll constantly be going after new women all the time. Some men enjoy this; for those men, a marriage like this would be acceptable. But if that doesn't sound fun to you, choose another option.

Unicorn Marriage

Unicorn marriages are quite rare and take a great amount of frame, strength, power, money, confidence, and relationship management skill to pull off. In a unicorn marriage, you have a second woman who actually lives with you and your wife in your home, either full time or part-time. This second woman is not a second wife. Your wife is still your only wife and is still clearly number one. Rather, this second woman is a sort of live-in FB. She's a trusted friend to both you and your wife. You have sex with your wife and her, either as threesomes or individually under a polyexclusive basis. Your wife can have sex with her as well if she's into that kind of thing.

A celebrity example of this was Hugh Hefner, who had a similar arrangement with his multiple live-in "girlfriends." He had one "girlfriend" who was essentially his OLTR wife and one or two other women he also called "girlfriends," but were actually just close, trusted live-in FBs.

As you can probably surmise, the likelihood of drama, jealousy, and problems in unicorn marriages is great. Having children in a unicorn marriage is also not really an option unless you're willing to do something highly unusual. These kinds of marriages are only for very experienced non-monogamous Alpha Males who really know what they're doing and are willing to take a risk. A higher income also really helps (and may even be mandatory).

Open Convenience Marriage

Open convenience marriages are also reasonably rare, but I have certainly seen a few, particularly in upper class or highly religious communities. This is a marriage where the husband and wife are married to each other for reasons that have nothing to do with love. Perhaps they are married for financial reasons, or for the good of small children they're raising, or religious reasons, and similar. The husband and wife don't love each other in the traditional sense and likely don't even have sex, but they more or less get along, don't fight, and are generally good partners.

The husband is allowed to violate the no dating rule in an OLTR Marriage and actually has real MLTRs or even a full-on girlfriend or two on the side. He not only has sex with other women but carries on real "with feelings" relationships with them as well. Sugar daddy arrangements in this kind of marriage are also not uncommon.

An open convenience marriage is almost never something a guy sets out to do on purpose. It's usually something he ends up with. It's more of a workaround to an unforeseen problem rather than something pre-planned.

I would prefer that you truly love your wife romantically and sexually and want to be with her and have sex with her because it's what you really want. I love Pink Firefly more than I have ever loved a woman. That said, I understand that strange things happen sometimes, and I have seen marriages like this more or less "work," at least on a mid-term basis. Like with a unicorn marriage, the open convenience marriage requires a very strong Alpha Male and is not for a beginner or typical guy.

Your Choice

You need to have a solid idea regarding which type of open marriage you want. My advice is to default to an OLTR Marriage, which is the primary thrust of this book, and then perhaps modify that marriage once you and your wife get into the groove of those techniques and systems several years down the road.

Chapter 3
THE OLTR MARRIAGE

Based on all of my research and experience over the past 13 years, I have come to discover that the OLTR Marriage is the best (or least bad, depending on your point of view) method the modern-day man has of settling down with a woman in a long-term cohabiting relationship. Again, I call this a "marriage" regardless of what legalities, paperwork, or sexual arrangements are involved, since once you live with a woman full-time in a romantic context, you're living the lifestyle of a married man whether you admit it or not.

The OLTR Marriage offers you the maximum amount of freedom possible while living with a woman while simultaneously providing you the maximum amount of protection against all the usual problems and risks most men incur from a TMM (or other non-monogamous marriage types that don't involve a separation of finances). It does by removing the two great weapons of TMM that a woman can and will use against you to control you and reduce your long-term happiness.

The Two Weapons of Traditional Monogamous Marriage

There is nothing inherently wrong with marriage, that being the act of living with a woman full-time in a long-term relationship that provides stability and companionship as well as a framework to raise children (if having kids is one of your goals). I think long-term pair-bonding is great, and I always have. It's also good for a stable society.

The problem with traditional monogamous marriage is not the act of marriage itself, but that it places two powerful weapons in the hands of your wife. She can use these weapons against you whenever she pleases. Sadly, you don't also get two weapons that you can use against her. Nope, she has these two weapons and you have none. You're completely outgunned in a very real sense.

These two weapons are *restricting sex* and *divorce ruin*.

Restricting sex means that, in a monogamous marriage, your wife has 100% complete control over your entire sex life. You are not allowed to have sex with anyone else but her and she decides when you're allowed to have sex with her. If she says no to sex, which of course she has every right to do, you go without sex completely. (You could then cheat on her, but that creates an entirely new set of problems, not the least of which is activating divorce ruin, the other weapon she has.)

This means she has the power to completely remove sex from your life whenever she pleases. This a vast and ridiculous amount of power. It means she can make all kinds of demands and threaten to remove all sex from your life whenever she wishes for any reason she wants. If you're like most men, you will comply with these demands so you don't have your only source of sex removed from your life.

Any marriage where the woman has the power to do this never includes a man with any freedom nor a great degree of long-term happiness (unless he has an unusually low sex drive, but for the rest of this book, I will assume that's not the case with you).

The second weapon she has is *divorce ruin*. In a traditional marriage (and in many nontraditional marriages), you have signed a civil license with your government, meaning that the government has total authority over how your assets will be divvied up during a divorce. Not you. The government.

In most jurisdictions all over the Western world, this means that if you get divorced, the government will force you to do one or more of these four things:

1. Give her half of everything you own, regardless of who earned it or who owned it originally. This is called "communal property."

2. Pay her child support if you have any children with her, even if the children are not biologically yours.

3. Pay her spousal support, traditionally known as alimony, meaning a monthly check you cut to her for a specified number of years (and in some cases, forever).

4. Pay divorce attorneys thousands upon thousands of dollars to fight

your wife in court over the above three items. As some men have observed, "You don't get half of your stuff after a divorce; you only get a third because the attorneys take the other third."

Unless you are extremely wealthy or extremely poor, these things will cause sweeping devastation to your financial life, your long-term future, and even your retirement. I have seen powerful, grown men break down in tears when they admit their savings and investments that they worked so hard for are now gone, or that they can't retire anymore, all because of a divorce.

If you refuse to pay your wife any of these allotments, the government can and will put you in jail. I have spoken with many men who went to jail specifically for that reason.

Even worse, most jurisdictions follow a system called no-fault divorce, meaning that you must give your wife all of these things even if you can conclusively prove in court the divorce was 100% her fault. She can steal your money, physically abuse you, carry on a secret affair with her boss, have his kids and pretend they're yours, and you can show conclusive records, photo, and video proof of all of this in court, and none of it matters. The judge just shrugs and tells you to pay her everything, or you go to jail.

Married women know all of this, or at least most of this. This gives them another weapon to use against their husbands. "You'd better to X and Y, or I'll divorce you and take half of your money!" Like restricting sex, divorce ruin is an extraordinarily powerful tool your wife can use to control you. She won't hesitate to use it once the honeymoon phase of the marriage is over (usually well within three years or so).

Picture two pistols, one labeled "restricting sex" and the other labeled "divorce ruin." In a TMM, your wife has these two guns on her at all times, and she can draw them and point them at your head whenever she wants you to do just about anything. Remember, you don't have these weapons. You can't threaten to take half of her money in a divorce because she probably doesn't have any, and if you threaten to not have sex with her, she'll just laugh.

That, in a nutshell, is the problem with TMM: these two weapons. It renders the entire concept of a TMM fundamentally unfair to men in the modern era.

However, there's an answer. All you need to do is create a marriage that is just like TMM except with the two weapons removed. That's the OLTR Marriage.

The OLTR Marriage

Very simply, the OLTR Marriage is identical to a TMM, except the two weapons aren't a part of the relationship. It's just like any other marriage with two key differences.

First, it is a sexually open marriage. The man (and the woman, if she really wants) are allowed to have sex with other people as FBs within a short and simple set of ground rules. This completely removes the weapon of *restricting sex*. Your wife can't threaten to withhold sex from you since you're allowed to get it from other women whenever you wish. Your wife can even stop having sex with you completely, and it doesn't threaten the marriage since you can still get your sexual needs met elsewhere. Interestingly, this actually helps the wife because she won't feel the constant pressure most wives in TMM feel to constantly have to sexually service their horny husbands. Statistically speaking, wives lose sexual desire for their husbands far sooner than husbands do for their wives, so having sex with a husband starts to feel like an obligation and a chore to wives in long-term marriages. A wife in an OLTR Marriage never needs to feel this way.

The second difference is that there are physical, legal, logistical, and in some cases, international barriers between his money and her money. There are enforceable legal agreements and documentation in place that ensures that if a divorce or breakup occurs, the man doesn't have to pay the wife anything (unless he chooses to). I emphasize the word enforceable since just getting a "prenuptial agreement" or the equivalent isn't enough to protect your finances in a divorce these days. In most parts of the Western world, prenups (or their equivalents) aren't enforceable at all, and most jurisdictions and judges will just throw them out if they are challenged. Instead, the OLTR Marriage includes multiple layers of financial protection that are extremely difficult, if not impossible, to violate. I lay out exactly how to create these protections in future chapters.

Other than those two differences, the OLTR Marriage is just like a TMM in all respects. To the outside world, everyone will view the two of you as if you're in a TMM. In an OLTR Marriage, you can still do things like:

- Get engaged
- Wear engagement rings
- Live in the same home
- Have a wedding
- Wear wedding rings
- Have her take your last name
- Introduce each other as husband and wife
- Live like husband and wife
- Have and raise kids
- Get medical coverage
- Take care of your wife financially (if you want)
- And so on

There is really no difference between OLTR Marriage and TMM except for those two aspects above. To illustrate this, here's a crazy example that happened to me many years ago. Way back when I was a beta male and in my first marriage (a TMM), there was a married couple who lived a few houses down the street from us. They had two boys and they were the happiest married couple on the entire block. They were very friendly and my wife at the time and I enjoyed them very much.

A few years after we moved away from that house but still lived in the area, I spoke with a friend of mine who still lived on that street. He revealed that this couple was actually in an OLTR Marriage. They had a wide-open marriage where the husband regularly had sex with other women, and they had some rock-solid prenuptial agreements in place (this was back when a prenup was all you needed; today you need more than that to protect your money). I was stunned. I had known these two people for years and had no idea.

Today, Pink Firefly and I live in a lower-upper-class neighborhood filled with very normal people. PF is friends with most of them, and none of them have any idea we have an OLTR Marriage. They all assume we have a TMM because that's exactly how we look to everyone. (This is doubly amazing considering that I'm a public figure talking about non-monogamous relationships.)

This is yet another advantage of the OLTR Marriage over other types of non-monogamous marriages I covered back in Chapter 2; it looks and feels "normal." As an outcome-independent Alpha Male 2.0, I personally don't give a shit about what people think about my marriage, but you might, and your wife (or prospective wife) almost certainly will. It makes things easier for everyone.

You can even raise kids in an OLTR Marriage, and many people do. We'll discuss that aspect in Chapter 22.

Having an OLTR Marriage isn't perfect and it's not a panacea, but it's far superior to having a TMM in just about every way. In terms of long-term cohabitation with a woman you love, it's as close to ideal a man can have in the Western world and in the modern era. The rest of this book will walk you through how to formulate and maintain your own OLTR Marriage. You'll be shocked at how great it is once you see the results in your life.

Chapter 4

THE THREE MOST IMPORTANT ASPECTS OF AN OLTR MARRIAGE

This chapter covers the core baseline for your OLTR Marriage. This is made up of three distinct concepts. These three concepts are foundational, and if you don't follow them, very little else will work in your marriage, at least in the long term.

Success in your marriage starts with a solid foundation that is based on Attraction, Mutual Harmony, and Freedom, three points on the triangle that are all equally important.

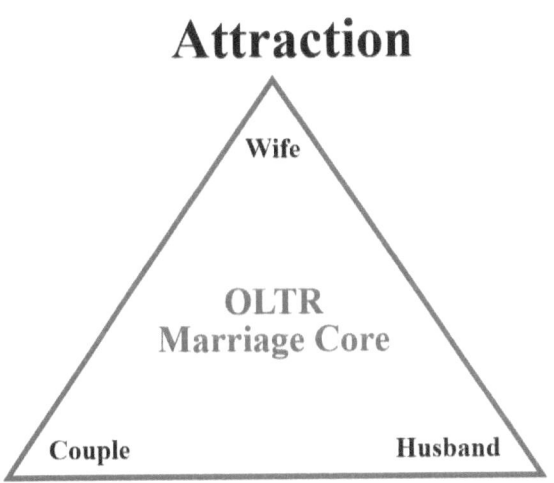

Attraction

Divorce is not the only way a marriage can fail. Another way a marriage can fail, and one almost as common, is a marriage that continues forever but without the spark or fire between the couple. They just stay together because getting divorced would be too much trouble. They end up simply tolerating each other. I know many old people with marriages like this, and likely you do as well. Society looks at these marriages as "successful," but they are anything but. They are just as big of a failure as a divorce.

Most marriages fail (divorce or sparkless marriage) for one reason: the woman eventually loses attraction for the man.

If you were to ask most people why marriages fail, they'd give you a bunch of other reasons, such as arguments over the kids, lying, cheating, fights over money, drama, and so on. However, *almost all of these reasons stem from the core catalyst of the woman losing attraction for the man.*

Yes, it's also true that the man can lose attraction for the woman. However, this is less relevant for two reasons.

First, it's not as common as the reverse. Divorce statistics clearly show that 70-80% of all divorces are initiated by the wife, not the husband. Women losing attraction for husbands occurs far more often than husbands losing attraction for their wives.

Secondly, a man losing attraction for his wife is more a problem in monogamous marriages than open ones. If you lose attraction for your wife in a monogamous marriage, that's a serious problem, and the entire marriage is threatened because you're not allowed to have sex with anyone else. However, if you're allowed to have sex with other women whenever you like, it's far less of a problem. I didn't say it's *no* problem (if you aren't attracted to your own wife, that's suboptimal regardless of anything else going on), only that it's far *less* of one. We'll discuss the concept of your attraction for your wife in a future chapter. The core concept of Attraction is the attraction your wife has for you.

When a wife loses attraction for a husband, several things occur:

- Arguments increase
- Complaining increases
- Frequency of sex drops, sometimes to zero
- Her stress level increases
- Her physical appearance starts to worsen (since she's no longer attracted to you, she doesn't feel the need to stay pretty or skinny in order to compete for you)
- Communication between husband and wife becomes less frequent and fruitful
- Husband and wife start spending less time together
- She starts to become more open to the option of divorce

Obviously, all of these things are severely detrimental to your marriage.

One of your core goals is to ensure that these things never happen. This is done by maintaining her attraction for you.

Attraction does not just mean physical attraction. One of the benefits of being a man is that women aren't quite as attracted to purely physical traits as we are. Also, the fact you're married means she loves you, and once a woman loves a man, the physical component of her attraction for him actually decreases a great detail (though not to zero). In other words, your physical flaws don't bother her quite as much as they would if she met you cold on a first date.

Attraction is her *overall* attraction for you as a man. She is attracted to traits such as:

- Confidence
- Masculinity
- Outcome independence
- Bravery

- Toughness
- The ability to take charge, especially in emergency situations
- Physical prowess
- Physical appearance
- Class (how well you dress, your grooming, etc.)
- Devotion to your goals and Mission
- Career or business prowess
- Social proof (how many high-quality friends or co-workers you have, particularly if they look up to you)
- Sexual proof (how many other women are sexually attracted to you, particularly if they are prettier or younger than your wife)

Attraction encapsulates all of those things. When she feels that you lack many or most of these traits, *or if she sees you demonstrate these traits less and less over time*, her Attraction will decrease. Then all the problems I listed above will begin to manifest.

This is why Attraction is so core and critical to your marriage. It must be heightened and then maintained at all costs throughout the length of the entire marriage.

The opposite of Attraction is Betaization.

Betaization

Betaization is a concept I've discussed a great deal in my other books. It is such an important concept that we're going to spend quite a bit of time in this book learning how to manage it.

Betaization is a hugely critical process that has major ramifications for your marriage. It permeates just about every marriage, yet the vast majority of human beings have no idea it exists. Once you understand Betaization, how it works, and how to avoid it, your life will be changed forever for the better. Just understanding Betaization will shed light on many of your past relationship problems and prevent you from experiencing them again in the future.

In an OLTR Marriage, it's double critical to avoid Betaization so you can keep Attraction at healthy levels. Think of Betaization as the inverse of Attraction; the more Betaization you allow in your marriage, the less Attraction you will have.

As I talk about in detail in *The Unchained Man*, we have bodies that were not designed for the modern, high-tech 21st Century. Instead, we have bodies and brains designed for the caveman era of 100,000 years ago. Because of this, we are full of Obsolete Biological Wiring (OBW) that tells us to do things that made perfect sense when we were cavemen, living a harsh world, dressed in furs and living in a cave, but that makes absolutely no sense in the modern, free, high-tech era we live in today.

One of these forms of OBW is how women attract and keep men.

Back when she was a cavewoman, a woman wanted to bear children, or at least was subconsciously compelled to do so by her biology. The world of 100,000 years ago was full of lethal dangers. Harsh weather, scarce food, saber-toothed tigers, ice ages, disease, volcanoes, and enemy tribes all threatened her life and the lives of her tribe on a regular basis. Therefore, her powerful biology instructed her to make babies with very strong men. The stronger the man, the more likely he would successfully protect the baby, and the more likely the baby would be strong and thus survive the harsh environment.

"Strong" in this case meant not only physically strong but mentally and emotionally strong as well. She was attracted to more confident, capable, bad-ass leader types. In other words, Alpha Males. She would then have sex with an Alpha Male or two (or perhaps many more than two) and get pregnant.

When the baby came, she was more or less incapacitated. She didn't have the physical ability to go out and get food, provide warmth, and protect the baby, all while raising the baby who was unable to live on his own. Therefore, she had to convince the Alpha Male father to stop running around the fields, hunting tigers, playing with his buddies, and banging other women so he could stand watch at the cave to protect and help feed her and the baby. Back then, masculine gallivanting around was dangerous behavior, and if he died, she would likely have no protection at all.

*http://www.alphamalebook.com/

So, through various feminine means, she had to convince, negotiate, trick, and/or coerce the Alpha to calm down, stay with her, and follow her instructions. She didn't want a strong, confident Alpha Male anymore. She now wanted a compliant, submissive beta male. In other words, *she had to transform the Alpha Male into a beta male* to ensure the survival of both herself and her baby. She had to "betaize" the Alpha.

Amazingly, women today have the exact same outdated biological urges as their cavewoman ancestors. When she's single or dating around, what attracts her are Alpha Male traits; confidence, strength (physical and otherwise), adventure, drive, motivation, masculinity, cockiness, sarcasm, roguishness, and rebellion. However, once she gets this attractive Alpha Male into a relationship and they start spending lots of time together, having sex on a regular basis, and start getting close, the process of Betaization starts to kick in.

When she actually moves in with this man, her Betaization dial cranks up to full blast! She now needs to completely betaize the Alpha and turn him into a beta. Now she wants beta traits like compliance, obedience, calmness, organization, peace, nurturing, reliability, and conformity.

Therefore, Betaization is the process by which a woman slowly and gently starts to transform a man she's living with from an Alpha to a beta. There is no malice or ill intent behind this desire; it's simply her stupid outdated biology kicking in. When she first had sex with you years ago, she wanted a bad ass. Now that you're her live-in husband (and remember, you're her "married" "husband" even if you never got legally married), she now wants a complaint, obedient little boy.

To be fair to her, *some* aspects of the compliant beta male husband are actually good for a long-term happy marriage, including a sexually open one. You're not going to have a very long-lasting and happy marriage if you're out getting drunk every night, having unprotected sex with random 19-year-olds, and smoking weed all day. Some measure of maturity and stability on your part is necessary.

The problem is the other 90% of the aspects her Betaization demands are things *that will turn her off and reduce her Attraction for you.* This is really bad, due to all the reasons and problems I listed above. Regardless of all the reasons for the Betaization traits she thinks she wants, she doesn't realize that if you do all of those things and comply with all of her Betaization demands, she will end up severely damaging and perhaps even destroying her own marriage because of the Attraction she will lose!

It really is a weird catch-22. Betaization has been confusing married men and enraging married women for decades for this very reason.

How, then, do you handle Betaization if your goal is to stay in a long-term happy OLTR Marriage?

It's quite simple. You give your wife just 10% of the minimal Betaization needed for a stable marriage, and then draw the line at that 10% and nicely and sweetly refuse to give her any more. This barrier at that 10% is called the Betaization Wall.

Here's an example. After living together for a few months, your wife asks you if you can stop leaving your socks on the floor of the bedroom and instead put them in the hamper. You say yes and start doing that. Later, she asks if you can brush your teeth before having sex with her when you've eaten a lot of onions. You agree to that and start doing that as well. Then she suggests that it would be nice if you texted her every evening before you come home from work to let her know what time you'll be home. You nicely tell her that you're not going to do that, but you'd be happy to let her know if you're going to be really late. She huffs and puffs and complains a little, but accepts it. Later, she implies that she would prefer it if you had sex with your FBs once a week instead of twice a week. You gently remind her that you're allowed to have sex with your FBs as often as you want and that you'll probably still see your FBs twice a week for the time being, but you'll try your best to schedule your FB visits when she's not home to help her feel a little more comfortable about it.

Don't get hung on up those specific examples. The point is that you give her just a little bit of Betaization and then drew a hard line and refused to give her any more, while still being very nice and understanding even when you say no.

Won't she complain when you say no to all of these things? She certainly will. A little complaining when she bumps up against your Betaization Wall is the small price you pay to maintain Attraction and thus keep a happy, long-term OLTR Marriage. Remember the list of severe problems you're avoiding by maintaining this Betaization Wall, even when your wife complains a little.

Don't worry. We will get into very specific detail about how to manage Betaization and how to enforce your Betaization Wall with minimal problems throughout this book.

Mutual Harmony

The next core component of your happy marriage is Mutual Harmony. This means that you are *both* pleased with the relationship you have together at least 90% of the time, ideally 95% of the time or more. It is meeting both of your needs and keeping you both happy or neutral the vast majority of the time.

The key there is *both* of your needs. If you're a dominant, overbearing bad ass, an Alpha Male 1.0 in my parlance, and rule your wife's life like an iron fist, doing everything the way you want, you won't have a marriage that lasts long-term in any pleasurable way. Regardless of how submissive your wife is, you're *eventually* in for either an explosion or a divorce.

The reverse is also true. If you're a good little boy and do pretty much everything your dominant wife demands (which is the standard for most marriages today), your marriage will also eventually fail (divorce or sparkless marriage) since Attraction will be destroyed.

This means that day to day and week to week, you both manage the relationship in a way that is conducive to *both* your long-term happiness and her long-term emotional stability. If you want a marriage that lasts a very long time in a harmonious way, you need to take into account both you *and* her.

Normal people do this via a concept called *compromise*. This is when she drags you to go see some chick flick that you'll hate, but she promises that next weekend you can take her to see the next Star Wars movie that *she'll* hate. That's a "compromise" because it's "fair."

An OLTR Marriage is very different. Instead of prioritizing compromise (which is just another way of saying "I'll punch you, then you punch me"), you instead utilize something called Zones.

There are three Zones in your marriage. There's Your Zone, Her Zone, and a Shared Zone. Your Zone is stuff you like and control 100%. Her Zone is the stuff she likes and controls 100%. The Shared Zone is stuff you both like a lot. Your Zone and Her Zone are very large. The Shared Zone is small.

She never expects you to enter Her Zone, and you never expect her to enter Your Zone (though you may enter into each others' Zones completely voluntarily if you really want to). Instead, you spend regular, weekly time in the Shared Zone, which you *both* enjoy. There is no compromise because neither of you is ever forced to or expected to do something you don't like.

Zones are not just metaphorical. They're also physical. In your home, you'll have to set up Your Zones, Her Zones, and perhaps a Shared Zone.

Most importantly, you have to minimize the Shared Zones in your home. This is very unlike a traditional marriage, where most of the entire house is a Shared Zone! This is *not* conducive to Mutual Harmony because you're 100% guaranteed to have disagreements and stupid arguments related to the shared kitchen, shared bathroom, shared bedroom, shared living room, and so on.

As an example, Pink Firefly and I have completely separate bathrooms and completely separate kitchens. I realize that might sound strange, but she and I literally *never* argue about *anything* related to a kitchen or bathroom. If you live with a wife or girlfriend, can you say the same? Do you know of any traditionally married couple who can say the same? I doubt it.

The only Shared Zone in our entire house our bedroom. Even then, I make sure to spend very little time in that room when I'm not sleeping *and* we have a spare bedroom I can use if there's ever a problem. Every other part of our house is either My Zone that is 100% mine or Her Zone that is 100% hers. Thus, our odds of arguments go way down, and our odds of Mutual Harmony go way up.

We'll discuss how to manage Zones (both metaphorical and physical) in an upcoming chapter.

Mutual Harmony also means the communication between the two of you is structured in a way to meet both of your needs. Men and women communicate very differently. The more masculine you are and the more feminine she is, the greater the difference will be in your communication styles. That certainly describes Pink Firefly and me; I'm extremely masculine and she's hyper-feminine, so we've had to really work hard regarding our communication.

You're going to have to learn and practice proper communication with your wife in order to make sure that both of you are getting your emotional needs met, particularly when there are disagreements. We will discuss exactly how to do this in future chapters.

Winning the War, Not the Battle

This is going to be a difficult concept to emotionally accept for most men, but it's absolutely critical to maintaining Mutual Harmony. Failure to understand and practice this concept means you will *never* have a relationship or marriage that lasts a very long time *and* is mutually happy.

When there is a disagreement, most married men focus on the *battle*. The "battle" refers to this current disagreement in this current scenario. She wants to send an angry email to her boss, and you don't think that's a good idea. She wants to check bags on your upcoming trip, and you want her to use carry-ons instead. And so on.

When there is a disagreement like this, men jack up their own egos and try very hard to win the battle by convincing or bulldozing the woman into doing things their way. The more Alpha 1.0 a man is, the more this is true, and the harder he'll try (though beta males are quite guilty of this as well).

Focusing on winning this battle causes several problems. First, it will create regular drama, conflict, and arguments. I don't know if you've noticed, but modern-day women in the Western world don't just bow and say "yes, master" whenever you disagree with them or give them orders. They get upset, offended, and fight back, even if they have more submissive personalities.

Therefore, if you're like most men and always focus on winning battles, you will *always* have regular drama and arguments in your marriage. This destroys our goal of actually being happy in our marriage and utterly murders Mutual Harmony.

Second, even if you get her to agree to your demand, you still haven't won. All this will do is create a seething, long-standing resentment in your wife that will result in an explosion down the road. I have personally seen this happen with many marriages and relationships involving a strong husband and a weaker wife. He bosses her around, fights her, and she grudgingly complies, over and over again. He beats his chest and brags about what a bad ass he is.

For a while, this is fine. She might even like it when the marriage is new. But over time, she becomes angry and resentful that she lives in such an unfair relationship in which she rarely gets her way. This resentment eventually (and it might take a year or two or longer) explodes within her, causing a major drama incident in the marriage, or a divorce, or she does something like cheat on him behind his back with a man like… me.

In other words, you will win the *battle* but lose the *war*. The "war" means *having a marriage/relationship that lasts well past two years where you are both still really happy with each other*. If you achieve this, you've won the war. We could argue about what the exact length the post-two-year marriage/relationship "should" be in order to constitute success, but that's a complicated discussion for another time. The focus here is getting it to last in a happy way much longer than two years, which I'm sure we can both agree is a valid goal. Any moron can have a decently nice relationship that lasts 6-18 months before a big breakup/divorce occurs and he has to start all over again with someone new, but won't help us. We're talking about *long-term* pair-bonding in this book (as in many, many years or decades). This requires a different set of goals and strategies.

The problem is that if you focus on winning 100% of all the battles, you are virtually guaranteed to lose the war. You'll either get divorced relatively soon or you'll both stay together but argue all the time. In either of these scenarios, you've lost the war.

This means you must have a constant focus on winning the war rather than having to win every battle. That doesn't mean you have to necessarily *lose* the battles either; you just don't have to win them. This is often done by making the battles irrelevant. I'll go into more detail about that later.

Focusing on the war instead of the battle is such an important concept to internalize that I'm going to come back to it again and again in this book. It's that important to Mutual Harmony.

Freedom

The last item in the core triumvirate is Freedom. Attraction addresses your wife. Mutual Harmony addresses both of you. Freedom addresses you.

One of the biggest, overarching reasons for unhappiness in a marriage is caused by the man feeling that he isn't free. As I talk about in great detail in *The Unchained Man**, the less free a man feels he is, the less happy he will be, at least in the long term. The freer he is, or at least feels he is, the happier he will be.

In TMM, men have extremely little freedom. Essentially every aspect of his life is either controlled or greatly influenced by his wife. His entire sex life is dominated by his wife. Most or all of his financial life is also controlled by her, at least to some degree. His day-to-day time, when not controlled by his boss at work, is controlled (at least to a degree) by his wife and her needs and desires.

Initially, this doesn't bother him much because he's so excited about the new marriage. During the "honeymoon phase," this drop in freedom doesn't even register with him. But over time, after three years at the most, when this temporary phase of happiness has passed, he's going to feel constrained. Men don't like feeling constrained.

This feeling of lack of freedom often manifests in the following ways:

- More arguments, often caused by the man
- Cheating
- Pornography
- Seeking emotional validation from women outside of the marriage (including carrying on an emotional relationship with another

**http://www.alphamalebook.com/*

woman)

- Hiding secrets from his wife
- Frivolous financial expenses
- Increased drinking or drug use
- Stress-related health problems, like headaches or ulcers
- Half-assed efforts to "get away" from the wife, like working longer hours, traveling more often, and so on

Obviously, these are all bad things that are not only going to increase your unhappiness but will also destroy your marriage. The way you avoid all or most of these things is to **ensure that you constantly have a high degree of real, personal freedom throughout your marriage.**

The commonly held view is that married men having a lot of personal freedom is somehow detrimental to a marriage, a family, or society. The reality is that it's usually the reverse. As long as you feel you have an extreme amount of freedom, your marriage will be better, not worse. You won't feel the stress and imprisonment most men feel in post-three-year TMM. You'll instead be a happier guy, which means you'll be a better husband to your wife and father to your kids (if you have any).

As a husband in an OLTR Marriage, you must have a high degree of Freedom in at least the following three areas:

- **Finances**. The ability to control exactly what you do with 100% of your money without ever having to check in with or get permission from your wife.

- **Sex**. The ability to have mutually consensual sex with whomever you want, whenever you want, within a few basic ground rules (that we'll cover later) without ever having to check in with or get permission from your wife.

- **Time**. The ability to manage your typical day-to-day schedule the way *you* see fit. You control your schedule, not your wife. That doesn't mean you never spend time with your wife; you will regularly spend time in your Shared Zone with her to maintain Mutual Harmony, but *when* that time is spent is *your* decision.

Many women reading the above statements (and a lot of men!) will be horrified by what I just said. How the hell can you have a proper marriage when the husband can constantly go out and do whatever he wants??? How can a marriage work if his wife can't control him???

The implication is that men are brutish, marauding barbarians who cause nothing but mass chaos wherever they go. Thus, men "need" women to control them so they can be set straight and become proper citizens. This is a very common belief in society.

I admit there are a few men like this, but these men are the exceptions to the rule, perhaps 5% of men. The vast majority of men in the world are pretty nice guys, Alpha Males included. I have no desire to go crazy, treat people like garbage, or ruin my life, and you probably don't either.

Instead, you and I want to be married, but we also want to make sure that marriage doesn't feel like a prison. More importantly, if it *does* feel like a prison, our marriage will suffer, and that will harm our wives and children.

In this book, we're going to discuss numerous methods that will enable you to live a high degree of Freedom while still being a kind and supportive husband to your wife. You can, indeed, have both at the same time.

Oneitis

The final aspect of Freedom is being able to love your wife without also having Oneitis. Oneitis is a term I've used a lot in my other books and one that is important for you to understand. I have several chapters on how to avoid it in *The Ultimate Open Relationships Manual**, and I strongly recommend that book for that reason. Here, I will quickly summarize the concept.

Oneitis is a common though hugely dangerous and destructive emotional condition. It is a set of actions and behaviors where a man does things in order to *get* one particular woman or *keep* one particular

*http://www.haveopenrelationships.com

woman at the expense of pursuing other women and/or at the expense of his own freedom and happiness.

A man struck with Oneitis will have stress and neediness skyrocket. He loses his outcome-independent frame and starts acting like a pussy. If he's a beta male, he starts getting sad, whiny, frustrated, and worried. If he's an Alpha Male, he becomes jealous, territorial, overly domineering, stressed, and angry.

There are several different types of Oneitis I describe in *The Ultimate Open Relationships Manual**, but the one relevant to married men is Relationship Oneitis, which is the most common type. This is when a man is dating or married to a particular woman, and he's very concerned (if not downright terrified) that she'll leave him if he does certain things she may not like.

She gives him drama, and he puts up with it. (If he's a more confident guy, he may fight back, but he'll still put up with it; the point is, he won't leave her.) She makes demands of him, and he complies. If they have arguments, even huge ones, he always goes back to her no matter how horrible they were. If she leaves or threatens to leave him, he cowers, says he's sorry, and he makes whatever promises he can to keep her.

His life is full of *major compromises that he would never normally make just to keep her*. These compromises, in addition to the drama, eventually make him unhappy. Yet, because he has Oneitis, he doesn't care. He just continues to suffer like a pussy-whipped wimp (in the case of a beta male) or a high-drama, argumentative asshole (in the case of an Alpha Male).

Relationship Oneitis is the default setting for monogamous relationships and the societal default for most men (Alpha Males included) when they get into serious, traditional relationships with women, especially when they live together. It is horribly destructive to all aspects of a man's life, happiness, and masculinity.

If you suffer from Oneitis for your wife, if you're really worried that she might leave you or that you must make major sacrifices to ensure she doesn't leave, you cannot experience a full degree of Freedom, and now

*http://www.haveopenrelationships.com

your happiness and marriage will suffer.

The Opposite of Oneitis

The opposite of Oneitis is *the willingness to end the marriage if it's clear it will continue to make you unhappy <u>even if you still love your wife</u>*.

I'll give you my example. As I stated earlier, I love Pink Firefly more than I have ever loved any other woman. I love her more than I thought I had the capacity to love, and I mean that. My relationship with her has been the greatest and most rewarding relationship I've ever had with a woman in my entire life, and that's saying a lot since I've had some pretty good ones. Her presence in my life brings me joys I've never known. It's almost like she was custom-made by the universe as my ideal woman mentally, emotionally, physically, sexually, and spiritually. She is literally a dream come true for me.

And if she ever tells me she wants to leave me, I would immediately help her pack her bags and escort her out of my house within a few hours and have no regrets. I would be sad, and it would certainly be a rough day, but I would still do it without any hesitation whatsoever. That's because *I don't want to be married to a woman who isn't happy being married to me.* I'd rather go through a quick divorce than stay married to a woman who was unhappy being with me. (Since it's an OLTR Marriage, any divorce would indeed be very quick and legally painless. More on this later.)

The same goes for if she ever made any hard demands that I do things like stop having sex with other women, work fewer hours or less intensively on my Mission, or that we move to a certain area I didn't like. Again, I would nicely help her pack her bags, escort her out of my house, and file any necessary paperwork to dissolve the marriage within the next 24 hours. I wouldn't be happy that day, but I would do it with 100% conviction I was doing the right thing.

This is because *I have the ability to fully love a woman without having Oneitis.* I can love without fear. I can love and still be free. I can love and know I'll be happy no matter what happens.

If you can't love without Oneitis, this means two things.

First, it means that to you, love must always include *fear* and *neediness*. This fundamentally damages love as a positive emotion. Love is supposed to feel good, not bad! Love is supposed to be 100% good, not some good and some awful. Men who must always have Oneitis mixed with their love will never be completely long-term happy.

On the other hand, I can love without fear. I can love a woman fully without having this nagging dread in the back of my mind of "Oh no, what if she ever leaves me?" If she leaves, I will be sad for a little while, and then my amazing life will continue. I'll do what I can to solve any major problems in my relationship, but if they can't be solved or if they require me to sacrifice something major in my life that will make me unhappy, I won't hesitate to end it. It has nothing to do with love. It's about my long-term happiness.

You need to remember that there is only one person in this entire world who is 100% guaranteed to stick with you forever until the day you die, and that's *you*. Your mom, dad, brother, sister, best friend, children, wife… *none* of these people are guaranteed to be with you for the rest of your life and be with you at all times when you want or need them. Just you.

Therefore, if you damage your happiness just to keep your wife around, you're making a terrible mistake. You're damaging the happiness of the one person guaranteed to spend the rest of your life with you (you) for someone who could leave you at any time (your wife). Instead, you should be married to a woman who A) doesn't make you unhappy, and B) doesn't make any demands of you that would make you unhappy. It's that simple.

One of the most consistent observations I have heard from divorced men is that they waited too long to get divorced. They almost always say that they should have moved out and initiated the divorce from their wives two years, three years, five years, sometimes even ten years earlier than they actually did. This applies to my divorce as well; I should have had mine at least three years earlier than it actually occurred. It even applied to my parents, who got divorced just two years ago while in their seventies. My dad clearly said the divorce came about eight years too late. I have heard this over and over again from way too many men. It's something to think about.

The second result of being unable to love without Oneitis means that you will never have a decent amount of Freedom. This is because she can make pretty much any demand of you, and as long as she sounds serious, you'll do it because you'll be frightened that she might leave you if you don't obey. Moreover, if you have Oneitis for your wife (and most men do), *she'll know this*. She will *know* that she can snap her fingers and make massive demands and you'll obey them like a good little boy. Not only will this destroy Attraction, but it will also ensure that the demands will never end. One demand will lead to another demand, and so on until within a few years, you're essentially her slave. This is the norm in most long-term marriages.

All of this is yet another reason for the Betaization Wall. It not only maintains Attraction, but it also maintains Freedom. It shows her that there is a limit (and a strong one) to the demands you will agree to. And, of course, if this is unacceptable to her, she should end the marriage immediately (which as a man without any Oneitis you will let her do) so she can go marry a beta male she won't have much Attraction for.

If you don't have the solid, emotional ability to walk away from your marriage if it's clear it's going to make you or her unhappy to stay married, many of the techniques in this book won't work, namely because you won't have the balls to do them. "Oh, my wife won't like that, and she might divorce me, so I don't think I'll..."

When I say "walk away" from your marriage, that doesn't mean you don't sit down and try to resolve problems. If there was a major problem in my marriage, *of course* I would attempt to work with Pink Firefly and our third-party relationship counselor (more on that topic in a future chapter) to resolve it unless the scenario was highly unusual. I'm saying that if it was clear that Pink Firefly would remain unhappy in the marriage regardless of any problem solving, or if the only way to make her happy was for me to make a major compromise that would make me unhappy, I would end the marriage immediately. I would be sad, but I have no regrets.

You need to work very hard to cultivate this frame and attitude if you don't have it already. You must learn how to completely love a woman without having any Oneitis. We'll discuss how to do this in future chapters.

Chapter 5
MAINTAINING ATTRACTION

As we discussed in the last chapter, if you want a long-lasting, harmonious, non-monogamous marriage, one of your required objectives is to maintain a high degree of Attraction for the entire length of the marriage.

One of the largest and most common catalysts for martial problems, drama, and divorce is directly due to the wife's loss of attraction for her husband. Some of this is unavoidable over time, and for the rest of this chapter, I'll call this loss of attraction "her fault." That said, *most* of this possible loss of attraction is indeed within your control. I'll call this "your fault."

Your objective is to keep the loss of attraction that is your fault to absolute minimum levels at all times throughout the length of the marriage. If you want your marriage to last the rest of your life, then yes, that means you need to keep doing this for the rest of your life. That bad news is that this will take some level of consistent effort on your part, effort that most normal men don't worry about (though these men pay a heavy price for that). The good news is that the things necessary for maintaining Attraction have multiple and layered benefits for your life that reach far beyond your marriage. I'll explain all of this in a moment.

If I were to roughly guess based on my experience and research, I would estimate that as much as 70% of this possible loss of attraction is directly within your control, i.e., your fault. The other 30% is going to be her fault based on her female psychology, and you have very little control over that as the marriage ages. In other words, even if you handle that 70% perfectly, you could lose as much as 30% attraction, which is her fault.

However! That doesn't really matter since you can lose that entire 30%, keep your 70%, and still have a long-lasting marriage that is reasonably harmonious. So while only 70% is in your control, that 70% is more than enough to carry the entire marriage in a positive way.

Moreover, that 30% that's her fault doesn't mean you're guaranteed to be screwed on that 30% no matter what. I'm just saying that 30% is outside of your control. It's possible that half or a fourth of that 30% attraction is never lost. It's also possible that no loss of attraction ever occurs in that 30% (though that's unlikely).

This means that if you maintain your 70%, and perhaps lose half of her 30% (as just an example), that's a total long-term Attraction of 85%; more than enough to maintain a long-lasting and very happy OLTR Marriage, especially when you consider that the typical married guy in a very long-term TMM maintains an Attraction of 10-20% or less (sometimes even 0%).

Unfortunately, the flip side is also true, in that it's possible you could maintain your 70% perfectly for many years and then suddenly end up divorced for various other reasons completely outside of your control. There are no guarantees in any marriage these days, non-monogamous or not. All you can do is to put the odds in your favor as much as humanly possible, and one of the most effective ways to do that is to maintain maximum Attraction at all times.

Your Fault

What do most men do in normal marriages? It's pretty simple: they get complacent. For the first one to three years, most do a decent job of maintaining whatever level of masculinity they had when they first got married. However, after a few years, they stop thinking that they have to continually put energy into their marriage and start to subconsciously think that their wife is pretty much going to be there forever no matter what they do.

Slowly, ever so slowly, they start to do the following things:

- Agree to more and more rules set by the wife
- Take on more and more responsibilities assigned to them by the wife
- Start compromising more
- Get into more stupid arguments with the wife

- Allow arguments with the wife to go on longer
- If there are children, engage in more "motherly" activities with them
- Start gaining weight
- Start dressing more shabbily around the house
- Start letting their grooming go
- Start threatening things when they're angry with zero follow-through
- Complain more often

All of these things drive Attraction downward. Over time, unsurprisingly, the wife starts to get bitchier, more demanding, less attractive, and less sexual. It can't *not* happen. And it's the husband's fault (or at least 70% of it).

You can keep your 70% Attraction at maximum levels throughout the marriage by doing two very simple things:

1. Maintaining masculine attractiveness most of the time

2. Maintaining the Betaization Wall

We'll discuss those two things in the following sections, but first, we need to cover the part that isn't your fault.

Her Fault

I explained the biological reasons for Betaization back in Chapter 4. The summary is that, like you, your wife's brain is, more or less, the same brain of the cavewoman she was 100,000 years ago. Her brain is designed to react to certain external stimuli regardless of what you do or don't do. Much of this is outside of your control, even if you do everything right.

This means that as much as 30% of her Attraction for you (and again, that's just my estimate, but I think it's very close) is completely outside of your control. This 30% is instead controlled by these factors, in order of importance:

1. Her female biology (mostly her brain chemistry)

2. Her personal history, including and especially what happened during her childhood and adolescence

3. Her personality

4. Negative external factors, such as medication, health issues, drug use, problematic children, health issues, work stresses, extended family problems, and so on

5. Luck

As you can see, you have little to zero control over any of those things regardless of the possible negative influences they have over her Attraction, her happiness, and your marriage. I have seen married men do a pretty good job at maintaining Attraction only to get their marriages sideswiped by one or more of the above factors.

For example, one of the biggest reasons my first marriage failed was because I was a beta male in a TTM, so I murdered my own Attraction. However, the actual divorce was set into motion by the fact that she was going through a horrible bout of premature menopause (heath issues, in the above list) that really made her crazy, as well as some depression meds she was on (drug use), and on top of that, she was going through horrible relationship problems with her mother (extended family problems). The loss of Attraction was completely my fault, but those three things were completely outside of my control and would have been problems in our marriage even if I had my 70% Attraction maximized.

The only small thing you can do with regards to the 30% "her fault" Attraction is to try to marry a woman with an easygoing personality and a relatively pleasant childhood. This won't guarantee anything (because women can and will change), but it could help tip at least a little of that 30% in your favor. (Obviously, if you're already married and your wife had a shitty childhood, you probably don't want to divorce your current wife tomorrow and find a new one, so you'll just have to do the best you can.)

Don't be delusional about your ability to change things in the 30%.

Some guys, usually younger men, think they can somehow force a wife or girlfriend to regularly report to a therapist, get off her meds, or stop talking to her problematic father forever. Sorry, but this is very unlikely. Of course, you can strongly suggest your wife do these things, but if she doesn't want to, she won't. Just assume that the 30% really is outside of your control (because it is) and instead focus on what you *can* control, that all-important 70%.

Maintaining Masculine Attractiveness as a Husband

The first of the two aspects of maximizing your 70% Attraction is maintaining your attractiveness as a husband most of the time. I say "most of the time" because I'm not asking you to dress up in a suit and tie every day, seven days a week, for the rest of your life. *Of course* you're going to have downtimes in your own home when you need to relax. *Of course* you're a guy, so you're going to do "gross guy stuff" like burp and fart in front of your wife sometimes. That's fine. It's your home, so you have every right to relax, and you should. As a matter of fact, showing your wife you have the balls to relax like this in her presence is actually helpful to Attraction.

That said, going too far with this stuff is what normal men in TMM do, and that will murder your Attraction. Instead, you need to maintain a certain level of attractiveness with your wife most of the time. This is done by doing the following things:

1. **Dress "up" just a little, even around the house.** Again, I'm not saying you need to walk around your house in slacks all the time. Instead of wearing jeans that show your butt crack and a ripped T-shirt every day or night, wear jeans that are a little nicer and wear a cool T-shirt, or even a really comfortable button-down shirt if that's your style. Be comfortable, but don't dress like a bum every day. Just keep your level of dress up a notch or two around the house most of the time.

2. **Smell good.** Find out what kind of cologne your wife likes, and if you like it too, wear it daily. You should always either smell *good* or have *no* smell. Never have any bad body odor around your wife. Also, change up your cologne every once in a while so you don't smell the same forever.

I almost never wore cologne before I got married and often didn't even wear deodorant. Now I wear deodorant and very nice cologne every day, seven days a week. It's not a sacrifice because I like how it smells. And she does too, which helps keep Attraction high.

3. **Stay as physically fit for the rest of your life as much as is possible based on your age and genetics.** In my opinion, you should do this anyway, married or not. But if you're married, you need to exercise three to five times per week (that means stretching, cardio, *and* resistance training, all three!) and watch your diet at least six days per week. Don't be the typical married guy and start allowing yourself to start getting soft and chubby. Stay as lean and muscular as you can for the rest of your life. I exercise *hard* five days a week, watch my diet as carefully as I can most days, and I fully intend on doing this for the rest of my life, all the way into my eighties. I'm actually leaner and more muscular today than on my wedding day.

4. **Do <u>everything</u> listed in Chapter 16.** That's the chapter on how to avoid Oneitis. Just about every technique listed in that chapter will help you maximize your masculine attractiveness to your wife, so you should do everything listed there.

5. **Follow all the sexual guidelines I talk about in Chapter 15 in regard to having sex with your wife.** You need to sex her well and never get complacent about that.

6. **Do romantic stuff <u>occasionally</u>.** Romance is tricky, and it's understandably confusing for a lot of men. Doing romantic stuff with your wife *all the time* will actually start to drive down Attraction. Many extreme beta male husbands are guilty of this, especially when they marry women who are very attractive. They constantly slather on the fancy dates, limo rides, fancy gifts, rose petals in the bathtub, and so on, all the time, non-stop. Initially, the wife loves this stuff and loves him to death for it. Eventually, though, it starts to bore her, and Attraction starts to drop.

On the other hand, if you are never doing anything romantic with your wife, this will *also* eventually start driving Attraction downward because she won't feel as loved and will start to feel jealous of other wives who have more romantic husbands.

The sweet spot is to do really romantic stuff with your wife *occasionally*. Not all the time, but not never either. If you have no idea what to do, just Google around and you'll find all kinds of ideas that women love (and that we more masculine men think are stupid, but hey, this is part of being married).

Romantic stuff has the most power when it's *unexpected* and *not attached to any specific event* like a holiday or birthday. Just last weekend as of this writing, for no reason at all, totally out of the blue, I had Pink Firefly dress up in one of her nicest dresses, I wore a full suit and tie (even though it was a Sunday), and I got a limousine to drive us to a nice steak restaurant downtown. She was ecstatic. My Attraction was boosted very nicely because A) it wasn't attached to any specific event or reason, and B) it had been a few months since we had done anything like that (I make sure not to do it all the time).

7. **Never stop having sex with side women**. As long as you're still having sex with side women, especially if your wife knows these women are attractive and/or young, this alone will help maintain a decent amount of Attraction (even if it still frustrates your wife a little). The instant your wife senses that you're not having any sex with any other women (and trust me, she'll know), your Attraction will take an instant hit even if she reacts with temporary outward satisfaction. Going monogamous in an OLTR Marriage is very, very dangerous. Don't do it. More on this later.

Maintaining Your Betaization Wall

Just as important as maintaining your masculine attractiveness, perhaps even more so, is maintaining your Betaization Wall. Remember this golden rule:

Attraction is maintained by saying, "No." Attraction is damaged by saying, "Yes."

Every time your wife requests or demands something of you, particularly if it represents a permanent change in your behavior, she leaning hard into your Betaization Wall and hoping that she can push it three or four feet in the direction she wants so she can continue and intensify the Betaization process. We already talked about why this is horribly bad for your marriage in the prior chapter.

If you say yes to this demand, she successfully pushes your Betaization Wall further down the Betaization path, and the Betaization process continues. She smiles in satisfaction… and her Attraction for you drops just a little bit. She'll do it again next week, and the week after that, and the week after that…

If you instead say no to this demand, your Betaization Wall doesn't budge an inch. She leans on it and pushes, but it doesn't move. Granted, this will piss her off a little, so you'll have to say no in a very gentle, caring, and loving way. Worst case, you may have to give a little in other areas. Regardless of her frustration, her Attraction for you stays high, and you've won, at least for now, until she tries to push again, which she will.

Your wife is going to spend the first two to six years gently pushing on your Betaization Wall repeatedly. Remember, this doesn't come from a place of malice. It doesn't mean she's an evil bitch. She's just doing what her 100,000-year-old cavewoman DNA is telling her to do. It's perfectly normal and natural.

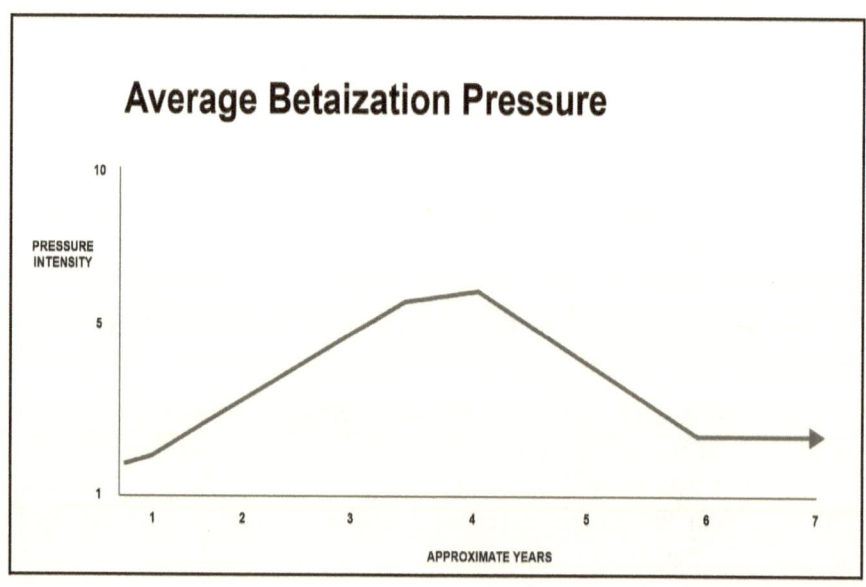

You can refer to the Betaization Pressure Chart to get a good idea of how hard she's going to push the Betaization based on the length of the marriage. Initially, her level of Betaization pressure is going to be low. However, the instant you two move in together, it's going to jack up in intensity. It's going to keep increasing in power until around the four-year mark. This means she's going to pressure you more and more to comply with her demands and damage Attraction by being a more beta male gentleman.

If you keep steady with your Betaization Wall, at around four years or so (this is just an estimated average; every woman and marriage is different), her subconscious mind will finally "get the point" that you aren't going to budge much. At this point, she will begin to try less hard (though she will still try). At around the six-year mark, her Betaization pressure will reach a new low and will sustain more or less indefinitely.

Note that her Betaization pressure will never go to zero. That's not how women work. She'll *always* try to Betaize you to some degree you as long as you live together. It will just lessen in intensity after about six years if you keep steady with your Betaization Wall. The only time after six years that she may intensify her Betaization is when your children grow up and move out (if you two ever have any). That will represent a temporary spike and then drop again.

This is all assuming you keep steady with your Betaization Wall. If you're like most husbands, you'll get lazy and/or complacent and drop your Betaization Wall completely within the first three to four years. With no Wall to stop it, her Betaization will run wild, go on overdrive, and sustain a very high level forever until she divorces you.

In order to keep up the Betaization Wall, you need to get into the habit of gently and lovingly saying no over and over again until she reaches a point where her biology understands that you aren't moving that damn wall.

Assuming you're doing everything else this book recommends, you'll likely end up with a very nice, happy, non-monogamous marriage where your wife maintains a high degree of Attraction for you despite the mild frustration that occurs when you say no.

That all being said, you actually *do* need to move the Betaization Wall just *a little bit* in order to maintain a happy marriage. If you want to stay married and maintain Mutual Attraction, you can't literally say no to everything your wife asks.

The best way to visualize this is by using the Betaization Scale. This is a one-to-ten scale that measures your degree of Betaization with your wife. A one on the scale means you're an extreme Alpha Male with 100% independence who doesn't give a rat fuck about what she wants. A ten on the scale means you're an extreme, Oneitis-filled beta male who is basically her slave.

Here's the scale:

The Betaization Scale

Alpha ↑	ALPHA ZONE	1	You do anything and everything you want completely regardless of your wife's feelings and literally never do anything your wife requests. Your wife is furious pretty much all the time. Attraction is moderate to low. Divorce is just a matter of time unless the situation is unusual.
		2	You do anything and everything you want with the exception of two or three basic items you do just to keep your wife from being horribly embarrassed or going insane. Arguments and drama are regular occurrences. Attraction is very high.
		3	You do anything and everything you want with the exception of a handful of items your wife wants that you don't consider don't consider very important. Your wife is a little frustrated on a sporadic basis. Attraction is very high.
	COMPROMIZE ZONE	4	You have significant portions of your life that are 100% within your control and where your wife has no say but in every other area your wife has significant influence. Attraction is moderate.
		5	You and your wife compromise with each other on a regular basis but you generally get your way more often. Neither of you ever get their way in any significant manner. Attraction is moderate to low.
		6	You and your wife compromise with each other on a regular basis but your wife generally gets her way more often. Neither of you ever get their way in any significant manner. Attraction is moderate to low.
	BETA ZONE	7	Your wife is more or less in charge of you but she's not a bitch about it and you get plenty of "me time" away from the wife where you can do what you want to some degree. Attraction is moderate to low.
		8	Whenever you're together your wife is clearly in charge. Only when you're by yourself, which is not very often, can you do what you want as long as it doesn't violate one of many rules she's imposed or promises you've made. Attraction is low.
		9	You're a slave. Your wife is in complete control of your entire life outside of your work and perhaps some minor aspects of your finances. Other than that, she's pretty much your boss in literally every other area (your time, your household, your budget, your kids, what you do on the weekends, etc). Attraction is very low. Either a divorce or her cheating on you is inevitable if it hasn't already happened.
Beta ↓		10	You're a slave. You do literally everything your wife demands no mater how ridiculous and she micromanages every aspect of your life. Attraction is zero. Your wife is only married to you for logistical reasons.

Betaization Scale

Level 1. You do anything and everything you want completely regardless of your wife's feelings and literally never do anything your wife requests. Your wife is furious pretty much all the time. Attraction is moderate to low. Divorce is just a matter of time unless the situation is unusual.

Level 2. You do anything and everything you want with the exception of two or three basic things you do just to keep your wife from being horribly embarrassed or going insane. Arguments and drama are regular occurrences. Attraction is very high.

Level 3. You do anything and everything you want with the exception of a handful of items your wife wants that you don't consider very important. Your wife is a little frustrated on a sporadic basis. Attraction is very high.

Level 4. You have significant portions of your life that are 100% within your control and where your wife has no say, but in every other area your wife has significant influence. Attraction is moderate.

Level 5. You and your wife compromise with each other on a regular basis, but you generally get your way more often. Neither of you ever get their way in any significant manner. Attraction is moderate to low.

Level 6. You and your wife compromise with each other on a regular basis, but your wife generally gets her way more often. Neither of you ever get your own way in any significant manner. Attraction is moderate to low.

Level 7. Your wife is more or less in charge of you, but she's not a bitch about it, and you get plenty of "me time" away from the wife where you can do what you want to some degree. Attraction is moderate to low.

Level 8. Whenever you're together, your wife is clearly in charge. Only when you're by yourself, which is not very often, can you do what you want as long as it doesn't violate one of many rules she's imposed or promises you've made. Attraction is low.

Level 9. You're a slave. Your wife is in complete control of your entire life outside of your work and perhaps some minor aspects of your finances. Other than that, she's pretty much your boss in literally every other area (your time, your household, your budget, your kids, what you do on the weekends, etc.). Attraction is very low. Either a divorce or her cheating on you is inevitable (if it hasn't already happened).

Level 10. You're a total slave. You do literally everything your wife demands no matter how ridiculous and she micromanages every aspect of your life. Attraction is zero. Your wife is only married to you for logistical reasons.

I have personally known and seen men at all levels of the Betaization Scale. One of my closest long-term friends was at level ten with his marriage until his wife finally divorced him and took his house, business, and children. I know of a guy who was at level one for about a year before his wife attacked him with a kitchen knife. So, both extremes of the Betaization Scale are severely detrimental to both a happy marriage and a happy life and should be avoided.

The problem is that most married men, especially those past the three-year marks in their marriages, live in the beta zone of levels seven through ten. As you can see, this zone, while being the most societally acceptable, is absolute death for Attraction. You need to stay out of this zone at all times.

The middle zone of compromise (levels four through six) isn't nearly as bad as the beta zone, but it's still not anywhere near optimal. Guys in the compromise zone rarely have amazing marriages.

The Alpha zone of levels one through three is great for Freedom and Attraction but severely unfavorable for Mutual Harmony. Level one is for crazy bastards who should never have moved in with a woman in the first place. Level two is only for Alpha Male 1.0s who enjoy constant drama and arguments with women. (Many Hispanic and Southern European men sadly live at level two in Mediterranean Marriages.)

The best place to be for the OLTR Marriage and the Alpha Male 2.0 is the high end of the Alpha zone at **level three**. Level three is the sweet spot for maximum Attraction and minimal conflict. Note that I didn't say *no* conflict; you're married, so that's not in the cards. I said *minimal* conflict. Again, when your wife pushes on your Betaization Wall and you don't budge, she will be a little frustrated. Doesn't matter. If you live with a woman in a romantic context, you *must* be *somewhere* on the Betaization Scale whether you like it or not. So if you have to be there, level three is, by far, the least bad place to be. **Level four** is not as good as level three, but it's still technically acceptable in an OLTR Marriage if you're very careful and stay vigilant.

Therefore, two of your primary goals in your marriage is to:

1. Get to level three.

2. Stay there forever, no matter what else happens.

If you screw up a little and rise to level four, that's okay, but you need to be careful. If you keep rising to level five or above, you're in big trouble. Also, if you find yourself at level two, you're also in big trouble. Your goal should be to consider level three as the "thermostat level" for your marriage; always try to stay there or get back there as fast as you can if you wander into other levels.

Rank yourself on where are on the Betaization Scale. Be completely honest with your ranking and don't bullshit yourself. No one is going to see this ranking except for you. Once you know where you are, you'll know exactly what you need to do:

- If you're anywhere in the beta zone, you need to start working very hard on moving down to level three or four. I'll be honest with you; it's going to be painful for both you and your wife. Doesn't matter; it must be done. Otherwise, your marriage is in jeopardy even if it doesn't feel like it is right now, and I mean that literally. Frankly, if you're at level nine or ten, moving to lower levels with this woman might not even be possible and you may have to get a divorce. We'll discuss this in more detail later in this book when we talk about monogamous to non-monogamous marriage conversions (since higher levels like nine or ten mean you're monogamous.)

- If you're in the compromise zone, you need to move down to at least level four. This move is going to take some effort, but you won't need to work nearly as hard as men currently in the beta zone.

- If you're at level four, that's okay. I would strongly recommend you move down to level three to maximize your Attraction and to use level four as a buffer zone in case you screw up, but it's not required. Just make sure you never get lazy by moving up to level five.

- If you're at level three, congratulations. Now the hard part begins: you have to make damn sure you *stay* at level three for the rest of the entire marriage. Don't ever get complacent! This book will help you stay focused on remaining solid at level three.

- If you're at level two, you need to look at yourself in the mirror and ask yourself what you really want for your life and if your long-term happiness is an honest priority to you. If it's not, then do whatever you want. If it is, you *must* calm down, chill the fuck out, sublimate your ego just a little bit, and move up to level three; you have no other option other than divorce.

- If you're at level one, you need to get divorced. You're not ready to be married and you should never have moved in with a woman in the first place. Move out, live your life, be free, and do whatever you want. When you're a little older and calmer, you can try this marriage thing again if you want and use this book as a guide.

Chapter 6
MANAGING THE DAY-TO-DAY

A happy OLTR Marriage isn't something you work on for just a few weeks, declare that you're done, and then forget about and set on autopilot. That's what most men do, and it's no wonder that the real divorce rate among people who get married is over 76%. Instead, your marriage requires regular attention and management.

The good news is that if you follow all of the mindsets and techniques in this book, you won't need to work very hard or even work on it every day. Regardless, you will have to regularly pay attention to several things on a regular basis to keep your OLTR Marriage going in a positive direction.

This chapter covers several mindsets and techniques you'll need to use regularly. They are all important and they are listed in no particular order. If you keep up on these things, your odds of marital success go way up. If you fail to do them, the odds are overwhelming you're headed for drama, divorce, or both.

Stop Trying to Fix It

Many problems in marriages are caused by the husband's desire to *fix it*. As men, we are hard-wired to want to fix things. We're problem solvers. We want to make things better. It's one of the great things about being a man.

The problem with this approach is that your wife isn't a man. Women don't want to necessarily fix things, particularly married women. Women instead want to *emote* and *commiserate*. When your wife has a problem, all she wants to do is talk about how bad it is. She doesn't want any input whatsoever on what she did wrong, how her actions may have contributed to the problem, how she can fix the problem, or what she should avoid the future. As a matter of fact, if these topics are raised, it's just going to make her even more upset than she already is. I strongly recommend you watch the famous YouTube video titled "It's Not About the Nail" for exactly what I'm talking about. It's as humorous as it is accurate.

The challenge is that as a man, those are exactly the topics you're going to want to bring up when your wife starts complaining about a problem she has. You're going to want to help your wife by fixing it. You're going to immediately start explaining why she has the problem and what she can do to fix it ASAP. And that will upset her. All she wants you to do is **listen to her and agree with the emotions.** She does *not* want the problem fixed. I realize that this may be difficult for your masculine brain to understand. I had a hard time understanding it myself. Doesn't matter; that's how it is.

Here's an example of the typical husband wanting to fix it and what usually happens:

Wife: Look, honey! Look at this! I broke a nail again at work today! I had to wrap it in this band-aid again! It snapped off when I had to move one of the tables. Ugh! It hurts so bad!

Husband: Well, that's because your nails are way too long. You're a teacher and you're using your hands performing manual tasks all day. You shouldn't have nails that long. Next time you get your nails done, you need to get nails that are much shorter. That way, you won't keep breaking your nails at work all the time.

Wife: Excuse me? This fucking hurts! You need to be a little more supportive!

Husband: Uh, I *am* being supportive.

Wife: No, you're not! You're being an asshole! <big argument ensues>

Of course the husband is right, but that doesn't matter. He's trying to fix it, and that's not what she wants. He's trying to win the battle instead of focusing on the war. By trying to fix it, which is what he thought she wanted, he's just going to make her even more agitated and cause drama

Instead, he should just listen and agree. Here's an example.

Wife: Look, honey! Look at this! I broke a nail again at work today! I had to wrap it in this band-aid again! It snapped off when I had to move one of the tables. Ugh! It hurts so bad!

Husband: <approaches and looks carefully at her finger> Wow! Yeah! That looks like that really hurts!

Wife: Oh my gosh, it does! It hurt so bad today. Now it's just really tender. <sigh!>

Husband: That must really be frustrating!

Wife: It is! It's so frustrating!

Husband: Come here. <gives her a big hug>

By listening and agreeing, he's intelligently avoided a shitload of useless drama. Again, I realize it may sound very weird to do what I'm suggesting, and it is… to us men. You have to constantly remember that your wife is not a man and should not be communicated to like she is.

The only time you want to try to fix something with your wife is if the problem affects you directly or if she specifically asks for you to help her fix something in her life. This will be rare, since again, women really don't want problems fixed the way we men do. If she doesn't ask, just *listen* and *agree*. It will feel strange to you to do this the first few times, but eventually, you'll get used to it. It will make your life a lot easier.

Track Your Marriage Success

One of the biggest reasons why reasonably happy marriages (usually when they are new) slowly become worse marriages is because the man is unaware of the small, negative, incremental changes that are constantly taking place. Every month, the marriage gets a tiny bit worse. She gives him drama just a *little* more often. They have sex just a *little* less frequently. She is just a *little* less nice to him. These changes are so subtle that week to week he has no idea they're happing. However, many months or years later, when things have become really bad, *then* he suddenly notices. Often by then, it's too late.

You absolutely cannot let that happen! Problems in a marriage are far easier to fix and avoid before they start or when they are very small than when they are big and serious. This means you need to be regularly aware of any small problems in the marriage the instant they arise. One of my personal standards is that as soon as I'm aware of even a little problem in my marriage, I want to immediately pounce on it like a panther and get it addressed right then and there, rather than waiting around two or three years like most married guys before it becomes a massive crisis that damages my long-term happiness.

The only way I know how to do this is to track your wife's behavior on a regular basis. As my regular readers already know, I have tracked all aspects of my entire dating life all the way back to 2008. Dates, relationships, sex, problems, and many other things I have tracked in detail on spreadsheets for over a decade. This data has helped me immensely in improving and optimizing my woman's life. Being married is no different.

You need to track how happy your wife is and her level of drama on a regular basis. If she's happy the vast majority of the time, that's great! That's the goal. Regardless, you still need to keep tracking it so you can immediately know when she starts becoming problematic. When this happens, you (with the help of your marriage counselor; more detail on that later) can immediately address things and get back on course.

There is no right or wrong way to track this, and there are many ways to do it. You should do this in a way that makes sense based on your personality and style. I'll tell you how I track my marriage with PF, but this is just an example. Feel free to copy it, change it a little, or do something completely different.

I keep it very simple. I have a spreadsheet with dates listed in the first column, every day. About once every two to four days, I pull this spreadsheet up, and on each date for the last few days, I put in the word "Travel," "Good," "Normal," or "Problem." I have an optional third column where I can put in a brief note with more information on what happened that day if I feel I need to (and usually I don't).

"Travel" means I was out of town that day and PF was back home, so I didn't see her or have any contact with her other than perhaps a brief phone call. Having regular time away from your wife is extremely important for your Mutual Harmony. I'll explain that in more detail later in this chapter.

"Good" means that PF was happy that day and enjoyable to be with. It was a good day.

"Normal" means she was more or less neutral that day. She wasn't particularly nice or happy, but there were also no problems. "Normal" can also mean that I didn't see her much that day because our schedules were busy.

"Problem" means there was some drama as I define it, no matter how small or short-lived. I define drama in Chapter 9. It simply means there was an argument (not a *disagreement*, but an *argument*; there's a difference), or she snapped at me, or raised her voice at me, and so on.

My objective has always been to have 90-95% of my days when I'm not traveling to be either Good or Normal. Problem days should be very rare. I am very happy to say that as of this writing, that is exactly the case. The times I have to put "Problem" down for any particular day is usually less than 5% of the time, sometimes far less. Moreover, Good days usually days outnumber Normal days. This is light-years beyond the vast majority of marriages of people I personally know, where most days in the marriage are Problem days!

To be fair, our marriage wasn't always like this, particularly during the first year together when we had to adjust to living together. We definitely had more Problem days back then. Not many, but certainly more than now. Today, Problem days are rare. It is my goal to keep it this way for as long as I can.

When I first started tracking this, I instead used a scale of 1 to 10, but I quickly found that was too cumbersome. What exactly constituted a "4" day? What constituted a "7" day? It was too confusing. After giving it some thought, I came up with a much more simple and clear system of Good, Normal, and Problem days.

You can track your marriage on a daily basis like I do, or track it on a weekly basis if you wish. You can use my system or a similar system that makes more sense to you. Regardless of how you decide to track it, *make sure you track it.*

Do not track her days where she is very sick or in physical pain. She's probably going to be irritable those days, and you would be too, so that's not fair. On those days, I just say "Sick" or something like that and give her the day off. (However, there's no rule against you staying away from your wife a little more often when you know she's going to be irritable because of sickness or physical pain; this is called Strategic Avoidance, and we'll discuss that in Chapter 11.) That all being said, having her period, PMS, or "being really tired" does *not* count toward this exception. If she gives you drama because of those things, they definitely "count," so put them down.

Don't be lazy about tracking daily drama levels; it only takes literally a few seconds every few days. It's one of the most valuable things I've done, and it will help you immensely.

Don't Expect Transactional Fairness from Your Wife

Another key difference between men and women is the concept of fairness. Fairness is a logical, rational, masculine concept. It doesn't really translate into the realm of the married woman. This doesn't mean that wives are unfair either. It just means that they don't factor fairness into the equation like we men do.

Men should never expect transactional fairness from their wives. If you do, you'll be disappointed at best and have your feelings hurt at worse.

Here are some examples of what I mean:

- A husband brings home flowers to his wife once a week for three weeks in a row as a nice surprise for her. She loves them. After the third week, he gets upset because she hasn't surprised him with any small gifts whatsoever.

- A husband offers to out with the kids on Monday so his wife can take a nap, and she takes his offer. He offers to help her out again on Thursday so she can go have coffee with her mom, and she takes his offer. On Saturday night, when he's in the garage working on his car, she asks him to watch the kids really quick so she can run to the grocery store. He says he can't right this minute because he's in the middle of working on the car covered in grease. She gets angry and snaps at him, complaining that he "NEVER helps her with the kids!" WTF? He's bewildered. How can she possibly say that? He just helped her with the kids *this week*. Twice! Didn't that matter to her at all?

- A husband is home alone working one night while his wife is having sex with one of her FBs. She comes home and they have a nice dinner together. Four days later, he comes home in the evening after having sex with one of his FBs. When he arrives home, his wife immediately complains that she was "sitting here alone in the house at night while he's out fucking one of his little sluts" and how she felt lonely and neglected while he was "out having fun." Confused, he logically points out that just four nights ago, she did the exact same thing and he didn't complain at all. She responds by raising her voice and getting angry, and an argument ensues.

In all of these cases and hundreds more I could mention, the husband was expecting fairness from a wife. Wives don't really do fairness, at least not in the way we men do. It's not a concept wives follow very well. It's not even something they think about most of the time. Instead, women, particularly married women, live in the moment. When they feel bad, they focus only on the negative emotion they're feeling at the moment (anger, loneliness, resentment, disappointment, frustration, etc.) utterly regardless of what happened four or five days ago. If you bring up what happened a few days ago while she's feeling her negative emotion, you're simply going to heighten that emotion.

You may tell me that it isn't fair. You're right. It's not. If you want 100% fairness at all times, then get divorced and stay single or go marry another man. Marrying a woman isn't going to get you very much fairness. That's just the way it is.

The bottom line is this:

- Never expect fairness from your wife. Plan in advance that she's going to ask for things that you find aren't very fair.

- Don't expect to build any equity with your wife by doing nice or helpful things for her. Assume that anything nice or helpful you do will be completely forgotten by your wife within a few days. (The reality is that she won't forget. She just won't consider it relevant to her feelings.)

This doesn't mean that your wife will literally never be fair. If you married a nice woman, of course, she'll be fair sometimes, just not all the time. (And if you married a selfish bitch, then that's your fault and you need to get divorced immediately.)

It also doesn't mean that your wife will never thank you or appreciate the nice things you do for her. Unless you married a bitch, she certainly will. She just won't consider these things as relevant the next time she's agitated or upset for whatever reason.

Lastly, it also doesn't mean you should never do anything nice for your wife. You have to do some nice things on a semi-regular basis in order to maintain Mutual Harmony and to keep yourself at levels 3 or 4 on the Betaization Scale without dropping to levels 1 or 2.

All of this unfairness stuff isn't nearly as bad as it sounds when you first read this. Once you get used to the concept, it won't bother you very much. As I talk about in *The Unchained Man**, you should be an outcome-independent Alpha Male 2.0 focused on his Mission, so your wife's opinion on what is fair or not really shouldn't be something that bothers you (and if it is, you have more work to do on your outcome independence).

Identify and Use Zones

Back in Chapter 4, I discussed the concept of Zones. In this chapter, I'll discuss the metaphorical Zones. In Chapter 7, I'll describe the physical Zones.

It is extremely important that you have Your Zones, she has Her Zones, and that you both have a Shared Zone.

Your Zones are those areas of your life that are 100% yours and only yours. You have 100% complete control over them, and she has zero. She has nothing whatsoever to do with them. You never expect her to be a part of them in any way whatsoever. Examples of Your Zones could be things like:

- Your business
- Travel

*http://www.alphamalebook.com/

- Video games
- Spending time with your guy buddies
- Your investments
- Certain kinds of movies or TV shows
- Sports
- Your FBs
- And so on

Please understand that the items above are just examples. If you want your wife involved in your business (for example) and you work well together, that's great! That would be a Shared Zone instead of Your Zone. You could also have some types of TV shows that are Your Zone and others that are in the Shared Zone. Those would be the ones you watch with her. You could have some FBs in Your Zone (the women she never has anything to do with) and other FBs that are in your Shared Zone (FBs who you have threesomes with your wife or have sex with your wife).

You get the idea. The point is to identify one or more Your Zones that are totally yours and that you never expect her to be a part of. As a man and especially as an Alpha Male 2.0, you must have areas that are purely yours. It's absolutely critical to your Freedom.

If you were wondering what my Zones are, they are my work, most of my companies (though not all of them), my investments, my international travel and projects, my fiction writing, most of my FBs (though not all of them), most of the movies I watch, my fitness, and, during the rare times I play any, my video games.

She must also have Her Zones. These are areas of her life that are 100% hers. You have absolutely nothing to do with them and have no control over them whatsoever. They can be anything she wants. It's important you let her have Her Zones, and it's important you stay the hell out of them unless you are directly invited by her to get involved (which may never happen and that's okay). If you want an example of a wife's Zones, Pink Firefly's Zones are her girlfriends, her TV shows, her money and her monthly purchases, and her work in the childcare industry. These are things that are purely hers; I have nothing to do with any of them, nor do I want to.

You may notice that PF has a lot fewer Zones than I do. That's okay. I'm a much more independent person than she is. It's one of our differences that are good for our Attraction. The number of Zones you have as compared to her isn't relevant. The important thing is that she has Her Zones, you have Your Zones, and they're both clearly defined.

You also have a Shared Zone. These are things that you actually share together. You're both involved and you both *honestly* enjoy them. Unlike in a TTM where everyone is expected to "compromise," instead, you must *both* really enjoy *everything* in the Shared Zone, or else resentment will build and the marriage will later be threatened. If either of you don't enjoy anything in the Shared Zone, it should be either be eliminated completely or absorbed into Her Zone or Your Zone.

Anything you two can think of can be in your Shared Zone. Here are some random examples:

- You could both work in a business together

- You could travel together

- You could exercise/go to the gym together

- You could have regular meals together

- You could watch certain movies or TV shows together (you'd better *both* honestly like them though!)

- You could work on a project together

- You could spend time together during designated times, hours, or days of the week

- Your sex life with her is in your Shared Zone by default (including any FBs you both play with together)

- And so on.

You two can put anything in your Shared Zone you want. It's a fun thing to discuss. The only requirement is that you must both *honestly* enjoy everything in the Shared Zone. No compromising!

If you want an example from my marriage with Pink Firefly, our Shared Zone includes our sex life with each other, some of our international travel and lifestyle, regular meals together, working on maintaining our happy marriage, a very small number of TV shows and movies (it's a small number since we have very different tastes, but we manage to find some), and every Sunday.

Yep, we actually put an entire day of the week into our Shared Zone. Since I have many more Zones than she does, and since I'm a motivated, driven guy who loves working on his Mission and work, several years ago, I decided to put every Sunday into our Shared Zone so that Pink Firefly wouldn't feel neglected. I do absolutely no work on Sundays, and instead we spend the entire day together doing things we both enjoy. Usually, this means going to a fancy lunch, then doing something like seeing a movie (that we *both* really want to see), going for a walk, hanging out down by the waterfront, or something else. It's fun to plan during the week, and it's been extremely beneficial to our marriage. Feel free to be creative with your Shared Zone like this. Your Shared Zone should be really fun!

Once you've established the three Zones, here are the rules:

1. Don't ever expect her to enter into Your Zone.

2. Don't ever let her get involved with Your Zone. Your Zone is yours! (If you instead make a conscious decision to move a particular item from Your Zone into the Shared Zone, that's okay, but that's something you *consciously decide*, not something that just happens because you got lazy or because you're being a beta and acquiescing to her demands.)

3. Don't ever expect to enter into Her Zone.

4. Don't ever try to control Her Zone. Even if she completely screws up Her Zone, that's her problem. She's an adult. Leave it to her. (Of course, if she asks you for help with one of her Zones, that would be okay as long as it's not a long-term thing.)

5. The instant you start to dislike something in the Shared Zone, *immediately* stop doing it and do something else instead. Discuss it with your wife. Be open and honest about it.

6. The instant you detect that she dislikes something in the Shared Zone, or that she's doing it just to please you, immediately stop doing it and do something else instead. Again, discuss it with your wife.

The use of Zones is hugely important to your OLTR Marriage. They are critical for both Freedom and Mutual Harmony. They can even help Attraction a little bit (having your wife watch you work diligently at your Mission can often be a turn-on for her). One of the biggest reasons my first marriage failed was because my wife at the time had no Zones. Literally everything she had was in our Shared Zone. I had my own Zone, but the only thing in it was my work; everything else I had was in our Shared Zone. This kind of setup is standard for most modern-day TMM, and it's a huge mistake. It results in both people feeling like they have no Freedom, as well as creating an environment where you disagree and argue about all kinds of things almost all the time. Setting up Your Zone and Her Zone first and then putting a *few* things into a Shared Zone dramatically reduces the opportunities for both resentment and conflict. It's very powerful.

We'll discuss physical Zones (which are just as important as metaphorical Zones, if not more so) in Chapter 7.

Spend Regular Time Away from Her

A common thread among marriages that last a very long time *and* include a very happy, loving, and sexual wife are marriages where the husband and wife spend regular, extended time far away from each other. I've noticed that even with some TMM, those few marriages that are still very happy after 10+ years, with the wife still happy and horny for the husband, often involve the husband (or in some rarer cases, the wife) leaving town for weeks at a time on a semi-regular basis.

As for normal Attraction aspects, the wife may not love this, but it inarguably does do a fantastic job at keeping Attraction high and Betaization and drama low over the long haul, at least usually.

As I talk about in great detail in my other books, blogs, and online courses, the Alpha Male 2.0 has location-independent income. This means he can travel wherever he wants, whenever he wants and can stay there for as long as he wants with no limits. You need to take full advantage of this in your OLTR Marriage. Travel alone regularly. When you travel, stay gone for at least a week. Two or three weeks is even better.

While you're gone, maintain regular contact with your wife. A good phone or video call once every other day is all you need. (Daily phone calls are technically acceptable, but don't go crazy. Always remember the Betaization Scale!) If you want to have sex with FBs or one-night stands while you're gone, that's fine too, though it's not required provided you have a regular FB or two at home (which, of course, you should).

Can you overdo this and be gone too much to the point where it harms the marriage instead of helps? Yes. This means you need to keep this time apart within certain parameters. I don't know the exact parameters and I don't think anyone else does either, but based on my experience and the experience of numerous other men I've worked with in OLTR Marriages, here's a good set of guidelines to follow:

- Time "away" from your wife does not mean you work long hours at the office or whatever. It means you are away from your home for several days and nights without your wife. Just being gone a lot during the day doesn't count toward this dynamic.

- Being two or three hours away by car also doesn't count because your wife can simply get in a car and come see you more or less whenever she wants. You need to be far away, meaning she needs to actually spend several hours on a plane to get to wherever you are.

- As long as you're both away from each other for at least several days, it doesn't matter which is the one who is actually traveling. In other words, your wife can be the one who travels and you can stay home.

- Your typical trip should last at least one week (seven days or so). Shorter trips are okay as long as there are lots of one-week minimum trips as well.

- The absolute maximum length of your trip should be four weeks. I *try* to keep my longer trips to three weeks or less. If you're away from your wife for a month or more on a regular basis, your wife will start to lose her connection with you, and you risk divorce and/or her getting emotionally involved with another man. If you must spend this much time away, you can alleviate this by having your wife fly out to meet you after three weeks or so. She spends a week (or so) with you and then goes back home. Then the new 3-4-week timer begins before you should do it again or return home.

- I have found that being away has maximum impact if you're spending your time in places your wife doesn't really want to visit. If you're spending several weeks relaxing at the beach at a nice resort in the Bahamas, your wife is going to be resentful for obvious reasons. But if you instead spend several weeks doing business or having sex with women somewhere like Santiago, Chile or Dubuque, Iowa, that's great. I regularly spend a lot of time in countries like Panama, Hong Kong, Paraguay, and China. Pink Firefly has absolutely no desire to go to any of these places, so it works out perfectly. She doesn't feel like she's missing out on anything when I travel like this. If I go somewhere she really enjoys like Western Europe, she will usually accompany me, and that's fun too.

- Make sure she's aware of every long trip you're going to take well in advance. Sometimes I see husbands suddenly leave town for a week or longer with minimal notice and drop the news on their wives at the last minute. This is emotionally rough on a woman and will likely cause drama, so it needs to be avoided. I realize that if you do a lot of international business like I do, there will be rare exceptions to this rule, but do your best. I lay out my travel schedule an entire calendar year in advance. Once a year, I print it out a copy for Pink Firefly and go over it with her so she fully understands everything well in advance. This way, there are never any surprises.

- Make sure your wife has something to occupy her time when you're gone. Having your wife sit around the house with nothing to do while you're gone for several weeks isn't going to help anyone. This goes back to the importance of having at least two or three things in Her Zone that are meaningful to her; these should help keep her occupied while you're gone.

Managing YOUR Attraction

When I talk about Attraction, I'm referring to your wife's Attraction for you. We also need to address *your* Attraction for your *wife*. The reason I don't talk about this as much is that your Attraction for your wife is actually much less important than her Attraction for you. This is because, unlike men in monogamous marriages, you always have the option of having sex with side women if you ever feel like the physical attraction for your wife wanes. As long as you still love your wife and enjoy spending time with her, your Attraction can be satisfied in other ways. Divorce is also less likely since men hate divorce far more than women do. As I mentioned earlier, 70-80% of all divorces (depending on the region) are initiated by women, not men. Men tend to stick around more than women do.

Regardless, it's still optimal to be attracted to your wife. The Alpha Male 2.0 can't tell women what to do, so you can't command your wife to dress in certain ways, not gain weight, change her hair color, and so on. However, the Alpha Male 2.0 can *state preferences*. Make sure that your wife knows *exactly* what you like about her physically and sexually and what you wouldn't like if she were to change these things.

For example, Pink Firefly is my ideal physical "type." She's a fit, skinny, huge-breasted, long-haired, platinum-blonde, Playboy Bunny Barbie babe with no physical flaws. This is exactly what I like and she knows this. She also knows that if she were to ever do anything like dye her hair brown, gain 50 pounds, get breast reduction surgery, or cut her hair really short, I would be less attracted to her *physically*. I would still love her and still want to spend the rest of my life with her. I would not leave her or even consider doing so for that reason alone (again, we men don't like divorce). It's just that I would not be nearly as excited about having sex with her as I do now. I'm a guy. It's just how I am.

Again, to be clear, I have never told PF that she can't do any of these things. She's an OLTR wife, so she has complete Freedom to do whatever she wants. I will allow her to change her appearance in any way she wants at any time, and I will never complain. I'm not giving orders like an Alpha Male 1.0 husband would. Instead, I'm just stating preferences then leaving it completely up to her.

I've been asked several times if it's okay to have an OLTR Marriage where you aren't sexually attracted to your wife at all and never have sex with her. (You may recall that I mentioned a few marriage types like this back in Chapter 2.) After all, if you can have sex with side women forever, isn't it okay to never have sex with your wife provided everything else is okay with the marriage?

The answer is that an OLTR Marriage like that is *acceptable* but not *optimal*. Could I stay married to Pink Firefly for the rest of my life and never have sex with her assuming everything else was fine and just have sex with my FBs? Sure. Would that be the best thing for our marriage? No. A marriage is always better if there is a healthy sexual component between husband and wife. Every couple has a different sexual dynamic, and every man needs sex with a different level of frequency, so you don't have to have sex several times a week for the rest of your life like I do. It's just optional to have sex with your wife regularly. I'll cover sexual issues with your wife in Chapter 15.

I would set a goal to have sex with your wife *and enjoy it* until at least her early sixties. The only reason I state "sixties" is because that's when a lot of women stop having sex completely. The reason for this is, unlike men, women need to feel sexy in order to have sex, and most women don't feel very sexy after age 65 or so. But from now until then, it's best if you stay sexually attracted to your wife. That means that she maintains her physical appearance as best she can until then (her job) and you don't get sexually bored with her (your job).

One last point about this. For all of these things to work long-term, you can't be one of these men who mostly love their wives because of how they look. This is extremely common for Alpha Males who marry really attractive women. The biggest reason these guys married her was because of her looks. The biggest aspect of their love for their wives revolves around their looks. This is not ideal. Even if she's a perfect ten, her looks are going to fade over time as she gets older. If she's genetically blessed in this area (Pink Firefly is), then this will take much longer to happen (double that if you or she have the income to pay for cosmetic work for her as she ages), but it will still eventually happen. If you're going to get really disappointed as soon as your wife starts gaining a little weight or getting a few wrinkles, you're in for serious problems in your life, even in a non-monogamous marriage. It's okay if your wife is really hot and really turns you on sexually, but at the same time, *you must really love your wife for reasons that have absolutely nothing to do with her physical appearance*. That automatically resolves a lot of possible future problems you may have if your marriage lasts long enough for your wife to start getting noticeably older (which we hope it does!).

The only other option you have is to be one of those chaotic men who marry a hot younger woman, have a kid or two, divorce her as soon as she hits her mid-thirties (because she's "too old now") then marries *another* hot younger woman and repeats the same process forever, constantly getting married and divorced, married and divorced, over the course of many decades. (Many male celebrities follow this insane model.) This is definitely not the path to consistent long-term happiness.

Chapter 7
MANAGING THE DAY-TO-DAY

One of the biggest sources of drama, conflict, arguments, and resentment in marriages is how the couple's shared home is organized and managed. Indeed, one of the biggest reasons why marriages tend to be less happy than normal boyfriend/girlfriend relationships where the two don't live together is simply that; the married couple lives together and has to share a house or apartment every day of their lives, 24/7.

Societal Programming tells people in traditional monogamous marriages that the entire home is both "theirs" and must be shared. (Conveniently for most women, this is regardless of who pays most of the rent or mortgage). In other words, people in a TMM put their *entire home* in the Shared Zone, with the possible exception of a single room (or corner or room!) where the husband has some kind of workspace.

What happens then? Husband and wife then proceed to argue for the rest of the marriage about important things like the toothpaste on the bathroom counter, the mess left in the kitchen sink, where to put the couch in the living room, when the husband puts his dirty shoes up on the ottoman, and various other stupid shit. Putting your entire home into the Shared Zone actually creates drama and arguments. I'll explain why in an analogy I call The Shovel.

The Shovel

Let's say you have a next-door neighbor, and both of you need a good solid shovel for some outdoor projects. In order to save money, you both go in 50/50 for a really fantastic $200 shovel. You each kick in $100. Now you both co-own the shovel 50/50. You both decide to keep it over at your neighbor's house and just schedule with each other when you need it.

The day you buy the new shovel, you both admire it in your neighbor's garage. Damn, what a great shovel. You're both going to both get some serious work done with that baby. Even better, you both saved $100! You pat each other on the back and congratulate each other on your mutual genius.

For a while, it works out great, but soon, problems arise.

Sometimes you both need it at the same time. You're both buddies, so you don't argue about it. However, it does mean that one of you gets to complete his landscaping projects sooner while the other has to *compromise* (uh-oh, there's that word again!) and is unable to use it when he wants it. Not a major issue, but it sort of nags at you in the back of your mind that this wouldn't be a problem if you each had your own shovel.

Not a big deal, but eventually, things get worse.

One day you go out to your neighbor's yard to use the shovel, and you see him using the shovel to smash rocks on his concrete retaining wall.

"Whoa!" you cry, "What the hell are you doing? That's not what a shovel is for! You're going to damage it!"

"Whatever, dude," he responds, "It's my shovel and I can do what I want with it."

"It's my shovel too!" you scream, "And I don't want you damaging it!"

You now have **drama**. You argue.

It's a tough situation since you're *both right*. You both co-own the shovel equally. Both of you have differing opinions about how the shovel should be used. Since no man can use his own property "wrongly," neither of you has the moral high ground over the other. Since the ownership is exactly 50/50, one can't force or command the other to do anything.

So, you're both stuck. You simply continue to disagree and argue, getting more and more pissed off, until one of four things happen:

1. One of you finally throws his arms in the air, gives up, and acquiesces to the other. Therefore, one person gets what he wants and the other harbors resentment. This creates a permanent rift in your long-term friendship, which, prior to getting the shovel, was pretty much problem-free.

2. One of you uses shrewdness or strength of personality and verbally forces or tricks the other person into doing it their way. The other

person grudgingly goes along with it but still harbors resentment and feels defeated to some degree. Once again, the friendship is damaged.

3. One of you bribes the other person, promising some payment or service for going along with their way. But that's stupid! Why should you pay someone to use something that you already paid for and that already belongs to you?

4. Realizing it was a bad idea to co-own something with your friend in the first place, as he continues to scream at you, you hold up your hand and tell him to just forget it and give you $100. That way, the shovel will then be 100% his, and he can then do whatever he wants with it. The two of you won't ever need to argue about it again. Realizing that you're right, he agrees. He pays you $100, keeps the shovel, then you go to the hardware store and buy your own shovel. Problem solved, forever. No more arguing ever again, and your friendship remains solid and intact with zero resentment. More importantly, you've learned a valuable lesson about human behavior.

Now… what would have happened if instead of *co-owning* the shovel, you just *shared* it instead?

New scenario. Let's say you need a high-quality shovel for some landscaping you'll be doing. You purchase a beautiful $200 shovel. It's all yours, and you're very proud of it.

One day your neighbor and good buddy comes over and sees it in your garage. He comments on such a fantastic shovel and asks if he could borrow it sometime. He's a good friend and you know he's a trustworthy guy, so of course, you say yes. As a matter of fact, you tell him he's more than welcome to take it out of your garage whenever he needs it without asking you. As long as you aren't in the middle of using it, and as long as he doesn't damage it, he's free to use it whenever he likes. You even tell him he can keep it over in his garage if that would be easier for him.

He feels happy about the trust you place in him. You feel happy about how generous you're being and that you're helping a good friend. You both get a little endorphin rush.

Do you have any problems? Not really.

Any time you need the shovel, you get access to it instantly, with no arguments or compromising. It's your shovel. If you need it and it's over at your neighbor's house, you go and get it, and he hands it over immediately since he knows it's not his shovel.

Will your buddy use your shovel to pound rocks and possibly damage it? No. He knows it's your shovel, not his shovel, so he takes good care of it. Even if one of his kids damages or loses the shovel, he immediately buys you a new $200 shovel to replace it without a second thought.

There's never any argument over when to use it or how to use it. Because it's *yours*, not *both of yours*. You're *sharing* it, not *co-owning* it.

The only possible problem you might have is if your neighbor is an irresponsible dumbass and blatantly damages the shovel without compensating you for it. Whose fault is that? Yours. You shouldn't share expensive items with irresponsible people. I certainly don't. Regardless, assuming you're a decently intelligent person, you're only going to share your stuff with responsible people and refuse to share your stuff with morons. Thus, you'll probably never have a problem.

Share Everything, Co-Own Nothing

This explains one of my core concepts for long-term, serious relationships, marriages included. You should *share* everything with your wife, but you should *co-own* nothing. Assuming she's a responsible person, if you want to let her drive your car whenever she needs it, that's great. The odds of problems are low. However, if you both co-sign on a loan for a car you each own 50/50, then you are 100% guaranteed to argue about when that car is used and/or how it's used. If/when you break up or get divorced, you're going to have all kinds of logistical problems and possible legal disputes over how to liquidate the car or who gets the car.

I will explain this in much more detail in Chapter 18, where I lay out the financial parameters of an OLTR Marriage, in that you and your wife should have no co-owned assets, debts, leases, or accounts. For now, I'm just going to focus on your house or apartment, which brings us to the first rule in terms of managing your home.

The home in which you live with your wife must be 100% owned by *her* or *you*, not *both of you*. If you are renting the home, the lease must be 100% in *your name* or *her name*, not *both of your names*. (I realize that in some jurisdictions, the other person living in the rental property must be on the lease in some way, but that person doesn't have to be responsible for paying the lease nor an actual leaseholder. This varies based on the location and landlord; please check your local laws.)

Moreover, the person with the 100% ownership *must have enough income to pay the entire mortgage or rent payment completely on their own* even if they don't charge the other person rent. The reason for this will become apparent in a minute.

For simplicity purposes, I'll call this one person who owns 100% of the mortgage or lease the "owner" and the other person who owns zero percent the "boarder." It does not matter if the owner is you or her. If she wants to buy a house completely on her own and then the two of you live there as husband and wife, that's perfectly fine, as is the reverse. The point is that only one of you is the 100% owner and the other owns nothing (or is not responsible for the lease payments).

If the owner wants to charge the boarder monthly rent, that's fine as well; make any arrangements you want with your wife. If instead you are the owner and you want to financially support your wife and not make her pay any rent payments, that's okay too. Just make sure that whatever you decide is clearly understood by both parties.

Why do all of this? Because it's an absolutely necessary requirement of your Financial Barrier that I first mentioned back in Chapter 3 and that we'll discuss in great detail in Chapter 18. If you both share a mortgage, lease or ownership of a home, if/when you get divorced, you'll likely face legal problems, expensive financial problems, and emotionally draining logistical problems. I'm sure you've seen many couples who have experienced this during a divorce or cohabiting break-up. There's are big arguments about who will move out and who will stay. Then the two exes have to battle each other for months regarding how to sell the home, or how one person can buy out the other person, and so on. You're stuck in a scenario where you're dealing with a woman who is probably irrationally angry with you while you're trying to sell a piece of real estate. Worse, it's likely you weren't even planning on selling it at all.

It's a huge mess. You can't have this problem.

It's just as bad if you're both on a rental lease. You have a divorce/break-up and she instantly moves out. Now you need to pay the entire lease on your own. If you can't afford it, you're screwed. If she goes crazy and damages any part of the property before she vanishes, now you have to pay for it, or else you're in big trouble. Conversely, if you move out and she stays, then she decides to not to pay the rent (or she can't) and she gets evicted, the landlord then goes after *you* for the thousands of dollars in back rent even though you're not even living there anymore. Financial problems, credit problems, mass chaos.

I could go on and on with all kinds of problems that occur when a cohabiting couple splits up when they are both on the mortgage, deed, or lease. You *must* refuse to live with any woman under these financial conditions. Either you are the 100% mortgage/deed/leaseholder or she is – never both of you. If she insists on both of you being owners, she does not qualify for an OLTR Marriage and you'll probably have to look elsewhere for an OLTR wife. Yes, I'm serious.

Home Zones

Once you've determined which of you will be the owner and which will be the boarder, and you've determined if the boarder will pay rent to the owner or not, the next thing you need to determine is the Zones in the home. These are just like the Zones we talked about in the last chapter, only these Zones are actual physical locations in the home instead of conceptual or metaphorical ones.

As I mentioned above, due to Societal Programming, most normal married couples consider the entire home as a Shared Zone. The kitchen, bathrooms, bedroom, living room, garage, front yard, *everything* is within the Shared Zone. Both husband and wife share pretty much the entire house or apartment 50/50 (with possible small exceptions like a home office). This causes silly, useless, non-stop conflict in the marriage for multiple reasons I've already described.

People in an OLTR Marriage seeking long-term happiness need to be smarter than this. Since we need to keep Freedom and Mutual Harmony at maximum levels as much as humanly possible throughout the marriage, we need to split up the home very differently. As a matter of fact, this OLTR setup is actually the direct opposite of how a home would be configured in a TMM.

In an OLTR Marriage, most of the home is split up into Her Zones and Your Zones. Only the tiny bit left over is a Shared Zone. You can even have *no* Shared Zone in a home if you really want to, but that's not required.

Home Zones need to be split up by room. Every room in the house must be designated as Her Zone, Your Zone, or a Shared Zone. The goal is to have the minimum number of Shared Zones in the home. The more Shared Zones, the more potential for arguments and drama.

When a room is in Your Zone, that means you control that room 100% in all respects, and she controls zero percent. You can decorate and organize that room in any way you want, and she has literally no say in how you do it. If she hates how you're doing it, that's her problem. Everything in that room is also part of Your Zone, so everything in that room is considered yours, not hers, and not both of yours. Of course, she is allowed to go in that room and spend time in that room if she wants. As always, you're going to *share* everything with her, but you're not going to *co-own* Your Zone. She can spend time in Your Zones as long as she doesn't complain about them or leave messes in them.

Her Zones work the exact same way. They're under her complete, 100% control and you have absolutely no say in how she organizes, decorates, or manages them. You can spend time in Her Zones as long as you don't leave messes or complain about them, and so on, just like in the above paragraph.

Your Zones and Her Zones in the home have nothing to do with who is the owner and who is the boarder. Let's say you and your wife live in a house that you own 100%. Let's also say that you don't charge your wife monthly rent. She still needs rooms in the house that are Her Zones that she has 100% control over. These Zones are 100% hers until she moves out of your house. The owner/boarder distinction is only relevant to the finances and legalities, not Home Zones.

The Shared Zone in the home are rooms or areas that you both share together. You both have input on how these rooms should be decorated and organized, and both parties need to listen to and co-operate with the other on how these rooms should be set up and managed. It's best to *not* have these rooms controlled as 50/50 man/wife. The potential for disagreements is too great if this is attempted. I strongly recommend that each room in a Shared Zone be 60/40 or 70/30. This means that while both parties have authority over the room, one of you has a *little* more authority (and responsibility) regarding how the room is organized and managed.

As you might imagine, it is in the Shared Zone where the likelihood of arguments and problems is highest. This means that *you must absolutely minimize the amount of space in your home that is in the Shared Zone*. You could even have *no* Shared Zones in the home, which would be perfectly fine, although that is an extreme scenario and is not required.

Your wife, likely being a more normal person brainwashed with standard Societal Programming, will likely suggest that *lots* of areas in the home be in the Shared Zone. Do *not* agree to this. The Shared Zone in your home must be as tiny as possible. I know that might seem strange, but once you've been married for a few years under this scenario, you'll realize how nice it is for both of you.

There are even certain types of rooms that should *never* be part of a Shared Zone and must always be in Your Zone or Her Zone (or one of each). Here are the types of rooms that can *never* be allowed in a Shared Zone:

- **Your office (or work area).** Wherever you work in your home, this must be Your Zone. If she also works out of the home and your home is large enough, she can also have her own office in Her Zone.

- **Bathrooms.** You can*not* share a bathroom with your wife, period. This will cause too much stress, arguments, and/or resentment. A bathroom is used too often, and men and women are too different in their bathroom usage to make this work in the long term without any arguing. She must have her own bathroom and you must have yours, and they must be in different rooms. This means that those larger bathrooms with two sinks *do not count*. That bathroom must be hers or yours, not both of yours.

Sometimes I get asked how to handle this if the home you live in has only one bathroom. That means *you need to immediately move to a home that has at least two bathrooms* so you can each have your own. If you can't afford to do this, then in my opinion, *you can't afford to be married*. Yes, I'm serious. The *only* time you can have a bathroom in a Shared Zone is if your home has three or more bathrooms. That way, you have yours, she has hers, and the third bathroom can be shared.

Here are the types of rooms that *shouldn't* be in a Shared Zone but technically could be in a temporary pinch. Having any of the following rooms in a Shared Zone presents a danger:

- **The kitchen.** That's right; you need to have separate kitchens. Before you resist this idea, remember how many times you and your wife have had snippy little arguments and stresses about things in the kitchen. Leaving messes on the counters or in the sink, how to cook, where to cook, who starts or empties the dishwasher, where to put things away, who ate whose food, and on and on. Married couples are so accustomed to constantly arguing about kitchen bullshit that they don't realize how often it happens.

When I say "kitchen," you don't actually need two physical kitchens in your home. All you need is one kitchen and one other room with a sink. Just add a small refrigerator/freezer, a small microwave, and (optionally) a countertop burner to that room, and boom, you now have a fully functional kitchen. I'll demonstrate exactly how Pink Firefly and I handle this in a minute.

- **The living room.** Sharing a living room doesn't cause as many arguments and disagreements as sharing a bathroom or kitchen, but it still causes them. Don't share a living room. The main living room should be Her Zone or Your Zone. Frankly, I recommend you just give it to her and make it Her Zone since women tend to be cleaner and better at decorating than men, but that's just my opinion.

- **The front and back yard, if you have them.** You'll have far fewer problems if the front and back yard are in Her Zone or Your Zone rather than a Shared Zone. Usually, one person in a couple is more into how the yard looks and is more skilled at things like landscaping and gardening. Give the yards to that person.

- **The garage, if you have one.** The garage should be yours or hers, not both of yours. I recommend the garage be Your Zone since women tend to not care much about it as long as they can park their car in there (if they have one).

- **Kid's rooms.** If you have children, the kid's rooms should be in the Zone of the person who is the primary caregiver. This is almost always going to be your wife unless you are wealthy enough to afford a full-time nanny, and even then, the kid's rooms should be in Her Zone or Your Zone, not the Shared Zone.

What room is left after all of that? The master bedroom. This is the one place in the entire house where it's usually okay to have in a Shared Zone. This is where you both sleep. This can be a Shared Zone with "higher owner" (60/40 or 70/30), likely her.

It is entirely possible to have no shared master bedroom as well. Some OLTR Marriages follow the concept of having completely separate bedrooms. This concept was first suggested by Harry Browne way back in the 1970s. She has her bedroom in Her Zone and you have a separate bedroom in Your Zone. You can both sleep together in one of those rooms every night if you wish, but regardless, each room is hers or yours; you don't share one. As I said, this is not necessary, and Pink Firefly and I don't go quite that far. I'm just saying it's certainly possible.

To give you a real-life example of how PF and I handle this, I'll describe how we set up the Zones in our home. Please note that I'm a higher-income man and live in a decently large house, so don't get hung up on the size of the home, just how it's laid out using the above system.

As of this writing, I still live in the United States in a house in the Pacific Northwest. I rent this home since I'm moving out of the country in a few months and don't want to bother with selling or renting out a property that soon. The lease is 100% in my name, not PF's, though her name is on the lease as someone residing in the home (this is a legal requirement of my local region). I do not charge PF rent, but I have made other financial arrangements with her that offset this (the details of which I can't describe publicly for legal and privacy reasons).

It's a large, two-story house. The entire upstairs is Her Zone with two exceptions. One is the master bedroom, which is the only Shared Zone we have in the entire house. I consider that room a 70/30 shared room with her having a little more authority, since I don't care how the room looks (I spend very little time in there other than to sleep and have sex) as long as it's functional for optimal sleep. The second exception is the fitness room where I work out. That used to be a Shared Zone, but she stopped using the equipment in there, so now it's My Zone, since I work out there at least five mornings per week, sometimes more.

The master bedroom also has the master bathroom attached with a large closet. This is Her Zone. I have my own full bathroom downstairs.

Also upstairs and in Her Zone is the kitchen, her office, the third bathroom, the living room, the dining room, and the rear upstairs deck. I don't give a shit about any of these things and I have my own kitchen downstairs, so I gave all of these rooms to her when we moved in.

The front and back yards are also Her Zone. We have landscapers regularly take care of those. I don't give a shit about the yard and never have in any house I've owned.

The entire downstairs is My Zone, with one exception, which is a guest bedroom, which is Her Zone. I've used this room a few times, mostly for sex (both with her and FBs), and she almost never uses it, but it's still technically Her Zone.

The entire rest of the downstairs is My Zone. This includes my work area, my bathroom (a full bathroom with two sinks, toilet, and full shower), an entire second living room with my furniture and TV, several storage closets, the back deck, my kitchen, and a "playroom" where I have my books, toys, and where I film social media videos,

My "kitchen" is really a bar in the large downstairs living room with a countertop, a sink, and dishwasher (which I never use; I use mostly disposable dishes for time management purposes). I have also added a large microwave and a small refrigerator/freezer. This "kitchen" is awesome. It provides 99% of my kitchen needs without having to screw around with another human or compromise on anything kitchen-related. The only time I ever need to go upstairs to use PF's kitchen is if we're having some special event where fancy meals need to be prepared, which is very rare.

I eat lunch in my own kitchen by myself most days. For dinner, I'll prepare my food in my kitchen and then bring it up to the dining room (Her Zone) and eat with PF. Sometimes we prepare food together in her kitchen for special occasions.

This system, while it looks weird to other people, works shockingly well. Unlike just about every other married couple on the planet Earth, Pink Firefly and I have literally never argued about *anything* regarding a kitchen. Not once. It's beautiful.

Where to Live

The world is full of married men who love their wives, love their children, and absolutely hate where they live. They suffer on a regular basis because they would rather be living somewhere else, but because their wives won't let them move, or because they feel stuck because they have children, they remain in a home, neighborhood, city, or even country they can't stand.

Obviously, no place is perfect. There will always be things about where you live that irritate you, and that's fine. I'm only talking here about men who *very strongly* desire to live somewhere else. You can't be one of these men. You must live where *you* want to live. If your wife or prospective wife doesn't want to live where you want to live, she shouldn't be your wife. It's that simple.

One of the recurring themes in this book is that you do not exist to suffer for your wife. The Alpha Male 2.0 is here to live life to the fullest and to love his life. If you are married to someone (or want to be married to someone in particular) who will not let you do this, then this is not a woman who should be your wife and share your life. Instead, you should go find another woman who either wants to live exactly where you want to live or at least doesn't mind living there.

I really love the house and the neighborhood where I live. Pink Firefly loves it too. That's how this is supposed to work. There are aspects of living in the United States which irritate me, but as I mentioned earlier, I am moving out of the USA (at least as a full-time, twelve-month-per-year place to live) and moving abroad. PF doesn't love the prospect of living most of the year outside of the USA, but she's cool with it. Again, that's how this is supposed to work. We're also going to spend regular time back in the USA, which makes her happy.

One of the reasons my first marriage failed was because, several years into the marriage, my wife at the time woke up one morning and suddenly decided she wanted us to move to rural Nebraska to live near her family. I don't know if you've ever visited Nebraska, but the Gene Hackman quote from the movie *Unforgiven* is accurate: "I thought I was dead, but I realized I was just in Nebraska." Nebraska pretty much sucks. I would be miserable if I lived there, so I told her no. For the rest of the marriage, she was resentful that I didn't want to move there. It's one of the many factors that lead to our arguments and subsequent divorce.

Here's the bottom line: Live where you want to live, and if your wife/prospective wife clearly doesn't want to live there, remove her from your life and go live there. Every other option involves your long-term unhappiness, and that's not acceptable. Live with a woman who honestly wants to live where you want to live (or at least doesn't mind living there). Period.

Chapter 8
QUALITY COMMUNICATION

One of the biggest challenges you face in your marriage is the fact that you need to regularly communicate with an alien from another planet. That alien is your wife. She comes from the planet Woman (or Venus, if you read that book). Creatures from the planet Woman are very attractive, wonderful to be with, fantastic to have sex with, and can bring deep meaning to our lives (assuming the marriage is structured correctly, of course).

The problem is that these strange, beautiful aliens think and communicate in ways that are utterly alien (pun intended) to us men. You'll clearly say something to your wife and she'll respond with something that makes absolutely no sense to you. You'll say something in response and she won't understand what the hell you're saying. Because of this, she'll often think you're saying something you're not. For example, you'll say something you think is factual and helpful, and she'll take it as a personal attack and yell at you. She'll say something she thinks you need, and you'll take it as an insult and get defensive. This silliness happens to millions of married couples all over the world, every day.

One of the primary jobs of both you *and your wife* is to alleviate these communication issues. This is a hard job. It takes a lot of effort and a decent amount of time. It might even be several years before both of you fully understand the other's communication style *and* where both of you overcome the deep-seated communication habits you had before you were married to an alien. (Remember, you don't come from planet Woman, so she's married to an alien too.)

The more different the two of you are, the harder this job will be. As David Deida describes, all men and women fall somewhere on the masculine/feminine scale. Your wife is likely going to be your "mirror" on the scale. This means that if you're closer to the middle of that scale (not too masculine, not too feminine, but more balanced), your wife is will likely be more balanced as well. You and your wife are going to have a much easier time communicating than most other married couples. (Good for you!) If you're more on the masculine edge of the scale, your wife is more likely to be on the feminine edge. This means that while Attraction will be easier, communication will be much more difficult for both of you.

I am on the extreme edge of the masculine scale, so unsurprisingly, Pink Firefly is on the extreme edge of the feminine scale. As a result, while our Attraction is very strong and likely will be for a very long time, working on our communication with each other has been the hardest aspect of our marriage. Sex, non-monogamy, living together, spending time together, all of that has been pretty easy for us, but communication has taken a decent amount of work on both of our parts. Today, we're pretty good at this and our marriage is very good. Yet, we have more work to do, and we may never get 100% there simply because of our extreme personality differences.

Just be aware that if you're a more masculine man married to a more feminine wife, you'll have to work harder at this. If you're a more balanced man with a more balanced wife, the work won't be quite as difficult, but it's still something you must both master.

That "both" part is important. Unlike many other techniques in this book, working on the communication aspect is something both of you must do, not just you. If your wife is unwilling to work on improving her communication with you, this is going to be a serious problem in your marriage. I would even consider it a dealbreaker. Proper communication in a married couple is just too important, and *it will not work if just one of you is working on it*. Both of you must put in the effort; otherwise, it's pretty useless.

Communication between a husband and wife is a massive topic. Entire books have been written about it (some of which I reference in the bibliography and the end of this book). As I said, even I have room for improvement in this area. Regardless, in this chapter, I'll do my best to provide you a solid framework to get started. Don't consider this chapter your only communication resource, though. Consider it a starting point.

The Five Love Languages

The Five Love Languages is a concept first described by Dr. Gary Chapman back in the nineties. It is one of the few mainstream relationship techniques that actually works. The five love languages accurately reflect real human behavior, at least in my experience and the experience of those I've talked to about it. If you're aware of this concept, it will help you in all of your sexual and/or romantic relationships with women, but most especially with your wife.

The idea is that, by default, we "love" (love as in the verb, meaning to show affection, not the noun) others in our lives by the way we want to be loved, not by the way our partner(s) want to be loved. Everyone is different in terms of how he wants to give and receive affection.

Since opposites attract, it's overwhelmingly likely that you will find a serious partner who prefers different ways to love than you do. If you're lucky, there might be similarities, but even then, it won't be exactly the same.

The five "love languages" are the five ways in which people like to give and receive affection. Here they are in no particular order:

Physical Touch – This means you like to touch a woman non-sexually and be touched by her. This includes things like touching, hugging, holding, cuddling, squeezing, playful groping, playful wrestling, touching hair, caressing, and so on.

Acts of Service – This means you like to do little favors for your partner(s). An example is to make her coffee in the morning while she's still asleep, or a woman you're dating who likes to clean your house without being asked.

Quality Time – This means spending time together in an involved way, usually talking. Watching TV or a movie together may or may not count, but going to dinner, going hiking together or talking to each other on the couch for an extended time would definitely apply.

Gifts – This means you like to buy gifts for people and love to receive gifts from others, even if they're small and/or cheap. "It's the thought that counts," has real meaning for people with this love language.

Words of Affirmation – This means you like to give and receive verbal compliments, encouragement, sympathy, and support.

You don't just like one of these things. Instead, you have a hierarchy of the above five items. You have a strong favorite, a reasonably strong second favorite, one or two you sort of like, and one or two you don't care about at all.

To use myself as an example, my hierarchy is this:

1. Physical Touch

2. Quality Time

3. Acts of Service

4. Words of Affirmation

5. Gifts

I'm an extremely physical man, so Physical Touch is huge for me. I'm constantly grabbing, squeezing, holding, and crushing (nicely) Pink Firefly every day and I love it. I also love it when she touches me. (I like sex too, but remember that Physical Touch is normally not about sex. I mean, come on, we *all* like sex.) Quality time is also extremely pleasant for me. My favorite "dates" involve a woman and me talking on my couch or in my bed for a long time. Acts of Service are nice, but I don't really need them. Words of Affirmation are useless to me, and I just don't give a shit. I utterly dislike Gifts. I find buying them for people a tedious chore. I'm also in a place financially where I already own everything I could possibly want in terms of physical things one could purchase, so receiving gifts is more of a hassle for me than anything else.

That's just me. You are likely going to be very different in your hierarchy, and the women you date will also be different.

It gets even more complicated. Even if you both have Physical Touch (for example) as your number one or two, her "style" of touch may be very different than yours. Maybe you're a barbarian like me and love to grab, crush, squeeze, and hold, but perhaps she likes to be lightly caressed with gentle fingertips. This is going to cause some weirdness unless you're both aware of this difference.

Here are a few examples of how these differences have affected me in my past.

When I was a young man, I lost my virginity to a much older woman whose number-one love language was Words of Affirmation, and number two was Physical Touch. However, her physical touch was the light and gentle kind. I was always holding her tight and grabbing her, and she liked that somewhat, but she was also constantly telling me to touch her gently and lightly, both during and outside of sex. Being a beta male and near-virgin, I wanted to make her happy, so I tried, but it was extremely difficult for me.

We would also get into huge arguments (again, I was a young beta male at the time) because I virtually never said nice things to her. Words of Affirmation was her number one, but it's my number four, thus not something I ever think about.

Several years later, I married my first wife. Physical Touch was literally at the very bottom for her, number five. She liked sex to a degree, but outside of sex, when I held her or grabbed her, it did nothing for her. She would just stand there, arms limp, and look at me funny. At the time, I thought she was being cold. I was wrong; we just had stark differences in our love language hierarchies.

Acts of Service was her number one, and Quality Time was her number two. So we had the Quality Time thing down, but the Acts of Service thing (my number three) was a slight challenge sometimes as well.

Many years later after my divorce, I was in a long, serious relationship with a younger Asian woman I've called HBM. Luckily for me, her number-one love language was Physical Touch, just like me. She was also physically tiny and a more submissive woman, so she loved to be grabbed, crushed, and thrown around. We were a perfect match this way. It was one of the reasons she was my longest consistent relationship outside of my two marriages. Words of Affirmation was her number two, which was a slight problem, but Quality Time was her number three, which again matched me very well.

At one point, I was seeing an MLTR who was constantly bringing over the little gifts for me. I had no idea what she was doing (I hate gifts and never asked for them) until I remembered the five love languages. So every once and a while, not often, but every now and again, I would give her something cute and girly that I picked up at my grocery store. These things were almost always under $5, but when I would give them to her, her entire face would light up like a Christmas tree and she'd be happy all day. It was alien behavior to me, but Gifts was her number one. Of course, since she was an MLTR, I had to take it easy on the gifts to not get into boyfriend-zone, but because gifts were number one, I pushed the envelope a little bit more than normal, and it worked. (I just made sure not to do it all the time and keep the gifts obviously cheap.)

Today I'm married to Pink Firefly, of course. Her hierarchy looks like his:

1. Quality Time

2. Words of Affirmation

3. Physical Touch

4. Gifts

5. Acts of Service

This means that we share Quality Time as a key to our communication. It's my number two and her number one. One of the reasons PF and I fell in love is that, before or after having sex, we would just sit and talk with each other, sometimes for hours, and we both really enjoyed it. When we started getting more serious, she told me that, with the exception of her mother, there was no other person *in her entire life or entire history* who she could talk to like that – just me. The fact we both held Quality Time as high on our hierarchies was one of the reasons.

Here's what you need to do:

1. Identify your hierarchy. Rate the five items above in terms of what you like best or dislike. You may never have been aware of it until you read the five love languages above. Knowing your own hierarchy is extremely useful. It really helped me.

2. Identify the hierarchy of your wife. Ask her if necessary, but I suggest you guess first and then ask her if your list is accurate. That will give you a good idea of how well you know your wife and/or how well you can read her.

3. Notate both the differences and similarities between her hierarchy and yours. If you both share something in the top two (and hopefully you do), capitalize on that and do that often. If you don't share anything in the top two, make sure that you regularly engage in the number-one item on her list (even if you think it's weird, which you probably will) and encourage her to do the same with your number one.   Also, try to avoid doing anything for your wife that is fourth or fifth on her list. It won't really resonate with her.

Calibrate Based on One of The Three Woman Types

There are three types of women: Dominants, Submissives, and Independents. It is absolutely critical that you fully understand which of these types your wife is and that you adjust your approach with her to reflect what that type needs.

I go into greater detail regarding the three types in my primary dating book *Get To Sex Fast**, so I'm not going to repeat all of that here. Instead, I will simply summarize the types and then relay the basics of what you need to know about each type when in a cohabiting relationship. If you want more detail on the three types as it relates to meeting and having sex with new women (since all of your FBs will be these types as well), get the book *Get To Sex Fast**.

Dominants

The first of the three primary types of women, and by far the most common type in today's Western world, is the Dominant. Dominants are women with strong personalities and who possess a very clear and inflexible agenda. They know exactly what they want, what a man should and should not do, and exactly how dating and/or a relationship with a man should look. They are not interested, at all, in deviating from this agenda, even if they are strongly attracted to a man who won't go along

*http://www.gettosexfast.com

with it.

Dominants tend to be strong, bossy, proud, defensive, and argumentative.

I'm not saying all Dominants are bitches. Many Dominants are fun, enjoyable women who are very pleasant to spend time with in certain scenarios. Regardless, they're still inflexible to a strong degree.

As soon as a Dominant gets into a relationship with a man, or in some cases, even goes out on a first or second date with a man, she starts to directly or indirectly convey orders, standards, rules, and/or parameters. She expects the man to go along with all of these. If he does not, she gets frustrated, personally offended, or even visibly upset. It's not her way or the highway; it's her way, period. If it's not her way, she's going to be very upset that her standards weren't adhered to.

If it sounds like I'm painting a picture of a monster, I'm not. Don't misunderstand me; Dominants can often be very attractive, intelligent, fun women. Most of them also have higher sex drives as well. There's both good and bad in every type of woman.

Based on the research I've done, my own anecdotal experience, and talking to literally thousands of men and women over the last 13 years on the subject of sex and dating, I roughly estimate that 60%-65% of women in today's world are Dominants. In the Western world, it's become the norm and the new standard. Culture today celebrates the "bad-ass bitch" who "takes charge of her life," and most women are going right along with this societal messaging. Men today are also far more beta and submissive than they have ever been before, causing women to take up the slack and become more masculine and dominant.

Unless you currently have a monogamous marriage that you have not yet converted to something open, it is unlikely that your wife is a Dominant. The vast majority of Dominants would never agree to a non-monogamous marriage where a man can go out and have sex with women whenever he wants. That said, there are a few men with swinger marriages other non-OLTR, non-monogamous marriages who are married to Dominants. Regardless, it's more than likely that if you already have a non-monogamous marriage, your wife is either a Submissive or

Independent.

Submissives

The second type of woman is the Submissive. They are the polar opposites of Dominants in just about all respects. Submissives are extremely feminine women who prefer that other people make the big decisions and set the agenda. Things like decision making, directing others, and formulating plans make Submissives uncomfortable. They'd much rather leave these things to other, more decisive people. This way, they can go with the group and ensure harmony with everyone involved. They're most comfortable with a strong, kind man who takes the lead.

Submissives tend to be feminine, shy, flexible, and overly emotional. They tend to be submissive (thus their name) and compliant, which a lot of men like. They're also the most feminine of the three types of women, by far. On the flip side, they often have very problematic, chaotic lives, have a lot of silly drama with their friends, co-workers and loved ones, and can often be clingy and whiny.

When forced into a position of power, like at her job or with a more submissive boyfriend or husband, a Submissive will hate it but will do it for a while before she implodes with some kind of huge meltdown.

I'm not saying that all Submissives are weak little girls. On the contrary, many are very strong. Their key trait is not weakness, but that they prefer to not be the one making the big decisions in most scenarios.

Approximately 25% of today's women are Submissives. You can identify a Submissive on a date when she's reluctant to answer questions, give opinions, or/and make decisions. Common answers Submissives give will be things like "Whatever you want to do" or "Well, what would you like to do?"

This does *not* mean Submissives have no opinions. On the contrary, Submissives are still women, and if you do something they don't like or don't enjoy, then you'll hear about it. The difference is that with Dominants, you'll hear about it loudly and instantly, as soon as it happens; with a Submissive, you'll hear about it several days or weeks after it's happened, once she's had a chance to stress about it for a while.

Independents

The final type of woman is the Independent. These women are somewhat uncommon in society, representing only about 10%-15% of women. However, because of changing cultural and economic conditions, this is a growing demographic in the Western world. Expect to see more Independents emerge over the next few decades.

Independents are essentially flexible Dominants. Just like Dominants, Independents are strong, confident, organized, high-sex-drive women. Unlike Dominants, they're extremely flexible, relaxed, happy, and don't really care about what you do or don't do. They're not wedded to an ironclad agenda like their Dominant sisters, yet unlike Submissives, Independents are confident, self-assured, and decisive. They have no problems making decisions or taking charge when needed. They are very low drama women, extremely fun, and are a joy to be around.

If this sounds like the ideal woman, think again. As always, there are downsides. Independents are, by far, the most masculine of the three types of women, which can sometimes turn men off. (My theory is that Independents have higher testosterone levels than most other women.) They often have jam-packed schedules full of work, school, family, activities, and social events, which makes them very hard to pin down. Sometimes you'll get the feeling that you don't matter very much to an Independent (which may, in fact, be the case) because she has so much going on in her life. Lots of men find Independents irritating and/or hard to keep up with. Other men complain that Independents come off as a little cold.

Your Wife

If you're already in a non-monogamous marriage, your wife is likely a Submissive or Independent. If you're in a monogamous marriage and haven't converted yet, she is likely a Dominant. (There are, of course, exceptions to all of these assumptions.) Also note that there are different degrees of Dominant, Submissive, and Independent. For example, your wife could be an extreme Independent or a mild Dominant.

You need to fully understand your wife's category. From there, you need to calibrate your communication style in order to keep Mutual Harmony at maximum levels.

If your wife is a Dominant, then I'll be honest: you're in for a real challenge. Non-monogamous marriages, OLTR Marriages in particular, are extremely difficult for Dominants if not impossible. I don't recommend any Alpha Male 2.0 be in *any* serious relationship with a Dominant since the Freedom of an Alpha 2.0 simply won't be compatible with her need for control. For the rest of this section, I'll assume that you've already screwed up and married a Dominant and are now trying to make the best of things.

Your biggest challenge will be Freedom (though Mutual Harmony and Attraction are also going to be difficult). Dominants like to be in charge. They feel threatened by husbands who have a high degree of Freedom. You must make it clear, though your words and actions, that you must maintain a high degree of Freedom throughout the marriage. Your frame should be *that you'd rather get divorced and be single than sacrifice your Freedom.*

Make very sure your Dominant wife has plenty of Her Zones that she controls completely, and stay the hell out of them so she can get her need for control met in Her Zones rather than with you.

You also need to avoid contradicting her when she says things you disagree with. If what she's saying doesn't really affect the marriage, then just nod your head and keep quiet regardless of how much you disagree. If you vocalize your disagreement, even mildly, you're in for drama and arguments. Men with Dominant wives learn pretty quickly that it's best just to let most of what she says "go."

The odds for divorce when you are married to a Dominant are high no matter what you do. Do your best, but always remember that a divorce is always a valid option if you are really unhappy. Again, non-monogamous marriages really need a wife who is a Submissive or Independent.

If your wife is a Submissive, your Attraction will be very high, your Mutual Harmony will be fair, and your Freedom will be optimal provided you take a few extra steps. Submissives are fine with non-monogamous marriages as long as certain requirements are met. Submissives have a strong need for *security* and *social conformity*. When married to a Submissive in an OLTR Marriage, she's going to need to know two things:

1. She's secure in her relationship with you. That means emotionally secure, logistically secure, and financially secure. The idea of being alone, having major problems, or getting divorced terrify most Submissives. Drama and conflict will be an outward expression of her fear, so if a Submissive thinks any of these things are likely, drama and other problems are going to be frequent in your relationship. Drama with Submissives can be just as bad as with Dominants because Submissives tend to be very emotional women (as most feminine women are).

2. She's not going to be embarrassed by your open marriage. Submissives are hypersensitive to what their friends, family, and social circle think of them. Your Submissive wife is likely going to demand assurances that your marriage will look 100% "normal" to the outside world, so her mom, dad, grandma, or whoever has a positive view of her marriage with you. Submissives also have a high degree of "Disney," so trappings such as weddings, wedding rings, family events, pictures of you two together on social media and other such items are going to be very important to them. You must provide these things to a Submissive so she'll feel safe. Failure to do this will introduce problems.

The bottom line is that the safer and secure your Submissive wife feels, the happier your marriage will be. (If you were curious, Pink Firefly is a Submissive.)

If your wife is an Independent, Mutual Harmony and Freedom are both going to be fantastic, but Attraction is going to be a challenge. Independents are the lowest-drama women of all three types by far, and unlike Submissives, you won't need to do anything to ensure this (other than being an easygoing guy). Unlike a Dominant, she doesn't give a shit about what you do, so you can max out your Freedom with no problems at all.

The problem is that her Attraction for you won't be as effortless as it would be with a Submissive. You're going to have to work a little extra hard to make sure your Independent wife doesn't lose any Attraction for you or get bored, which is a common problem for Independents. They are free spirits and, unlike a Submissive, can quickly get bored or fickle and divorce you on the spot even if you've done nothing significantly wrong. (Dominants can divorce you too, but they'll do it with a lot of drama and you'll see it coming from a mile away.) It's your job to keep your marriage to your Independent wife exciting and interesting. Independents are amazing women, but they require a *lot* of energy. (If you're an Alpha Male 2.0, this shouldn't be a problem.)

The Great Paradox

As men, we have a strong psychological need to protect, nurture, and make our wives happy. When our wives are happy, we feel a sense of pride and accomplishment. When our wives are unhappy, we feel deeply uncomfortable, that we have failed somehow. Our need to *fix it* drives us to try harder to make her happy.

The problem is that, as I discuss in great detail in *The Unchained Man**, women *can't* be long-term happy. It's not how their brains are designed. Instead of consistent happiness, women desire to experience a *range of emotions*, both positive *and negative*. Being happy all the time, even if she were capable of such thing (and she isn't), would actually bore her after a while. She prefers to be happy sometimes, sad sometimes, joyous sometimes, angry sometimes, relaxed sometimes, frustrated sometimes, and so on.

What happens when you have a husband who constantly strives to make his wife long-term happy when she can *never* be long-term happy? This is the Great Paradox of marriage: men strive for a goal that is impossible to maximize his wife's consistent long-term happiness.

Even I fall prey to the Great Paradox sometimes. Pink Firefly will have something in her life (outside of me) that will be hugely stressful and frustrating for her. I love her, and I want her to be long-term happy like I am. So, without thinking, I will leap in and start to give her advice and help her out so that this problem will not only be fixed but will never happen again. I want her to be happy forever!

*http://www.alphamalebook.com

Then I catch myself and remind myself that Pink Firefly is an alien from the planet Woman, where consistent long-term happiness is impossible. As a man, especially as an Alpha Male 2.0, it's more than possible for *me,* but not for her.

Men caught up in the Great Paradox experience regular frustration at their inability to make their wives long-term happy. Here's how you can avoid this problem:

- Always remember that your wife's brain is hard-wired very differently than yours and that her emotional patterns are thus also very different, and always will be no matter how wonderful your lives become.

- When your wife experiences a negative emotion (which she will on a semi-regular basis because she's a woman), be there for her and to provide comfort and emotional support, but let her feel the pain. *Let her* be sad, angry, frustrated, scared, or whatever. Let her emote. That's what she wants and needs. If you don't try to fix something unfixable, it takes the stress off you *and* you won't inadvertently create drama by trying to fix it as I talked about in Chapter 6.

To be clear, I'm saying to let her emote, *not* let her give you drama. If she's furious about her boss or aunt, that's fine, let her be angry. But if she's furious at *you,* that's *drama,* and now we have a serious problem that needs to be handled very differently. We'll go into great detail about that in Chapter 10.

- Instead of setting a goal for your wife to be long-term happy (which is impossible) or virtually never be upset, sad, or frustrated (also impossible), instead set a goal (or goals) to work with your wife to constantly improve your lives as a married couple together. I regularly describe my goals regarding my future income, lifestyle, fitness, travel, Mission, and fun with Pink Firefly and ask for her input (if she has any) and her help (if it makes sense). The better your mutual lives become, the fewer things there will be to upset your wife. To repeat, your wife will be upset about *something* on a semi-regular basis no matter what you do, even if you become a billionaire, spend all your time with her, and look like Schwarzenegger in his prime.

My point is for you to focus on the overall quality of *your lives* and *your marriage* rather than *her overall happiness*. Those are things you can actually change and improve.

Work with A Marriage Counselor/Therapist

Your marriage is too important to work on all by yourself with your wife. Marriage is one of the few areas in life that, if it goes wrong, negatively affects *everything* else in your life (your money, work, health, happiness, children, recreation, future, and more). Moreover, you're not a marriage expert. Even if you do everything this book recommends and even if you've been married for over a decade, you're still an amateur at all of this. Being a lone amateur at something this critical to your life isn't a good idea.

On top of all this, regardless of how amazing you are or how much Attraction you have in your marriage, eventually your wife will stop listening to you in regard to what you think the marriage needs. Let's face it… often to her, you're her Big Dumb Husband that doofus portrayed in all the commercials on TV she watches. She sees your dirty underwear and rolls her eyes as you burp and fart around the house. She might listen to some of your martial opinions, but not all of them. However, listening to a neutral and expert third party… that's something else entirely. She'll listen to that.

All of this means you need to work with a professional marriage therapist/counselor. You need to start doing this immediately, even if you think everything is going fine. I started taking Pink Firefly to a marriage therapist as soon as she moved in with me, while everything was going great. My objective was and is to *keep* everything going great, not to wait until things are going horribly and then go seek a marriage counselor. As marriage counselors will often tell you, by then it's often too late.

Men, especially tough Alpha Males like us, often resist seeing marriage counselors. They feel like they're for pussies, or that the counselor will be a feminist and will constantly take their wife's side, or that therapy is bullshit or a scam and doesn't work. These are all valid concerns, and I'll address them in a minute. For now, let me tell you the three big reasons why you and your wife should see a counselor and why it will massively help you.

1. **It will minimize drama.** When both you and your wife (especially your wife) know that you have a regular standing appointment with the counselor, it often helps calm yourself and/or your wife because you both know you'll have a chance to vent everything at the next counseling appointment. Both you and your wife will be far less likely to start drama before then. Also, your wife isn't going to scream quite as loudly or irrationally when the counselor is in the room watching her than when she's with home alone with her Big Dumb Husband. Regularly seeing a counselor diffuses drama on multiple levels.

2. **It will provide you with tools customized to your particular scenario that you likely wouldn't have on your own.** If your counselor is good (and we'll get to that in a minute), he/she will provide you with tools you and your wife can use that really will help improve the marriage, particularly Mutual Harmony. Reading a how-to book on marriage like this one is valuable, and you should do that as well, but only a counselor can provide you customized solutions based on your specific situations.

3. **It provides a neutral third party to mediate disagreements.** This is huge. One of the biggest reasons I bother with going to and paying for a counselor on a regular basis is not necessarily to help the marriage (although it does help) but also to have a neutral third party in the room to A) help settle disputes and B) provide a third person in the conversation *whom your wife will actually listen to.* As I said, your wife may or may not listen to her Big Dumb Husband, but she *will* listen to the counselor. Many husbands (myself included, in both marriages) have had the experience of telling their wife something, having her snort and blow it off, only to have the counselor tell her the exact same thing, and then she nods in agreement and does exactly what he says. Humorous and unfair, perhaps, but it works, and it's very powerful. You simply don't have this kind of power without a counselor.

These three benefits are too massive to pass by. Hopefully, you now see why you need to go see a marriage therapist even if you think everything is going fine at the moment.

Here's a bit of interesting trivia about this. Well, after I started seeing the marriage counselor with PF, I read an article about Will Smith. Smith is pretty amazing, namely because he's a self-made guy and has an open marriage with his wife, Jada Pinkett. I was both shocked and pleased to read that as soon as he and Pinkett got married, Smith made them both start seeing a marriage counselor *three times a week*. He had been divorced once before and, like me, he wanted to start seeing a marriage counselor immediately, while things were going great, so as to avoid a second divorce. His wife was very confused at the time, as was mine. Why go to a marriage counselor when we're not fighting?

Did it work? Well, Will and Jada have been married for 23 years now(!), under an ostensibly open marriage. Even if they get divorced tomorrow, that's an amazing accomplishment, doubly amazing considering they're Hollywood celebrities who are usually dreadful at staying married. They really are an extraordinary couple. Clearly, seeing a therapist works.

You don't need to go overboard and see a therapist three times a week like they did. I recommend that if everything is going well in your marriage, you both go see the therapist (always go together) once a week for a while until you feel you've both got the hang of things, then drop it to once every two weeks, then later, perhaps drop it to once every three weeks. If things are going badly or you're currently experiencing problems with your wife, you should go at least *twice a week* and keep going at that frequency until the problem is alleviated. *Seeing a marriage counselor only once a week when there is a real problem in the marriage is not enough.*

Avoiding the Pitfalls

Now let's get to your concerns about seeing a therapist. Here are several things you need to do to make sure the therapist doesn't cause any new problems.

- Only work with therapists who have at least 10 years of experience. Twenty is even better if you find them. When you look up therapists online, it usually will state how experienced they are.

- Only work with therapists who specialize in couples/marital counseling. They can practice other types of therapy, but couples/marriage counseling should be their focus.

- Only work with therapists who have experience counseling non-monogamous couples. Just ask them on the phone during the initial interview if they have. Most older, experienced therapists in larger cities have extensive experience with this, but if for some reason they don't, move on.

- Once you find a new therapist, follow the Rule of Three. I use the Rule of Three whenever I hire an advisor or staffer of any kind for my businesses. The Rule of Three states that you may have to go through as many as three people before you find the one that works out. That means you may need to eventually fire this therapist and find a different one. Then you may have to fire *that* therapist too. The third one should be good. Sometimes you'll get lucky and only need to go through one person; PF and I had to fire our first therapist (who was a very nice person, but she just didn't cut it), but the second one we found was amazing. We still see her to this day.

- Your therapist can be a man or woman, but obviously, if she's a woman, your therapist can't be biased toward your wife's needs at the expense of yours. If it's clear that she's doing this (and you'll see it pretty damn fast if she is), no problem, fire and replace her as I explained above. Our marriage therapist is a woman, and I haven't had any problems with her being less fair to me. Indeed, often she takes my side, which means I have a powerful, neutral, third-party advocate my wife will actually listen to and obey, as I already explained above.

- On the other side of the coin, your therapist can't be too neutral, either. One of the reasons I had to fire our first therapist was because she was too nice. Every time PF or I presented a problem to her, she always considered it equally both of our faults, 50/50, every time, regardless of the scenario, because she wanted to be nice to both of us. That obviously won't work. Sometimes a problem really is the fault of one of you, and a good therapist has the balls to call that person out, regardless of it's the husband or wife.

- Do *not* let your therapist try to move you up the Betaization Scale. Sometimes this can happen to married men in marriage counseling if they aren't paying attention. What sometimes happens is, on a regular basis, the therapist (through the wife) asks the husband if he'd be willing to start doing X or stop doing Y. These are usually little, inconsequential things that rarely matter, so the husband agrees. The problem is if this keeps happening over many weeks, all of these things add up. Before you know it, your Betaization Wall has been moved or seriously damaged. *Always* maintain your Betaization Wall not only with your wife but with your therapist as well. If it seems like many counseling visits involve you agreeing to several small compromises and changes *without your wife doing the same as often*, call your therapist out on this, and make it very clear to both her and your wife that you're not going to keep moving that Wall on a regular basis *without your wife also making an equal number of changes that you want to see*. If you need to, consider having a one-on-one session with the counselor to explain to them exactly what you're doing and why you're doing it, so at least your counselor has some context to your concerns.

- Be aware of false psychology Societal Programming from your therapist. I believe in psychology as a real science (more or less anyway; of course, nothing is perfect), but every industry has its own bullshit Societal Programming, and psychology is no different. I know this well since my father was a psychologist, so I grew up in this industry. Every once in a while, you're going to hear some oddball stuff from any therapist, even good ones, that don't make a lot of sense. A common one I've heard regarding marriage from psychologists is that you'll have a bad marriage because you had bad parents or crappy upbringing, but they also turn around and tell people like me who had a good upbringing that I will *also* have a difficult marriage because I can't measure up to the good one my parents had when I was a child. Just keep your radar up for this shit and be aware of it when you hear it.

- Lastly, stand up to the therapist when you disagree with something he/she says. I like my marriage counselor, but I challenge her, often strongly, all the time. Make damn sure your therapist always justifies the techniques or mindsets he/she is giving you based on facts, science, and objectivity rather than opinions, biases, or Societal Programming. It's very important.

Chapter 9
DRAMA MANAGEMENT

The greatest long-term threat to your marriage is Betaization. However, the greatest threat to your marriage on a day-to-day basis is *drama*. This is a particular kind of conflict far beyond just having a disagreement or a bad day. It's absolute poison to your marriage and long-term happiness. Drama absolutely murders Mutual Harmony and places massive downward pressure on your Freedom. One of your primary overall objectives of your marriage is to keep drama to absolute, bare minimum levels at all times.

Drama does not equal disagreement. Any two normal human beings living together in the same house will eventually disagree on all kinds of things. Disagreement is normal, natural, can't be avoided, is to be expected, and there's nothing wrong with it. Drama, on the other hand, is very different. It's the level *beyond* disagreement.

One of the wonderful aspects of the OLTR Marriage is that its entire structure minimizes both the potential for drama and the severity of drama if it occurs. This is very unlike traditional monogamous marriage where drama is a normal and regular experience, as well as one of the biggest reasons for divorce and cheating. Over the next few chapters, you will learn exactly what drama is, how to avoid it, and how to handle it if it occurs.

The Definition of Drama

I have a very specific definition of the word "drama" when I use it in a relationship context. Per the glossary at my dating and relationship blog for men, blackdragonblog.com, drama is defined thusly:

Drama – Any harsh negative actions directed from a woman to man where the man is the target of said negativity. Screaming, nagging, complaining, arguing, demands, crying "at you," threats, ultimatums, the "silent treatment," refusing sex for nonmedical reasons – all of these things are drama, and there are many others. Drama is not "anything negative." Specifically, it must be harsh (sweetly lying would not be considered drama) and focused on the man (angrily complaining about her boss at work would not be considered drama). Drama is a female trait. (Men have Guy-Drama, which is different.)

You may notice that my definition may differ from your definition of "relationship drama," or perhaps the typical, societal definition of that term. Many people, men and women both, view drama in a relationship as "anything bad." She lied to me; that's drama. He burps loudly while he talks to me; that's drama. She badmouthed me privately to one of her girlfriends; that's drama. He didn't park where

I told him to park; that's drama.

The problem with these definitions is that they hold human beings to impossible standards. This makes it impossible to achieve a consistent state of happiness in any marriage. Of course she's not always going to do what you tell her to do. Of course she'll sometimes lie to you. Of course sometimes she'll have a really bad day and be a little bitchy. She's a woman. Women do this stuff. So do men. Even nice, kind, low-key people can occasionally be dramatic, bitchy, irrational, or dishonest. It's part of the human condition and you're never going to change this.

Moreover, you can sometimes be upset, cold, demanding, or an asshole. We're all flawed human beings. If you then demand that a woman act perfectly all the time, you will never be happy. Where I differ strongly from most other people is that when I'm in a relationship with a woman, I *expect* her to be flawed because that's how human beings are, myself included. I expect her to be irrational, at least sometimes, because that's how women are. I fully expect she will, at certain times, say things that make no sense. I also expect her to get flustered or angry about things that have nothing to do with me and/or are completely outside of my control.

Moreover, and this is important, I expect some of this no matter how old, intelligent, classy, submissive, low-drama, or educated she is. As in all things, I am rational about my expectations and adapt my expectations to the real world, not a fairytale.

When I'm married to a woman (and again, that means I'm living with a woman full-time in a romantic context regardless of the sexual arrangement or the legal paperwork signed or not signed), this takes on an extra dimension. As I stated above, I know that we're going to disagree about things occasionally as cohabiting partners. I also know that some of the powerful techniques I use to successfully manage drama in FB, MLTR, and non-live-in OLTR relationships I discuss in my other books (such as soft nexting, freezeouts, etc.) are no longer valid once I move in with a woman.

Yet none of this changes the core definition of drama, as I stated above. Therefore, if I'm spending time with my wife, if she:

- Gets really upset about something that has nothing to do with me and tells me all about it

- Tells me a little white lie that I know isn't true but is not a big deal

- Angrily screams at someone on the phone (who is not me)

... then all these things are perfectly fine with me. They aren't drama as I define the term since there is no harsh negativity directed at me. It's just her exhibiting normal female behavior that I can't do much about, even if I scream at her with a bunch of my own Guy-Drama and command her to never do that again (which wouldn't work in the long term anyway).

For a behavior to be drama, it must be all three of these things:

1. Negative

2. Harsh

3. Directed at you

Drama must have all three; if it has just one or two of the three, it's a negative behavior she needs to work on (which we will discuss in Chapter 12), but it's not drama. Here are a few examples to make this clearer.

Situation: Your wife angrily bitches for 30 minutes at the dinner table about how much she hates her boss.

Is it drama? No. It's negative and it's harsh, but it's not directed at you.

It's directed at her boss.

Correct action: You listen quietly and nod, occasionally agreeing with her, and let her emote until she calms down.

Situation: While your wife is washing dishes, she cuts her finger and starts screaming her head off about how furious she is about that, and how much she hates dishes, and how horrible her day has been.

Is it drama? No. It's harsh negativity, but it's not directed at you.

Correct action: Ask her if she needs a bandage and agree with her about how her day really *has* been shitty.

Situation: While your wife is washing dishes, she cuts her finger and starts screaming her head off about how furious she is about that, then starts yelling at you about how you didn't text her this morning.

Is it drama? **Yes!** It's harsh, negative, and directed at you. *This* is a problem and needs to be nipped in the bud fast before it gets out of hand.

Correct action: The Drama Corrective Procedure described in Chapter 10.

Situation: While hanging out with you at your home, your wife receives a call from her mom, and a huge, angry argument ensues with her. She screams at the phone as she is sitting next to you on the couch.

Is it drama? No. It's not fun to listen to, but it's not directed at you. Let her scream at her mom all she wants. That's her problem, not yours.

Correct action: Sit for a minute or two and chill, nodding in agreement when your wife says something, and if the argument keeps going, quietly leave the room and let your wife keep screaming if she wants.

Situation: Your wife implies (or flat-out says) that one of your FBs is a "dumb slut."

Is it drama? No. It's certainly not cool but it's not directed at you. She can think whatever she wants about your FBs. That's completely irrelevant to you, your wife, and your FBs.

Correct action: Shrug and say something like "Eh," then change the subject.

Situation: Your wife sees a text hit your phone from one of your FBs. She immediately gets uptight and starts pelting you with questions about her. As you answer them, she starts angrily bitching at you about how she thinks that FB is a "dumb slut" and that it really pisses her off that you "see someone like that."

Is it drama? **Yes!** It's harsh, negative, and directed at you. It's also Betaization, making it a double whammy of bad.

Correct action: The Drama Corrective Procedure described in Chapter 10.

Situation: Your wife is upset with you regarding an argument you had yesterday and gives you the "silent treatment." She refuses to talk to you or answer any of your questions, or if she does, it's in cold, one or two-word answers.

Is it drama? **Yes!** It's negative, clearly directed at you, and it's harsh. No, it's not "harsh" in the traditional sense in that she's screaming at you or calling you an asshole, but it's still harsh in that she's shut down communication with you because she's upset with you. The silent treatment is *classic* passive-aggressive behavior. Therefore, it's drama. Many married men seem to think that is the silent treatment perfectly fine. Some even use it as a technique against their wives. Wrong. The silent treatment will damage your marriage just as certainly as a screaming argument will. Make no mistake: **the silent treatment is just another form of drama and thus unacceptable.**

Correct action: The Drama Corrective Procedure described in Chapter 10.

Situation: Your wife is steaming, quiet, and clearly upset. When you ask her what's wrong, she screams, "Nothing's wrong! Everything's FINE!!!"

Is it drama? Yes! It's negative, harsh, and directed at you. This is childish woman-theatrics and it's definitely drama. Granted, it may be very brief drama; perhaps when you ask her a second time, she calms down and tells you what's wrong in a normal tone of voice. Or she escalates the drama and gets worse. Drama is drama, regardless of how long or quickly it lasts.

Correct action: The Drama Corrective Procedure described in Chapter 10.

Situation: Your wife comes to you in a quiet tone of voice and says, "Hey Joe, the other day when you said my sister was a bitch, that really bothered me and hurt my feelings. Could you not say things like that?"

Is it drama? *Absolutely not.* It's negative and it's directed at you, but it's not harsh. She's keeping a calm tone, isn't yelling, isn't crying, is not visibly upset, and isn't threatening you or insulting you. Not only is it not drama, your wife is doing a fantastic job at keeping her cool. This is exactly how you want her to behave if she disagrees with something you've said or done. *Remember, disagreements handled like a mature adult are not drama; harsh attacks thrown at you are.*

Correct action: If you really did say those things, sincerely apologize to her.

That last scenario is important. If a woman comes to you in a quiet tone of voice to bring a problem with you or the relationship to your attention and does so without insulting, threatening, crying, or raising her voice, that is not drama and is perfectly fine. Your wife should know with absolute certainty that she can come to you with any problems she likes as long as she keeps a normal tone of voice and doesn't threaten, insult, yell, or cry. When she presents a complaint to you in a normal tone like this, she's trying to solve a problem with you, not give you drama. That's perfectly okay.

There's a limit to this, of course. If she's complaining about something you're doing, that's still a negative behavior even if it isn't drama. It's possible it's Betaization too. If she's nicely complaining about your behavior all the damn time, you've got a relatively serious problem in your marriage. Therefore, I'm not saying negative behavior is acceptable if it happens all the time. I'm saying that non-drama negative behavior is acceptable as long as it doesn't occur too often. Actual drama is *never* acceptable.

The Reason for Drama Is Always Irrelevant

Because you will allow your wife to bring problems in the relationship to you whenever she wants as long as she does it like a calm adult, this means that *whenever she gives you drama, the reason for the drama is always irrelevant.* This is a critical point that many people have a hard time understanding.

Many times, women will justify their drama because of their reasoning behind it. Most women are under the impression that if you do anything they don't like, they have the "right" to throw drama at you. You will often hear statements from women like,

"Yes! Yes! I AM screaming at you! I'm screaming at you because you..."

"Well, I called you an asshole the other day because you..."

"I gave you the silent treatment because you..."

No! **The reason for the drama is irrelevant**. Disagreements are fine, but drama is *never* justified. If she has a problem with you, she can bring it to your attention without screaming or insults. Therefore, if she is screaming at you, it doesn't matter why she's doing it; it's unacceptable and you will have to take corrective action immediately. As soon as she starts raising her voice (or insulting you, or threatening you, or whatever), she instantly loses the moral high ground, and now the reason for her anger is null and void.

Sometimes men will ask me, "What if she gives you drama, but she's right? What if she has a point?" If she's screaming at you, it doesn't matter. The reason, at that point, is irrelevant. *Every woman in the world who is not mentally insane has the ability to take a few deep breaths and calm down before she opens her mouth.* If she's giving you drama, she has *chosen* not to do this. She has made a choice. That choice is drama, and drama is unacceptable.

Chapter 10
HOW TO HANDLE DRAMA

In this chapter, I'll lay out a very specific system for how to handle drama whenever it occurs in your marriage. In the next chapter, we'll discuss how to minimize the possibility of drama starting in the first place, but in this chapter, I'll show you how to deal with it if it occurs despite your best efforts.

When It Really Is Your Fault

Before we get into how to deal with drama when it's not directly your fault, first we have to cover the scenarios when it is. It's very rare to see a marriage where 100% of the drama is 100% the wife's fault. You're human, and you're going to screw up in your marriage, probably a lot.

Let's say a woman complains to you about something you did in a non-drama way. This is not drama, so it's perfectly okay if she does this. How do you respond?

First, I'll reiterate that if she's complaining about something you did and she's yelling at you about it, this is drama, so even if it's your fault, it doesn't matter. In that case, you'll have to take the corrective procedure I outline in the next section.

However, if she's coming to you in a calm, collaborative, adult-like tone, complaining about something you did, there are only three valid responses to this:

1. If she's wrong and you didn't actually do what she's saying you did, correct her. Be nice and calm but show her that you didn't do it without getting defensive. Show her proof if you can.

This scenario is rare, since usually if a woman is complaining that you did something, you probably did it (though mix-ups can occur sometimes).

2. If you did it, and it was clearly something that wasn't very nice, then

man up and *apologize*. Be sincere. Tell her that you'll *try* not to do it again.

Never tell a woman that you'll "never do it again" because we're flawed creatures, and keeping a promise to literally "never" do something wrong is difficult, particularly if it's a habit you've had for a long time. For example, I'm an extremely outcome-independent smart ass with very little filter, so I have a long-standing habit of being very blunt and saying whatever I think. Sometimes, I go too far with this and might hurt Pink Firefly's feelings. When this happens, I sincerely apologize and instead of saying that "I'll never do it again" (because I honestly may not be able to keep that promise), I tell her, sincerely, that I'll be more aware of my actions and more careful about it in the future (and I usually am). That's all one can expect. If you're clearly sincere, she'll accept your apology.

Do *not* get into a conversation about it. Admit you were wrong, apologize, and *move on*. Negative extended conversations like this can too easily become drama. *Once you've admitted you've done something wrong and you've sincerely apologized for it, there is no need for further discussion on the matter.*

3. If you did it and *it wasn't* anything unkind or rude, just something she didn't happen to like, then she is likely attempting Betaization. Your job, as always, is to maintain your Betaization Wall. This means you need to clearly state that's the way you are, you do that a lot, and you'll never change. It's her job to accept it (not *like* it, just *accept* it). She won't like it when you say that, but you have just passed her "shit test" with flying colors, maintained your Betaization Wall, and maintained or even boosted Attraction. A total win... even if she looks a little frustrated for a few minutes (which she probably will).

If you are unable to say that to your wife, **you have Oneitis**. It means big problems are coming to your marriage soon (if not already). I have indeed said things like this to Pink Firefly (and other women I was dating before her), and I meant it 100%. (Of course, a *few* adjustments in your behavior need to be made when you live with a woman, but we've already discussed those in prior chapters.)

The Drama Corrective Procedure

Here is the step-by-step procedure you need to follow whenever you encounter drama from your wife. Unfortunately, we married guys don't have some of the more effective drama management tools available to us like soft nexting (since you can't soft next someone you live with full time). Instead, we have to rely on property structuring our OLTR Marriages to minimize the possibility of drama occurring in the first place and a specific procedure that is most likely to diffuse drama as fast as possible.

I call this the Drama Corrective Procedure. It's a combination of martial communication tools created by multiple marriage experts and therapists I've read and spoken to combined with my own Alpha Male 2.0, OLTR Marriage aspects. It's been approved by several marriage therapists I've had review it. While no procedure works every time (let's face it, all bets are off when there's an angry wife standing in front of you), it will work the best (or least badly) of any other procedure I've ever seen.

You initiate this procedure as soon as your wife gives you any form of drama. Again, drama is harsh negativity directed at you, per the definitions and examples in the prior chapter. You do *not* execute this procedure when you both have a simple disagreement and neither of you is agitated. That's not drama.

It's important that your wife buys into this procedure before you ever execute it. You need to go through this procedure with her first, before any arguments occur. Just verbally summarize it to her; she doesn't actually have to read it unless you really want her to since my verbiage and tone is targeted toward a male audience, and being a woman, she may not appreciate it. If you need to discuss this with your wife in the presence of your marriage counselor, that's okay too. Just make sure your wife agrees that this is the system you will both use when there is drama (or even a very strong disagreement). You can't just "spring" the Drama Corrective Procedure on your wife when she has no idea what you're doing. Instead, she must be ready for it, and she must have stated verbally that she agrees to it in advance. That way, it has power.

Here is the Drama Corrective Procedure:

Step 1: Immediately self-correct and/or apologize *if it's applicable.*

If there was a direct cause-and-effect relationship between why she's giving you drama and something you just did *and* what you just did is one of the following:

A) Something clearly rude

B) Something you've promised in the past to not do

C) Something you knew in advance would have pissed her off, but you forgot or got lazy

…then immediately apologize for what you did. It could be something as simple as saying in a sincere tone of voice, "Ack! Sorry! I shouldn't have said that." Often that alone can immediately stop the drama from progressing.

It's important you actually state this as sincerely as you can. Women are far more perceptive and intuitive than men, so she will be able to quickly ascertain if you're saying this just to placate her. She'll pick up on things like your tone of voice and facial cues if you're doing this as a "technique." This will actually make the drama worse, so be sincere.

If she immediately calms down, great. Mission accomplished. If she doesn't calm down or if the drama has nothing to do with anything you did or said (sadly, this will be the case sometimes), then continue on to step two.

Step 2: Immediately remind yourself that your goal is to win the *war,* not the *battle.*

As soon as they're verbally attacked, men's bodies and brains go into a mild but immediate form of fight or flight mode. When your wife starts screaming at you, insulting you, threatening you, snapping at you, or any other form of drama, your entire body is going want to *fight back*. "Fight back," in this context, means to defend yourself, show her she's wrong, and/or tell her to calm down and shut up. That's the *battle*.

Because of all this, you must stop, pause, take a mental beat, and remind yourself that the battle doesn't matter. You're here to win the *war*, meaning maintain a long-term happy marriage. The battle doesn't mean anything. Likely, in three days (or less), whatever she's upset about won't matter to either of you. But the *war* has a huge and sweeping influence on your entire life, positive or negative.

Stop for just a split second and think to yourself, "Everything is okay. I don't need to win this. It doesn't matter to me. I'm here to win the war, not this battle. I'm here to have a fantastic, long-term marriage. That's it."

Step 3: Listen and Repeat

Next, you need to make it very clear to her that you're listening to her. One of the biggest causes of big arguments with married couples is that *the wife doesn't feel like the husband is listening to her or understanding her.* Therefore, you need to make it blatantly obvious to her that you are hearing everything she's saying and understanding what she means. Of course, you really *do* need to understand what she's saying, but even if you think you understand her 100%, she needs to know this with absolute certainty.

Here's what you say: "I heard you say...." then repeat what she said. Then say, "Is that right?" It's extraordinarily important to *keep your voice very calm* while saying this. This is doubly important if she is raising her voice. If you aren't paying attention, you'll mirror her and raise your voice also, which will cause her to raise her voice even more, and now you're arguing. Stupid. On the flip side, if she's raising her voice and you're speaking very calmly and quietly (but strongly and clearly), it is more likely to demonstrate to her that *she's* being the crazy one and that she should probably drop her volume a little so she won't look insane. Most modern-day women are sensitive to looking crazy or hysterical since they know that's the stereotype men have about women. Use this to your advantage by staying calm and acting like the adult.

She will answer you either by saying no, you didn't hear her correctly, or yes, you got it right. If she says no, ask her to explain what she means so you can get it. Play dumb if you need to but listen carefully. Then say it again, "Okay. I heard you say... Is that right?"

If she says yes, then nod your head thoughtfully and say, "Okay, got it. That makes sense. Is there more?" If she's only mildly irritated, she'll probably say there is no more or simply repeat what she already said. If that's the case, proceed to the next step. If she's angrier, she may keep bitching about something else. That's fine. Keep repeating the "I heard you say... Is that right?" question on everything she says until she either says she has no more or keeps repeating what she already said. Then go to the next step.

Step 4: Validate

Next, you need to validate what she just said. *Validating is not agreeing.* Validating means that you understand why *she* would think that from *her* perspective. It doesn't matter how crazy her perspective is, it's still valid *to her*. If a mentally insane person sees a monster that isn't there leap out of a wall and attack him, and he yelps and runs away, you have to agree that's a valid response *to him*. Right? Therefore, so you can validate something without agreeing with it at all. This means your wife could say the most irrational, insane shit you've ever heard, but you can still validate it.

Here's what you say: "I can understand that." You could also say, "That makes sense to me because..." and keep the rest *very* short. "I can understand that," is usually safer.

Step 5: Empathize

Next, you need to empathize. This is going to be hard if you're a more masculine or analytical guy (like me), but I've made it very easy for you. All you need to say is, "Tell me how that makes you feel." Then listen for the answer. Let her have her say and don't interrupt her, *even if she makes no sense* and *even if you 100% disagree with her*. Your goal right now is not to argue. It's to diffuse the drama.

Once she's done, say something like, "I'm sorry I may have done something inadvertently to make you feel that way; that was not my intention." As always, use your own words to say that if that doesn't sound like you.

Even if you feel it wasn't your fault (and it may actually not be your fault), you need to make it clear that perhaps you did something or said something that may have triggered a negative reaction. Remember, validation and empathy don't mean you agree with her. It just shows that you are listening to her and taking her feelings into account. Women are all about feelings!

Step 6: Take Her Temperature and Continue or Terminate

Now that you've done literally everything a woman wants a husband to do when she's upset (you've listened, verified you understand, validated her feelings and empathized with her), you need to "take her temperature" and see if she's calmed down and returned to a state where the drama is over. If she has, and if she is no longer raising her voice, insulting you, threatening you, or exhibiting any other type of drama, you may continue the conversation and do your best to resolve the problem as quickly as you can, if that's required (and maybe it isn't; you might be able to just stop the conversation right there).

As quickly as you can is the goal here. Don't sit there and complain about how you feel or throw orders at her. Keep your tone calm, quiet, rational, and stick with the facts. Get to the solution as fast as you can so you can end the conversation and return to harmony as fast as possible.

It's also possible that listening, verifying, validating, and empathizing didn't work and she is *still* giving you drama and is *still* in an irrational state. You can tell she's still in an irrational state if she's still doing any of the following:

- Raising her voice (yelling or screaming)
- Saying things that literally make no sense
- Repeating herself over and over again
- Insulting you in any way
- Snapping at you
- Threatening you or the marriage in any way

- "Non-sad crying" (this is when a woman is crying for any reason *other* than sadness, like when she's crying because she's angry, frustrated, exhausted, or trying to manipulate you)

If she's still doing any of this crap at this point, it's time to *temporarily* end the conversation. Continuing to talk to her while she's like this is just going to create more drama and anger, waste both of your time, and damage the marriage. Instead, you need to end things right now and give her (and you!) 24 to 48 hours to cool off. Then you can both resume the conversation as rational adults instead of irrational children.

Say, "I understand how you feel. Right now, we're not in any condition to keep talking about this. I'm going to end the conversation now, but I want to resolve this. Let's talk about this again at…" then give her *a very specific time* in the next 24 to 48 hours. For example, "Let's talk about this again tomorrow right after dinner." Or, "Let's talk about this on Saturday morning after I work out, around 10:00 a.m."

You say, "*We're* not in any condition," because if you say, You*'re* not in any condition," you'll just set her off even more.

You say, "I want to resolve this" because if you say you want to end the conversation without that, she'll accuse you of not wanting to resolve the problem.

You give her a specific time to resume the conversation because she's going to *hate* the fact that you're ending the conversation when she's not done yelling at you, uh, I mean, expressing her concerns. She's *got* to know that you really are going to circle back at some point in the next day or two to address her disagreements. That's why you need to provide a specific time – so she knows you're not just blowing her off.

Step 7: Leave the Room

End the conversation immediately. There's no more discussing it right now, no matter what she says or tries.

If she's in a cool mood at this point, just change the subject and talk about something else. If she's still heated and upset, physically leave the room and go do something else. If she asks where you're going or why you're leaving, just state that you'd rather not spend time with her while she's like this and keep walking. *Don't talk any more. Just get the hell out of there.* This is hard for a lot of men since most men will want to keep responding to her attacks and defending themselves in order to win the battle. You must exert self-control here; *shut up* and *leave*.

Common Questions Regarding the Drama Corrective Procedure

What if, when you leave, she physically follows you and keeps trying to argue with you? This often means you've done the procedure incorrectly or have skipped over one or more of the steps. (You kept talking too much, you raised your voice, you didn't validate or empathize, etc.) That's your fault. Do better next time.

If you've actually done everything in the procedure perfectly and she still does this, then we have a serious problem. You're being a good guy about all of this and she's not following through on the procedure she agreed to follow. Make the best of it, leave the house if it gets really bad, and make a note (written if you have to) regarding when this occurred and what she did, and bring it up next time you see the marriage counselor.

If she keeps doing this as a pattern of behavior, despite repeated counselor visits, then we have a Catastrophic Problem. I'll talk about that in the next section.

What if you're out at dinner or in the car and can't leave? If you're at dinner, wrap it up as fast as possible. Bag the food, get the check, go home, and stay away from her for the rest of the evening (or until she calms back down). If it's in the car, just stop talking. Likely she'll stop talking too, which is good. Turn on the radio and just stay quiet until you both get home.

I follow the procedure, but at the end, she just changes the subject to something else she's upset about and talks about that. What do you do then? Yes, this is a common behavior some women do when they're upset. When they're in an agitated state, they pull up all the stuff they're pissed off about from their "frustration database" and throw it at you.

If she's doing this in an irrational way, then when you take her temperature in step six, you can terminate the conversation in step seven. Once she's irrational, the conversation is over and you must end it. If she then says, "Wait, I want to talk about X now!" you just keep on walking out of the room, perhaps with that one statement of how you don't want to talk to her when she's like this.

If she's constantly changing the negative subject *and* doing this in a calm and rational way (which is extremely unlikely), then just tell her something like, "Sweetie, I'm honestly a little overwhelmed. We've already talked about <problem 1> and <problem 2>. Let's talk about <problem 3> on Sunday. I'm out of energy on this." Then terminate the conversation per step seven.

What if she gets physically violent? That's a Catastrophic Problem. We'll address those in a minute.

What if she threatens divorce when I leave the conversation? Let her threaten whatever she wants. Stay strong and leave anyway. Just say, "Okay, I understand," as you're walking out of the room, and *keep walking*. When people (and women in particular) are angry, they threaten all kinds of things they don't mean. If any threats really become a concern, take them up at the next counselor visit.

Catastrophic Problems

Most problems in a marriage can be fixed with a conversation or two, with or without the marriage counselor. However, some rare problems are so serious that a simple conversation or two won't fix it or are so egregious that having a conversation isn't even relevant because of the damage already done. This type of thing is a Catastrophic Problem. A Catastrophic Problem is a problem that actually threatens the marriage all by itself. It makes getting an immediate divorce a valid option. It may not *require* getting a divorce, or it might, deepening on the specific scenario.

Catastrophic Problems are rare in properly managed OLTR Marriages, especially if you do everything this book recommends. Yet, they are still possible no matter what you do. You and your wife are human beings and are thus imperfect and subject to change. Moreover, you and your wife might be great right now, but 20 years from now, one or both of you could change for the worse.

A Catastrophic Problem can be caused by you or your wife. For the rest of this section, I'm going to assume none of these types of problems will be caused by you, since I'm going to assume you're a normal, clear-thinking person who knows that doing things such as physically assaulting your wife, impregnating her sister, and robbing banks are things you should never do for any reason, and that any normal man would expect his wife to divorce his ass as soon as he did any of these things. Obviously, if you are engaged in horrible behaviors like any of this, you've got serious problems that are outside the scope of this book.

That all being said, examples of Catastrophic Problems include, but are not limited to, when your wife does the following:

- Physical violence against you
- Physical violence against your children if you have any
- Knowingly putting your children in direct harm or probable harm
- Committing crimes, especially violent ones
- Drama as a pattern of behavior (she does it over and over again despite your repeated efforts of working with the marriage counselor and use of the Drama Corrective Procedure)
- Falling in love with another man (which means she knowingly violated OLTR Marriage rules)
- Getting pregnant by another man
- Addiction to hard drugs or alcoholism
- Ongoing and severe mental issues that are not being resolved or improved (these can range from extreme bi-polar behavior to gambling addiction and everything in-between)
- Stealing (or otherwise using or wasting) large amounts of your money without your prior permission

In most cases, if you encounter a Catastrophic Problem from your wife, you need to get a divorce. (I would say the same thing to your wife if she encountered a Catastrophic Problem from you). Remember that the legal aspect of a divorce in an OLTR Marriage is a pretty simple procedure that often takes 30 days or less in most jurisdictions.

If you decide not to get divorced, then at a bare minimum, you must set a hard deadline for improvement. This is an **actual date on the calendar** where you need to see the problem either vanish or improve massively; otherwise you will *immediately* initiate a divorce on that date with no more second chances. Be sure to inform your marriage counselor of the date as well so it's "on the record," and your wife can't later say you changed the date or lied about it if/when the divorce actually occurs.

Remember, if you don't have the balls to divorce your wife if and when it needs to happen, you have Oneitis, and that's a severe problem you need to work on. I walk my talk; even when I was a beta male when my first wife became violent with me, I moved out of the house within 48 hours and initiated divorce procedures. It was scary and painful, but I did it. And I would have no hesitation to do it again with Pink Firefly if it was ever needed (not that I anticipate it would be; if PF and I got divorced, it's very unlikely it would be due to a Catastrophic Problem).

Hopefully, you'll never encounter a Catastrophic Problem in your marriage. Lots of men don't (they can still get divorced, but the divorce is amicable; sometimes the ex-wife just becomes an FB!). But if you do have one, you need to have the balls to take the correct action.

Chapter 11
HOW TO MINIMIZE DRAMA

The absolute best way to handle drama in your marriage is by minimizing the odds of it ever happening in the first place. We've already talked about many ways in which to do this (keeping Attraction high, using Zones, maintaining the Betaization Wall, etc.). In this chapter, I'll get into specific techniques you need to employ on a regular basis to ensure that you rarely have any drama. They are all equally important and you need to do all of them.

Don't Use Guy Logic

In my writings, I refer to a concept called "guy logic." It's a technique men employ when arguing or disagreeing with women that virtually never works. Guy logic works great when talking to other men, but your wife doesn't give a shit about logic from her Big Dumb Husband. Your logic will just irritate her, even if you're right (and, in some cases, *especially* if you're right).

The problem is that most men have a strong need to get our wives to understand logical concepts and to repeat them back to us to demonstrate to us that they understand our wonderful, intelligent, rational guy logic. The problem is when a woman is upset, emotional, scared, or nervous, she doesn't have the ability to do this. Therefore, you must combat *your own need for her to understand your guy logic*. You must just calm down, relax, be outcome independent, and let her be irrational. Maybe later you can explain your guy logic if you really want to (though you shouldn't want to, nor need to), but certainly not while she's agitated.

Be Outcome Independent!

This is huge. If you really get this and integrate this into your mindsets, it will have a positive effect on everything else in this book and in your marriage.

You must stop giving a shit about stuff. If you're a highly anal-retentive, picky guy regarding many details in life, it's going to be very hard for you to have a low-drama marriage. Frankly, guys on the extreme end of that spectrum should just live alone.

Having a disagreement with your wife on a major life issue is one thing, but most arguments between married couples are over stupid, little things that won't matter to either person just a few days later. If you don't care at all these little things, you'll never have these arguments. It's that simple. Honestly, one of the biggest reasons I have such little drama with Pink Firefly is that I don't give a shit regarding just about everything. I'm serious. I care a lot about the big picture items, but those are within my Zones, so I don't need to worry about them. Everything else? The color of the curtains in the living room? Where Pink Firefly goes this afternoon? What my mom and PF talk about when they talk on the phone (even if they talk about me)? I just don't care. I'm too focused on the important things: my work, fitness, and Mission.

Stop giving a shit about all the details. Calm the hell down. Relax your ego. Let your wife be in charge of all the little stuff, even if she's a Submissive. If you have a disagreement over a detail in your life, particularly if it's not in one of your Zones, just let her have her way with it. You have more important things to concern yourself with, or at least I hope you do.

My theory, and so far it's worked, is that if I let PF get her way on most of the details (which I don't give a shit about anyway), I have much more ammo when I refuse to move my Betaization Wall. If instead I fight her (and win) regarding a lot of these details, she's going to be even more upset and less flexible when I refuse to move my Betaization Wall regarding the big things.

Details are part of the battle and you're here to win the war. Calm down and let her win those stupid battles. Speaking of which…

Always Focus on the War, Not the Battle

One day a while back, PF had a really bad day at work. Since she's a woman and thus not outcome independent like I am, she was absolutely furious about it and bitched about it for a long time. Since it wasn't drama, I patiently listened. A full 75 minutes later, she was still ranting. It was getting late and I needed to get ready for bed, so I finally said, "Hey, I don't want to interrupt you, so keep going, but just so you know, I need to go get ready for bed in about five minutes."

Since she was already agitated about the work stuff she was complaining about, she immediately got upset. She angrily snapped at me and left the room (which is *good*; this is what I *want* her to do when she's mad – *leave*). I shrugged, smiled, and went downstairs to my Zone to get ready for bed.

The next day, she was still a little mad about it and mentioned it. My masculine need for guy logic wanted me to immediately attack, to set her straight and logically explain to her that I listened to her in a very supportive manner for 80 fucking minutes… and she really has the gall to be mad at me about *that? How stupid!* Not only did I have my need for guy logic, but I wanted transactional fairness (which you should never expect from a wife), and I wanted to win the battle (which is the wrong focus).

Instead of doing that, I practiced what I preach. I walked up to her and said, "I'm sorry. I know you had a really bad day yesterday. I love you." Then I gave her a big hug. She smiled and hugged me back, and that was it, no more drama. I forgot about the battle and continued to win the war.

Had I acted like any other husband and followed my default masculine tendencies, we would have screamed at each other for a good hour. (I know, because that's what I did in my first marriage and that's exactly what usually happened.) I would have won the battle, but damaged (or even lost) the war.

You might think that doing what I did above was a pussy or beta male move. Taken in complete isolation outside of the context of my OLTR Marriage, it was. But as a single piece of a much larger OLTR Marriage puzzle, it was the smartest thing I could do. I was a nice guy while keeping my Betaization Wall rock-solid and intact. I'm one of the most Alpha Male married men you'll probably ever meet. The very next day after this event, I had sex with a model-gorgeous 19-year-old for almost an hour, and today I'm still very happily married to Pink Firefly.

Forgetting about the *battles* and focusing on the *war* really works. I know it's hard to do, but do it. You'll see what a difference it makes.

Behavior Is Trained

Behavior is *trained*. This is neuroscience. When you argue with her a lot, you train her to argue with you more often. On the other hand, when you notice when she does something you like and slather her with compliments or gifts when this happens, you train her to do more of that.

Therefore, *notice* whenever she does something you really like and apply her number-one love language to her when she does it.

For example, when many weeks go by with zero drama (and I know this objectively because I track this every day as I talked about back in Chapter 6), I will reward Pink Firefly with a special dinner out of the blue or buy her favorite flowers. I will tell her why I'm doing it too, something like, "You have been so nice and so wonderful lately. I wanted to give you a surprise."

Never Expect Logic from An Angry Woman (or an angry man, for that matter)

One of the biggest mistakes men make is when their wives (or girlfriends) are really angry and say insane things, the men take these things at face value. They will be surprised when such an intelligent woman could say such stupid or nonsensical things. Worse, they actually will attempt to respond to these things as if they are valid (in an effort to win the battle).

Neuroscience again. When you get really mad, higher brain functions actually shut down. You get stupid and irrational. You stay stupid, insane shit. (This is one of the many reasons why you shouldn't ever get really mad in the first place. I never do.) This applies to men and women, including you, and including your wife.

Therefore, whenever your wife is really mad (hopefully a very rare occurrence), and she says insane things, just treat it as if she drunk. Yes,

I'm serious. Just say to yourself, "She's drunk, she doesn't know what she's doing/saying." Don't take anything she says seriously until the next day when she calms down and gets back to normal.

It should go without saying that you shouldn't verbalize any of this. Just remind yourself of it mentally. For goodness sake, don't ever say something to your angry wife like, "Oh, you're just mad right now and you're not thinking straight, so I'm sure you don't mean that." You're in for nuclear explosions if you're dumb enough to say something like that. Just follow the Drama Corrective Procedure in the prior chapter.

Don't Discuss Contentious Topics

Some couples can discuss highly sensitive, contentious topics with both keeping their cool. Other couples can't do this and get heated when these topics are brought up. Still other couples can discuss just everything and be fine except for one or two key areas where tensions may flare.

You need to figure out which category you and your wife are in. Pink Firefly and I are in the third category. We can talk about pretty much everything, and even if we completely disagree, we're both okay. However, religion is a hot-button issue for her. She's a practicing Christian and I'm an agnostic bordering on atheism (though not quite all the way there). If we ever discuss our religious differences, she can get agitated, quickly turning the disagreement into drama. Therefore, a year ago, we made a mutual agreement that we won't discuss religion with each other. It's just not worth the drama. (And once again, I don't care about this topic anyway, so this is by no means any sort of compromise for me.)

You must understand exactly which topics set off your wife (or set *you* off, but ideally, you shouldn't have any of these as an outcome-independent Alpha Male 2.0) and then make a pact with your wife to never discuss them. Examples of these topics can be religion, politics, certain family members, certain people you both know, certain events in the past, and so on.

Use Strategic Avoidance

There will times when your wife is in certain emotional or physical

134 | *How to Minimize Drama*

states where drama is more likely. You need to be aware of these states and stay away from her (or at least spend less time with her) when she's in these states. These states include:

- When she's angry (regardless of if she's angry about you or something else)
- When she's agitated or irritable (for any reason)
- When she's sick
- When she's in physical pain or severe physical discomfort (headaches, infections, bad PMS, etc.)

Strategic Avoidance means that whenever your wife is in these states, you do your best to stay away. Be busy. Go do something else. If you're both home together, spend your time in another part of the house. Even better, go out to appointments. You get the idea.

You also must avoid and even perhaps cancel any logistical scenarios where you'll be stuck with her for a prolonged period of time while she's in one of these precarious states. If she has a pounding headache and she's furious at something her best friend just did, then dude, this is *not* the day to take a three-hour drive with her to the beach. You're essentially *asking* for major drama. Cancel it and reschedule it for another day. Just tell her that she's clearly not feeling well and you'd probably both rather have a day together when she's feeling good so you can both enjoy it. No, she won't like that at all, but hearing her complain for two or three minutes that you rescheduled the beach trip is going to be far better than having massive drama for hours on end in a car where you can't escape.

Doing this kind of thing takes balls, but it's worth it. Also, make sure that when you practice Strategic Avoidance that you are very nice about it. Be kind and understanding, but do it.

Read Between the Lines

Often, if not usually, what she says she's upset about, arguing about, or complaining about is not what's actually making her upset. For example, her best friend said something really rude and hurtful to her that morning. It infuriates her and ruins her entire day. Two hours later, not knowing any of this has happened, you make a quick joke about the omelet she made. She absolutely loses it, starts screaming and ranting about what an asshole you are, and wants to argue about that for the next 30 minutes. Maybe you shouldn't have made that joke, but her arguing about you actually has nothing to do with you. It's about what her friend did.

Another example I've heard from men is that she may be complaining about non-monogamy or your FBs in general, when in fact, she's actually upset about one particular FB you're seeing for some specific reason because she thinks that particular FB is prettier or skinnier than she is. She doesn't say this, though; she instead bitches about you "fucking *all* of your FBs all the time."

Never assume she's upset about what she says she is. If she's able to keep her cool, probe a little bit and try to uncover the real reason she's upset. She might really be upset about what she's saying, but often it will actually be something else. Many men take their wives' word for it and waste a lot of time trying to fix problems that really aren't the problem.

Plan Difficult Discussions in Advance

When you need to bring up a topic that you know will result in strong disagreement (or even drama) from your wife, plan it out in advance. Do it on a day when she's not upset about anything else and feeling good. If that day comes and something else happens in her life that upsets her, defer that discussion to another day.

Also, **never, ever** start any difficult discussion when you can't logistically leave, like while having dinner with her at a restaurant, driving with her in the car, or on a trip in a hotel. (We've all been guilty of screwing that one up, haven't we?) Wait until you're both home.

Diverting Drama

You can't tell a woman to never have drama. That's impossible. Women must engage in some drama occasionally; they're women. Even very happy, low-drama women have bad days where they need to bitch at someone. The good news is that you can train the women in your life to divert their drama away from you and direct it toward someone else.

Numerous times in my relationships over the years, a woman I'll be dating will suddenly get upset with me, and instantly turn around, leave the room, call someone on her phone, and scream at them. As humorous as this sounds, I think this is great. Every time it happens, I smile and get back to work, since that's exactly what women should do. Screaming at someone else on the phone over on the other side of the house is not negativity directed at me (even if it's *about* me); thus, it's not drama. Moreover, it gives the woman an outlet for her drama. Win-win.

When I was a kid, I used to create little rivers in my huge sandbox. I would carve out a trench, give it a little angle, then turn on the garden hose that was laying on the high end. The water would flow through the trench and I'd watch the little river I had created. Then I would dig another trench attached to the first one and watch as the water was diverted from the main river to my new secondary river. This was a lot of fun for me when I was little, and I used to do this kind of thing for hours in the summertime.

Women's drama works the same way. It's an unyielding river that never ends. Some women have big rivers (obviously you shouldn't marry women like that), and some women have little trickles (*those* are the ones who qualify for OLTR Marriage). Through all the techniques in this book, you can reduce the size of this river, often substantially. Yet, you can never dry it up completely. Much of what remains, you can divert away from you, around you, and "aim" it toward other areas in her life.

Here are three ways you can do this. I have personally field-tested all of these techniques over many years with numerous women of various ages and personality types, including Pink Firefly, and I can tell you for a fact they all work.

1. Encourage her to call her friends or family members and yell at them whenever she's upset.

This is the best technique by far. If a woman is pissed, she needs to yell at *someone*. Why does that someone have to be you? It doesn't. Let her go scream her head off at one of her girlfriends, her mom, or her sister, who themselves are women and thus will enjoy the drama, gossip, and attention to some degree. Let those people take the brunt of the damage while you relax or work on your goals.

Women, especially women who are married or live with a man, are under the mistaken impression that their man is the default repository for any anger or frustration she has because she's in a bad mood, or is having her period, or had a bad day at work. Wrong! She needs to clearly understand that when she's upset for some irrational reason, the last person she has the right to scream at is her husband. Her girlfriends, guy friends, sisters, mother, friend zone guys, and co-workers should all be people she yells at *first*. Not you, her partner in life.

2. Completely ignore her if/when she says bad things about you to other people.

Outcome independence!

This is a tough one for men. I admit I had trouble with it in the beginning. Years ago, when I was first attempting non-monogamous relationships, occasionally I'd have women complain about me in a very public way on their social media. As you might imagine, I got a little upset. At one point, I even found myself getting needy and telling women to "not say bad things about me." However, I caught myself and realized how outcome dependent I was being. I made a pact with myself that I would never, ever tell a woman not to complain about me or badmouth me to other people. I would be completely outcome independent and not give a shit.

It worked. Soon, I didn't care. My drama went down, my happiness went up, and I felt better as a man.

Let your wife say whatever she wants about you to anyone she likes. Diverting her drama is not going to work if you freak out every time she bitches about you to one of her friends or family members. Hey, she's a *wife*. Occasionally complaining about the Big Dumb Husband is what wives do. You're never going to stop this, so just accept it. Get used to it, stop giving a shit, and ignore it. You'll live a much happier life. (Also remember that you'll get much less of this than the typical beta male husband, who gets it constantly, near all the time.)

Just remember I'm talking about badmouthing you *to other people*. If she badmouths you to *you*, that's drama, and now it's time for the Drama Corrective Procedure.

3. Strongly encourage her to spend lots of time with other women.

I have experienced overwhelming evidence that strongly suggests the following: *the amount of drama a woman gives you is inversely proportional to the amount of time she spends with female friends*. If a woman has "no friends" or is one of these women who dislikes other women and only has a bunch of guy friends, then at least in my experience, she is more likely to throw drama at you, *and* the more intense the drama will be.

However, if she spends a lot of time with female friends, this seems to allow her to vent her drama on her girlfriends like that hole on the top of a steaming teapot. By the time she gets around to spending time with you, she's already vented her frustrations and is less likely to give you drama.

As an Alpha Male 2.0, I never tell a woman what to do, including my wife. However, I always encourage the women in my life, especially my wife, to spend more time with other women in social settings.

The more time she spends with female friends, the better. Men who get upset when their wives spend "too much time with their girlfriends" are making a huge mistake. You *want* her spending time with her girlfriends, trust me! In my experience, women who spend a large amount of time with other female friends are the lowest-drama women out there (in terms of how much drama they give you, that is – their girlfriends get plenty of it).

Guy Drama

Obviously, one of the best ways to keep drama with women to a minimum is to not start any drama yourself. Men are not innocent victims when it comes to relationship drama. Often, they start it up themselves.

Men often have their own form of drama called Guy Drama. Per my glossary, this is the definition:

Guy Drama – A particular form of drama directed from a man to a woman. Unlike drama, which is feminine and takes many forms, Guy Drama takes the form of a lecture issued in order to correct behavior. "Setting her straight," "straightening her out," "laying down the law," commands to "respect" him, or issuing "rules" are all forms of guy-drama. Guy-drama is extremely ineffective at managing a relationship. It simply creates more drama, or at best, simply delays (instead of preventing) future drama.

Guy Drama is when men attempt to boss a woman around. It should be obvious by now that most of the techniques described in this book that are most conducive to long-term and low-drama non-monogamous marriages are based around *not* telling women what to do (through the use of things like Zones, outcome independence, and so on).

Guy Drama, as I stated in the definition, does not prevent drama; it simply *delays* drama. If you're a strong man and boss a woman around, she may follow your orders in the short-term, particularly in the initial phases of the marriage when things are still new and exciting. However, assuming she's a Western woman (or a non-Western woman living in the West), she will, guaranteed, soon start violating your orders and rules. You'll get upset at her, she'll get upset back at you, and congratulations, you're now in a normal marriage where drama is the norm.

This all comes back to our friend, outcome independence. If you're a more controlling, domineering guy (the Alpha Male 1.0), you'll have to learn to stop giving a shit and soften your approach with your wife. I strongly recommend you read *The Unchained Man** if you have not already, since that book shows you how to become a happy, outcome-independent Alpha Male 2.0 who never tells women what to do because he doesn't care (and has so many women!).

The Case Against Drama

Depending on your personality and the culture in which you were raised, you might be wondering why I'm focused so much on keeping

*http://www.alphamalebook.com

drama levels to an absolute minimum in a marriage. This is because, as I talked about in detail in *The Unchained Man**, the goal of life is consistent long-term happiness (as consistent as possible within the real world, of course). Unless you are an extreme sociopath, you can't experience relationship drama with a woman and be happy at the same time; it's literally impossible. Therefore, if you tolerate drama in your life (from anyone!), *you are less happy*. This violates the primary goal of life, at least in my opinion.

Moreover, as I said above, putting up with a woman's drama (or responding to it in kind) is a form of *attention* and thus trains her to keep doing it, even if it's negative attention. She craves your attention, so if you give it to her whenever she behaves poorly, this encourages her to give you more drama in the future.

In the normal world of needy, Societally Programmed people, "putting up" with drama from a woman you care about is considered a noble thing. When you put up with her regularly bitching or screaming at you, that means you really love each other. It means you're committed to her through thick and thin. You really care about her. To argue is to be human, and being human is a good thing, right? I mean, come on, if you're with someone for years and almost never fight, that means you're two boring robots! No one wants to be a robot!

I'm sure you've heard women say things like, "If you really love me, you'll put up with me being a bitch." Or that's what "a good husband does."

Often, men are just as bad. There are men who honestly believe that big, regular fights are healthy and good for "self-expression" in a relationship. You want her to yell at you when something is bothering

her; otherwise, she'll be repressing her emotions, and oh dear, we can't have that. And of course, everyone knows you are the only place she has to dump all her negativity. So yeah, it's much better for you to be her emotional trash can and constantly be a receptacle for all of the negative shit she's feeling in her life.

Moreover, other men will advise that, when she screams at you, you need to man up and scream back at her. Otherwise, you're a pussy! You're

*http://www.alphamalebook.com

not going to just take that, are you? Fuck no! You need to logically tell her that her behavior is unacceptable and she needs to shut the fuck up and calm down right now! That's what a real man does!

With these kinds of beliefs, is it any wonder why most people have regular drama in their relationships?

I'm going to give you the exact opposite of what you've been told your whole life. When you allow the woman in your life to give you drama, **you are hurting her**.

1. You are not helping her express her feelings. As a woman, she has many other ways of expressing feelings besides calling you an asshole or bitching about you getting a text from one of your FBs. She likely has many other people in her life she could be yelling at in order to express her negativity. It doesn't have to be you, nor should it.

2. You are not becoming more "human" together. If her dog dies and she cries in your arms, that's human. If she gets a new job, and you cheer and celebrate with her, that's human. But if she's had a bad day at work, then angrily screams at you about how you were eight minutes late picking up the pizza, that's not human. If she calls you an asshole because you didn't help her in the kitchen fast enough, that's not human. These things make both you and her *less* human; her behavior is pulling both of you down to our furry primate ancestors.

3. You are not building closeness. Being happy together builds closeness. Spending time together builds closeness. Overcoming *real problems* together can also build closeness. Her bitching at you because you forgot to close the garage door is not a *real problem* in this context. That kind of garbage does not build closeness; it instead builds a wall between you. It builds anger, jealousy, and resentment, regardless of her reasons, real or stated, for the drama she's giving you. It also compels you to start hiding things from her, which is the exact opposite of what you should be doing.

4. As I said above, drama trains her to give you more drama, not less. More drama won't bring you closer together. Indeed, the opposite is likely true (unless you're both dysfunctional drama addicts).

Chapter 12
THE SIX NEGATIVE BEHAVIORS AND THEIR CURES

Not everything bad in a marriage is drama. There are other problematic behaviors that don't fall into the drama category or don't quite rise to the level of full-on drama. While not as serious as drama, they are problems nonetheless, thus they should be avoided and managed. Otherwise, they will damage both Mutual Harmony and Freedom.

I call these problems the Negative Behaviors. There are six of them. Three are usually caused by the wife, and three are normally caused by the husband (though there can be exceptions to either).

It the job of both you and your wife to ensure these behaviors are whittled down to their absolute minimums. In some ways, reducing Negative Behaviors is even harder than reducing drama because the Negative Behaviors are deeply rooted in long-term habits and masculine/feminine psychology within both you and your wife. Drama is reasonably serious; thus men and women are usually both aware they probably need to avoid it, but the Negative Behaviors seem more normal, and in some cases, even helpful, meaning the pressure on you (and your wife) to address them is far less than actual drama.

We'll cover her Negative Behaviors first, then yours.

Her Negative Behavior #1: Snapping

As you already know, the definition of drama is *harsh* negativity directed at you. Snapping *quick* negativity directed at you. Unlike drama, it happens very fast, often just a few seconds, and then it's over.

When a woman snaps at you, she throws one or two quick, negative attacks your way and then quickly moves on. It's not an argument, nor is it drama, though it can certainly create these things. It's just a shitty little snipe.

Here are some examples of what snapping looks like:

Wow. You never fucking listen to me.

<yelling> Hope you had fun with your FB!

Maybe that would be a problem if you weren't so disorganized all the time.

There are thousands of examples I could give, but you get the point. She makes a quick attack and then moves on to other topics. (If she continues after the snap, then it's not snapping; it's drama.)

When your wife snaps at you, calmly make her aware of it by pointing out her behavior, then move on. An example would be, "You just snapped at me. I'd appreciate it if you didn't do that. Or, "You just snapped at me. It's not helpful." Make sure you state it in a calm tone of voice with a neutral expression on your face. Don't worry about whether or not she acknowledges or admits she just snapped at you; that isn't the point. The point is *to make her aware that she's doing it*. Most wives get into the habit of snapping at their Big Dumb Husbands simply because either the husband never calls it out *or* because the husband immediately counterattacks and creates a huge argument. Both of these approaches are silly. Instead, just make her aware of it, move on, and if it becomes a habit (track it if you need to), bring it up at the next meeting with the counselor.

Her Negative Behavior #2: Complaining

You know what complaining means. It's when your wife bitches and moans about something. It's not an attack; it's just a complaint.

I separate complaining into two distinct categories, both of which must be handled differently.

The first category is when your wife complains about something that has nothing to do with you. This is normal. Women process the world by talking. Complaining about everything is a core part of female psychology. As I've alluded to in prior chapters, you need to be cool with the fact that part of your "job" as a husband is to occasionally listen to her complain about the things that happen in her life that the dislikes. Moreover, as I explained back in Chapter 6, she will be the direct cause of many of these problems and she *won't want them fixed*. She just wants to talk about them and have you feel bad for her.

Therefore, there's nothing wrong with listening to your wife complain about things that have nothing to do with you occasionally. It's part of the deal. The only caveat to this is the word "occasionally." If your wife is complaining about things all the time, non-stop, every day, then obviously that's a problem. She needs to make some changes and probably needs to go see a therapist, counselor, or coach. (Remember, *you* can't fix these problems, nor does she want your help. Stop trying to fix it!)

If she refuses to change anything in her life but keeps complaining to you constantly, this is a serious problem, and you need to bring this up with her and your counselor. If there are *still* no changes, you'll have some difficult decisions to make. Your wife needing to complain about things is one thing. Your wife using you as a daily trash can for all of her never-ending negativity is unacceptable.

The second category of complaining is when she complains about *you* or *your actions*. Stronger women (Dominants and Independents) will usually complain clearly and directly; weaker or more passive women (Submissives) will usually complain indirectly, but it's still about you.

When your wife complains about you, this is a mild form of drama and needs to be handled using the Drama Corrective Procedure. If this complaining persists despite your best efforts, this is a serious problem that you need to bring up with the counselor.

Also, remember that you're going to get *some* complaints about you every once in a while because of your Betaization Wall. Her complaining that you're not becoming a beta male that her Betaization needs is not only normal but a strong indication that you're doing things correctly. Again, she can't complain about this stuff constantly or all the time, but hearing this stuff every once in a while is normal and natural.

Her Negative Behavior #3: Nagging

Oh boy. This is a tough one.

Nagging is when your wife verbally corrects you, reminds you regarding something obvious, or repeatedly urges you do something you already promised. Here are some examples:

- She reminds you to "remember to take out the trash tonight" for the second or third time in a row.

- You tell her you're going to call your sister regarding an upcoming holiday tonight around 9:00 p.m. and at 6:00 p.m. she asks you if you've called your sister yet.

- Any time she's being a "back-seat driver" when you drive and she's in the passenger seat. Examples would be when she asks, "Why are you parking *here?*" or when she complains you're driving too fast/too slow, or when she tells you to make sure to turn left at the next light when it's obvious you're looking right at Google Maps. Back-seat driving is a *huge* source of wife nagging in married couples.

- When you make an honest and blatant mistake and she points it out to you (like you didn't already know), especially when she brings up that mistake more than once.

Of all the negative feminine behaviors in this book, nagging is the one hardest to crack. This is due to a core difference in female vs. male psychology. When a wife nags her husband, she honestly views it as being *helpful*. When a man hears his wife nag him, he views it as *criticism*. She views it as assistance and he views it as an attack.

Here's what often happens. The wife wants to help her husband because she is honestly worried he'll forget to do something or do something wrong. So she'll nag him. She won't view it as nagging; she'll view it as a friendly, helpful reminder. When he gets nagged, the husband immediately bristles and becomes irritated. He'll usually either snap back at her, causing an argument, or he'll grumble angrily and just take it, building up a lot of resentment that will blow up later.

In some cases, he'll even counterattack by saying things like, "Don't treat me like I'm stupid" or "I don't need your fucking help." In my first marriage, I used to angrily counterattack with "Don't nag me!" Early on with Pink Firefly, I used a more Alpha Male 2.0 counterattack by smiling and saying, "Thanks, *Mom*."

Wives respond to these counterattacks by stating that they're not nagging you, they're helping you, and they have no idea why you're getting upset and "being mean to them" when "all they're trying to do is help." An argument then ensues.

Again, a classic masculine/feminine difference.

The only way I know of to handle nagging is to sit down and explain the above concept to your wife. Do *not* do this when she has just nagged you; that will just cause drama. Instead, do it when you're having a good day together. Don't call it "nagging." That will just make her defensive. Instead, call it something like "obvious reminders" or "corrections."

Be aware that regardless of how intelligent your wife is, she will have difficulty understanding this concept. Again, she views nagging as being a good, helpful wife. Just do your best to explain to her that while you love her and appreciate her help, when she nags you, er… *corrects* you, since you're a man, you take it as a personal attack and would rather she just either stay quiet or say something else.

Then, *gently* remind her next time she does it, something like, "Remember when I talked to you about those corrections? You just did one. It's no big deal, I just want to help point it out to you." See? *You* are reminding *her* now, so if she gets irritated about this, you can point out to her, "Perfect, now you see how it feels."

As always, if none of this works, bring it up at the next meeting with the counselor.

That covers it for her Negative Behaviors. Now we'll move on to *your* Negative Behaviors as a husband.

Your Negative Behavior #1: Anal Retentiveness

Being "anal" is when you have such an attention to detail that it becomes a frequent catalyst for your own unhappiness. It causes you to bitch, complain, issue orders and commands to others, and even start drama on a semi-regular basis. Women can sometimes be anal too, but in my vast personal experience, being anal is mostly a masculine trait.

When a guy lives alone, he can be as anal as he wants. No one is in his home or yard screwing up his perfect systems. However, when he lives with a woman, and certainly when he has children and/or lives in a family neighborhood, a man's anal retentiveness often becomes a never-ending source of arguments, drama, and pain for all involved.

I'm quite sure you've seen many examples of this from married men, but I'll give you a few off the top of my head.

When I was a kid, one of my chores was to wash both my parents' cars. When I was all done, I'd put everything away, and then an hour later, my dad would angrily barge into my room and tell me that I washed his car "wrong." He would then take me out and show me a tiny spot that I had missed on the side of his car and forced me to get all of my washing equipment back out to fix it.

When my kids were small, I lived on a street where one of my neighbors had two small children of his own. This guy would regularly fly into a rage any time anyone drove in front of his house even one mile per hour over the speed limit, screaming about his kids, even if his kids were inside. Many times, I saw this guy scream at slowly passing drivers. Soon he started putting up cones in the street and other obstacles even when his kids weren't out playing.

Similarly, I live close by to a guy who actually runs out of his house and screams at people if they walk their dogs on the sidewalk in front of his house, which is public property. Pink Firefly and I have seen him do it with several people, including Pink Firefly herself. This guy is so terrified that a dog turd might end up on the sidewalk (not his yard, mind you, just the sidewalk) that he's willing to alienate pretty much everyone else in the entire neighborhood.

Being anal is not the path to happiness nor a good marriage. I have several chapters in *The Unchained Man** about cultivating outcome independence and reducing the number of things in your life that make you unhappy. If you're an anal guy, I strongly recommend you read it. Also remember that you can be as anal as you want within your Zones, which is one of the many reasons you utilize Zones.

Calm the hell down. Focus on your Zones and *relax about everything else*. Let your wife be as disorganized as she wants in her Zones. Frankly,

**http://www.alphamalebook.com/*

if you're anal as hell, you should be living alone, not with a woman (or anyone else, for that matter).

Your Negative Behavior #2: Territoriality

Women are jealous, men are territorial. As I talk about in great detail in *The Unchained Man**, a man's territoriality is when he views other people as his property. As a man, you have Obsolete Biological Wiring that strongly signals that your wife is a slave whom you own. According to your caveman brain, this means that:

1. You *must* take care of her fully (financially, and so on).

2. You *need* to run her life.

3. No other man is allowed to touch her sexually (or else you must kill them).

In an OLTR Marriage, you must understand that *you don't own your wife*. You own yourself 100%, and she owns herself 100%. She lives with you, sure. At the same time, she is a completely independent person who can do whatever the hell she wants. Since she's part of a cohabiting OLTR couple, the only things she's not allowed to do is to get romantically involved with another man (though she can FB-only have sex with another man) or do anything that directly threatens your finances, property, health, or Zones. Outside of those two basic rules, she should be allowed to do whatever she wants. If you have a problem with that, that's tough shit. That's a very small price to pay for the Freedom, financial protections, and numerous other benefits of an OLTR Marriage.

As I've talked about in prior chapters, your frame with your wife is that you're going to be a good husband, but you're also going to do whatever the hell you want, and if she has a problem with that, she needs to divorce you and go marry someone else. *That door swings both ways.* As long as your wife isn't doing anything that is breaking one of the few core rules of an OLTR Marriage, she can do whatever *she* wants, and if *you* have a problem with it, that's *your* problem.

Sexual jealousy is a component of territoriality. I cover how to deal

*http://www.alphamalebook.com/

with that in Chapter 17, but the key point is that your jealousy is your problem, not hers. Just because you're irrationally jealous doesn't mean she can't be allowed to do certain things. (There may be odd exceptions to the rule where jealousy is warranted, but we'll cover those in Chapter 17.)

Your Negative Behavior: #3: Lording

Lording is an extension of territoriality. This is when your inner Alpha Male 1.0 comes out and you attempt to boss your wife around like she's a child or a servant. You order her around and set up numerous rules for her to follow, getting upset when she doesn't follow them (which, of course, will be all the time).

Normal women (Dominants) lord over their beta male husbands all the time. It's a societal norm. However, we're not talking about a normal marriage here; we're talking about your OLTR Marriage. The odds are high that your wife isn't a Dominant and is instead an Independent or Submissive. Therefore, if anyone is doing any lording, it's probably you.

When it comes to long-term cohabiting with a romantic partner, I follow something I call the 10% Rule. This means that when you are married to someone, there is about 10% of that person you're going to hate. This 10% will never be fixed. It will always be there. Your choice is to put up with that 10% for the rest of the marriage or get divorced and be single. Marrying someone else isn't an option for the 10% Rule because if you marry a different woman, there will simply be a *different* 10% about *her* that you'll hate, and you'll be right back to square one. (Of course, if you hate *more* than 10% of your wife, you're married to the wrong person and need to get divorced immediately.)

This means two things. First, your wife needs to accept the 10% of you that irritates the hell out of her and she needs to keep quiet about it. It also means that *you* need to accept the 10% of *your wife* that you hate and never bother her about it again. Let her do or say stupid shit. Let her make mistakes. Even let her be messy (in her Zones, of course). Let her do things wrong. Remember that Mutual Harmony is the goal, not correcting your wife all the time. In many respects, lording is the male version of nagging.

If you really are a dominant guy with a harder Alpha Male 1.0 personality, get your lording needs somewhere outside of the marriage. Lord over your staff in your business. Lord over your FBs during sex. Lord over your friends if you really have to. But don't lord over your wife. Even if your wife is a Submissive, that isn't going to work long-term.

Chapter 13
GROUND RULES

As I've talked about in great detail in my other books, your goal is to have the minimum number of rules to follow in any relationship you have with a woman. Your marriage is no different. The more rules you have, the more effort your relationship will take, the more drama you will have, the more disagreements you'll encounter, and the more stress you will both experience. The absolute minimum number of rules is the order of the day.

That all being said, when you live full-time with a woman, *some* rules are needed. Not many, but some.

These rules fall into two categories: the Cardinal Rules and Ground Rules.

The Cardinal Rules

If you've already read *The Ultimate Open Relationships Manual**, you know what the Cardinal Rules are. These are a set of several rules you must follow in an FB, MLTR, or OLTR relationship so you can maintain a pleasant, sexual, fun, drama-free relationship with a woman for a long as possible. Each relationship type (FB, MLTR, OLTR) has its own unique set of Cardinal Rules.

The OLTR Marriage has these Cardinal Rules, listed below. You must follow these rules at all times, with no exceptions. They are listed in no particular order.

- No actual dating or romantic feelings for side-FBs is allowed, for either of you – just sex.

- Always keep sex pleasurable for your wife.

- Never lie to your wife.

- Have your own life.

*http://www.haveopenrelationships.com

- Always maintain your Betaization Wall.
- Always be having sex with at least one other woman.

Here's a description of each rule and how to do them correctly.

No Dating or Romance with FBs

This is pretty straightforward. It means that you are both allowed to have sex with other people, but you're not allowed to date or get romantic feelings for other people. An OLTR Marriage is where you are sexually open but emotionally exclusive. If you don't want to be emotionally exclusive, you're deviating from the OLTR Marriage model. This *might* be okay depending on your circumstances, but it must be discussed in advance with your wife *before* you do it. (I already discussed emotionally non-exclusive marriage types back in Chapter 2.) For the rest of this section (and book), I'm going to continue with the assumption that you're following OLTR Marriage parameters, which is the easiest and simplest form of non-monogamous marriage to have for most people.

When you (or your wife) are spending time with your FBs, this means you're talking, relaxing, and having sex. That's it. This means, with FBs:

- No dates.
- No going out to lunch, dinner, movies, or other events.
- No spending the night.
- No going on vacations.
- No long phone calls.
- No "spending the day" together.
- No lovey or romantic talk.

If you do any of these things with your FBs, you're jeopardizing the entire marriage. I have personally seen (and heard of in the media) many cases of people with open marriages who started doing those things with side-FBs, and it rapidly destroyed the marriage. On the flip side, I have *never* seen an open marriage couple get divorced for these reasons when they stuck with the above rules.

When you (or your wife) start "dating" or engaging in dating-type behaviors with your FBs, it opens the door to possible feelings between you and her. If you value your marriage, that's a door that should always remain closed.

To be clear, I said no *romantic* feelings for your FBs. You can certainly be friends, even close friends. My FBs are really wonderful people who I care for deeply and consider very close friends. They are wonderful, special people to me, and I want the best for them, but we aren't romantically involved.

Always Keep Sex Pleasurable for Your Wife

As we've talked about already, sexual boredom is something that is always looming over both you and your wife (though mostly your wife) as the marriage ages. A standard Cardinal Rule for FB and MLTR relationships is to always make the woman orgasm every time you have sex. This not only keeps her happy but keeps her coming back to you over and over again, even when she knows you're having sex with other women.

When you're married, this takes on a different dimension. You don't necessarily need to make your wife orgasm literally every time you have sex. Unlike for men, orgasms are a lot more "work" for a woman. There will be times your wife is perfectly fine just having sex with you and not cumming herself.

However! This is not a license for you to eventually become sexually lazy, like most husbands. Every time you have sex with your wife, you need to make it pleasurable for her. Make her orgasm unless she clearly tells you she doesn't need to. Do whatever you know your wife likes (you know what she likes), and do that every time. Also, change things up so you don't fall into the typical trap of having sex the exact same way every time. Every once in a while, utilize different techniques, positions, sex toys, role play, whatever. Keep things new and interesting for your wife. *It's your job to keep your wife sexually engaged.* Remember, you need to keep Attraction high at all times! Sexing her the way she likes goes a long way to this end.

Never Lie to Your Wife

Most men in relationships stupidly think that lying to their wives or girlfriends prevents drama. They are wrong. Instead, lying *delays and amplifies* drama.

Here's what I mean. If your wife asks you a difficult question, one where you know the answer is going to upset her, if you answer truthfully, sure, you'll likely get some drama because she won't like your answer.

If you instead lie to her and tell her something false but that she wants to hear, sure, you won't get any drama *at that moment*. She'll nod her head and move on, and you'll *think* you've won. But you haven't. Several weeks or months down the road, the lie will eventually come out (or she'll at least encounter evidence of the lie and bring it to your attention), and *now* she'll give you drama. However, now she'll give you much more drama than she would have given you originally had you just come clean in the first place. By lying to her, you didn't prevent any drama at all. You simply amplified it by several times and shoved it into the future. Not smart.

This means that if you want near-zero drama in your marriage for the long-term, you can never lie to your wife. It's that simple.

Normal married guys "need" to lie to their wives about all kinds of things, particularly when they cheat on her or need to get away from her because they lack any Zones of their own. However, the Alpha Male 2.0 in an OLTR Marriage has no need to lie. He's structured the marriage and his life so that he never needs to lie in the first place. I never lie to Pink Firefly and never have. I'd love to say this is because I'm an honest and ethical person, which I think I am, but the main reason is that I simply don't *need* to lie to her about anything. I'm an outcome-independent Alpha Male 2.0 with zero Oneitis in an OLTR Marriage. Everything important for her to know about what I'm doing, she already knows. If she doesn't like it, she can leave. I don't need to lie.

To be clear, "never lie to your wife" does not mean "tell your wife literally everything about everything." *Honesty* and *disclosure* are two different things. You can let your wife know that you're going to see your FB next Thursday, but there's no rule stating that you have to also disclose your FB is a super-hot 18-year-old girl with a pussy tighter than hers. You can let your wife know that you put money into savings or investments every month, but you don't have to sit down with her and show her exactly where the money is going, which accounts it's going into, and so forth.

D*isclosure* is another topic entirely. Every woman is different, and each couple has their own unique dynamic regarding disclosure (which we will discuss in the next chapter). Use your own judgment on that. *Disclosure* is what you say or don't say. *Honesty*, which is what I'm talking here, means that whatever you *do* say to your wife is the 100% truth at all times.

Have Your Own Life

This is standard advice I've given many times before in my other books and blogs. As a man, you must have strong meaning and exciting motivations in your life that have literally nothing to do with your wife, your children, or your marriage. Your work, your hobbies, your fitness, your external sex life, your spirituality, your projects, and so on. One or more of these things should be the bulk of your life, and many of these things should have literally nothing to do with your wife. Some can if you really want; you could work with your wife or share your spirituality with your wife, as just two examples. But if that's the case, then you should have something else major in your life that is 100% yours and nothing whatsoever to do with your wife.

Many married men, including married Alpha Males, make the mistake of having nothing significant outside of their wives to hold their time or their passions. They work with their wives, spend all evening with their wives, raise kids with their wives, and so on. They have nothing significant outside of their wife.

This is a huge mistake. You *must* have your own life. My relationship with Pink Firefly is one of the most important things in my life. At the same time, my work, my Mission, my international projects, and most of my hobbies have nothing to do with her. PF and my marriage to her is *one* of the most important things in my life, not *the* important thing. I have a huge, exciting, and meaningful "life" completely outside of her.

You need to have a strong "life" outside of your wife too.

Always Maintain Your Betaization Wall

I've already covered the importance of this and how to do it in prior chapters. Just remember that keeping that Betaization Wall up at all times is one of the Cardinal Rules. Don't ever forget it. Don't ever get complacent or lazy and let that Wall drop. When it drops, so does your marriage, at least eventually.

Always Be Having Sex With At Least One Other Woman

This is a difficult one and the most controversial Cardinal Rule of them all. I get a lot of objections regarding this particular rule, as well as a lot of questions about it.

It's likely that you're already having sex with other women right now. That's great. The problem is the odds are decent that that at some point down the road, in a few months or few years, you're going to start getting lazy about this.

Over the past 13 years, I've seen it literally hundreds of times with men in OLTRs or OLTR Marriages. For a while, the men have a great time having sex with FBs on the side while with their OLTR girlfriend or wife. However, over time, they start getting complacent. One day they wake up and realize that, oops, it's been five months (or longer!) since they've had sex with anyone other than their OLTR.

This is called **de facto monogamy**. It's when you're sexually monogamous to a woman without verbally promising it. These de facto monogamous men think they're in non-monogamous or open relationships, when in fact, they aren't. *They're actually just as monogamous as any beta male, at least now.* It doesn't matter who you were having sex with six months ago. All that matters is who you're having sex with *now*.

Though they don't realize it, they've taken their Betaization Wall and smashed it with a sledgehammer.

When someone like me points out the real and multiple dangers of what they're doing, they start throwing out excuses. They start making excuses about how busy they are with work. They make excuses about how much time or effort it takes to have FBs (which is silly, since FBs take virtually no work or time; that's the beauty of FBs). They complain that their FB isn't as good-looking as their OLTR (then get a new FB, dumbass!). They make excuses about how sweet or low-drama their OLTR is and how well and/or often their OLTR has sex with them, so why do they need to have sex with anyone else?

By rationalizing these excuses, they solidify themselves as monogamous beta males. As I've explained in my other writings, monogamy works *for a while*. So *for a while*, their newly de facto monogamous relationship works fine. Eventually, the fact these men have no more Betaization Wall causes these men to start slowly rising on the Betaization Scale. Then demands, drama, and arguments begin. Things get worse and worse until they finally break up or get divorced.

An even worse outcome is that during this time, the men start having sex with side women again, but because they've established a de facto monogamous relationship or marriage, their wife now views their outside sexual activity as *cheating*.

Their wife explodes as a result, and the man idiotically responds with a bunch of Guy Logic about how he used to have sex with other women and it was okay with her; therefore, it should still be okay with her, which doesn't resonate with her feminine feelings at all. As he drones on with his Guy Logic, she just screams and throws a frying pan at his head.

Ceasing *all* sexual activates in your OLTR Marriage with side women is one of the dumbest, most destructive things you can do. It converts your entire relationship into a monogamous one utterly regardless of what you have said, what you think she knows, what you have *haven't* promised, or what she *did* promise. It smashes your Betaization Wall to pieces. It causes you to rise several notches on the Betaization Scale (not today, not tomorrow, but eventually). It eventually murders both Attraction and Freedom. It will likely contribute to the downfall of your entire relationship.

So please, just don't fucking do it. Regardless of how satisfied or lazy or busy you feel, *always* keep having sex with at least one FB on the side, no matter what else is going on in your life. I can tell you for a fact that even if PF and I stay married forever, I will keep having sex with other women consistently until I am at least 80 years old (and perhaps even after that).

This leads to the issue of *frequency*. You are certainly allowed to have side-sex less often as you get older and as the marriage matures. I certainly have less side-sex and with fewer women now than I did five years ago, and I'm sure I'll have even less five years from now (but it will never go to zero!). So dropping the activity level, the frequency, and/or the number of side women you see over time is perfectly acceptable, perhaps even preferable. One of the big benefits many older men seek by getting OLTR married in the first place is being able to dial down their crazy sex lives a little, especially if they spent many years having sex with an extreme number of women (like I did). That's understandable, particularly as we men get older and our priorities change.

What, then, are the absolute minimums? Every man is different, so it's difficult to give precise numbers that will apply across a broad spectrum of men. That said, based on my strong opinion which is sourced in observing hundreds of men in these kinds of relationships, I believe your minimum should be to have sex with at least *one* woman on the side at least *once every six weeks*. Once you let 30 days go by without having any sex with anyone on the side, you're in a danger zone. Once you let more than 45 days go by, you're essentially de facto monogamous, and now you're in big trouble. If you just make sure you have sex with some side woman (an FB, a new woman, or a one-night stand) once every 30-45 days or so at the most, you'll be in good shape. Your Betaization Wall will remain, and you'll never get de facto monogamous.

As usual, I walk my talk. I have never *once* gone more than two weeks without having sex with one of my FBs since the day I started seeing Pink Firefly over five years ago. I can't see myself dropping below that frequency at any time for many, many years, and I will *never* let it go below once every 30 days. My low-drama, happy, non-monogamous marriage is too important to me.

Ground Rules

The Cardinal Rules apply equally and across the board to all men in all OLTR Marriages. Ground Rules are different in that they vary from couple to couple. Ground Rules are customized, mutual agreements that you and your wife have, which are unique to your marriage and your situation.

Unlike with the Cardinal Rules, I can't give you a list of Ground Rules to follow because most (or all) of them may not apply to your particular situation with your wife. Every couple is different, and every couple has a different set of Ground Rules.

In Chapter 28, I cover this topic in more detail, but for the moment, I can give you a few examples of Ground Rules I've heard from other OLTR couples. Again, these are just examples. I'm *not* recommending you have any of these rules because they may not make any sense in your individual situation. They're just *examples*. That's why you'll notice that some of them are opposites. Here are a few.

- Never tell anyone about the open aspect of the marriage.
- Always use condoms when having sex with FBs.
- Never have sex with any FBs who are under the age of X.
- Only have sex with FBs who live far outside the neighborhood.
- Never bring any women home to the house.
- No ongoing FBs – short-term FBs or one-night stands only.
- No one-night stands or short-term FBs – long-term FBs only.
- STD blood tests required for both husband and wife every X.
- STD blood tests required for any long-term FBs
- And so on.

As I talk about in *The Unchained Man**, Ground Rules in an OLTR Marriage are acceptable, but *you can't have very many*. One to three

*http://www.alphamalebook.com

Ground Rules is all you need in most cases. (PF and I have only two. The first is that while I can have sex with my FBs whenever I want without having to check with her, I can't bring my FBs over to our house unless PF grants permission first. I use a side location instead. More on this in Chapter 25. The second is that I've promised to verbally tell her any time I have sex with more than two FBs in a single week. That's it!)

If your wife starts throwing out endless numbers of Ground Rules, you've got a problem, and you may have married the wrong woman. Similarly, you can't throw out a mountain of Ground Rules either. The more Ground Rules you have, the less Freedom and Mutual Attraction you will have in your marriage. *A minimum number of Ground Rules is the order of the day.*

Section Two
Sexual Aspects

Chapter 14
MANAGING THE OPEN ASPECT WITH YOUR WIFE

When you're regularly having sex with women who are not your wife, you need your wife as an ally in managing this part of your life. Doing this incorrectly will either cause drama with your wife or will cause you to rise on the Betaization Scale, both bad things. Doing this correctly will ensure a smoothly running marriage.

The Five Disclosure Levels

You and your wife need to decide on the level of disclosure regarding your sexual activities with your FBs (and her activities with hers, if any). As I talked about in Chapter 13, you must be 100% honest with your wife at all times. She will know you're having sex with FBs or one-night stands on a regular basis, and you will never lie to her about this. However, how much specific information you reveal to your wife about your sexual side activities is another matter.

Every couple is different regarding this. Some couples love to talk about sexual details when they have sex with other people; it turns them on, and they enjoy talking about it. Other couples are the opposite. One or both of them don't want to hear anything about any side-sex and get agitated when the topic is brought up. Yet other couples are somewhere between these two extremes.

This can vary wildly from woman to woman. Before I met PF and I was dating HBM, she was fine with having an open relationship with me, but any time she discovered any details about any women I was having sex with she would get very agitated and upset (unless she was directly involved, like we were having threesomes or she was helping me have sex with her girlfriends). I learned to keep my mouth shut about details about my FBs when around her.

Years later, when I started getting serious with PF, I slowly realized that she was the exact opposite. If she didn't know about exactly who I was with and when, she'd get agitated and concerned. If I explained exactly who the woman was, showed PF pictures of her and described her in detail, suddenly PF would calm down. If PF actually met the woman in real life, then she'd completely relax and even encourage me to go have sex with her on occasion(!).

It's your job to discover what level of disclosure your wife is most comfortable with, and what level you are most comfortable with if your wife has FBs of her own.

This brings us to the five disclosure levels. Your wife (and you) will be most comfortable at one of these levels. Here they are:

Level 1: You never need to disclose to her anything about your side sexual activities, you likely never do, and she's never allowed to ask you about it.

Level 2: You never need to disclose anything about your side sexual activities. However, if she asks a few basic questions here and there, you will answer them, but you avoid detailed conversations about it.

Level 3: You disclose what you're doing in general, even without being asked. You answer all the questions she has about your side-actives with no limits regarding the details.

Level 4: You are required to tell her whenever you have sex with someone (and she's required to tell you if she does) within reasonable expectations. She has a decent understanding of all or most of your regular FBs, who they are, how they look, and so on. She may even know some of them personally.

Level 5: You usually tell her literally everything you're doing down to the minutest of details of your side-sexual escapades (and she tells you all about hers), and you and your wife both really enjoy talking about this stuff.

You need to discuss these disclosure levels with your wife and pick one you think would maximize the highest amount of Mutual Harmony in your marriage, mostly based on your wife's personality. If your wife is a little more on the jealous side, you'll likely have to be (or at least start) at the lower levels. If your wife is more into open relationships or polyamory, you can be at the higher levels.

You can start at lower levels and slowly move to higher ones as your wife becomes more accustomed to the open aspect of the marriage. Over a long period of time, a woman can "earn" levels by showing you she won't give you any drama when you reveal more info about your other women. For example, you could start at Level 2, and if she never gives you drama or complaining when you answer her questions, you can go to Level 3 and try that out.

Here's my example. Since Pink Firefly had zero open relationship experience when I first met her, I started her at Level 1 when we were casual. When we started getting very serious, I moved her to Level 2. When I realized she was more comfortable knowing more data about my FBs, I carefully moved to Level 3. Today, after several years of being together and living together, we are at Level 4, and that seems to work best *for us* (though I know what I just described would work badly for some other couples). We will never go to Level 5 because I know that wouldn't work *for us* (though I know Level 5 works great for some other couples). You may be very different than me, and your wife may be *extremely* different than Pink Firefly. Find which level works best *for you*.

Scheduling Logistics

As an Alpha Male 2.0, you have the right to have sex with your side women literally whenever you want. You should never need to ask your wife for permission for when to do this nor the frequency of which you have sex with other women.

That all being said, there is still the issue of Mutual Harmony. If you and your wife are having a wonderful evening together at home and then you suddenly say, "Well, I'm going to fuck one of my FBs now!" and then just leave, clearly this will cause a problem in your marriage (unless your wife is uniquely unusual). Just because you're allowed to do something doesn't necessarily mean you should do it in any context you feel. There are other factors at play.

There are no hard and fast rules here. Just do what you think would maintain Mutual Harmony best in your marriage. To give you an example of what I do, I *try* to not to see any of my FBs in the evening most of the time, since that's when Pink Firefly is home from work. PF generally works during the day on weekdays, so to be nice to her, I *try* to schedule my FBs during those times. It doesn't always happen that way, but it usually does. Sundays are also in our Shared Zone, so I never see FBs on a Sunday (unless PF and I are seeing one together).

Once again, come up with a system that works best for you and your wife.

When She Is Having More Side-Sex Than You Are

Most of the time and in most cases, your wife will not have nearly as much sex with her FBs as you are with yours. In many cases, your wife won't sleep with other men at all, particularly if she's over the age of 40 or so.

However, I have spoken with some men in open marriages who are exceptions to this, where their wives are having quite a bit of sex with their own FBs. In some cases, the wives are having more side-sex than the husband. A question I get is if the man needs to have sex every time his wife does to ensure a level of equality and thus maintain Attraction.

The answer is complicated. *Ideally*, yes, you should be having side-sex as much or more than your wife. If she's having more side-sex than you are, it's usually bad for your frame as a man, an Alpha Male, and as a husband.

If Pink Firefly was having lots of sex with men on the side (she doesn't, but if she did), I would certainly dial up my activity to match or exceed hers. However, I'm an extremely high sex drive man who really loves sex. Some men are not like this. Some guys have legitimately lower sex drives than the average. Other men have lower sex drives than their unusually high sex drive wives. In these cases, it's acceptable if your wife is having more side-sex than you are. It's not ideal, but it's acceptable. However, for this to be acceptable, the following conditions must both be true:

- You are still having at least some side-sex with women at least once every six weeks, just as I described back in Chapter 13. If your wife is having sex with FBs and you're not having sex with any FBs *at all*, this is a serious problem and will likely get worse (barring rare exceptions to the rule) since this will drive Attraction downward regardless of the logical reasons you come up with to justify it.

- You have *always* demonstrated a lower sex drive with your wife, so it's something she's accustomed to and always has been since you were first dating. If you were the hornier one for years and then over time your sex drive dropped, this is almost guaranteed to make you rise on the Betaization Scale. However, if you were always a lower sex drive guy and your wife dated you and married you under those conditions, it's different since you're not "losing" any sexual power or masculinity you had before (at least in that respect). Opposites do indeed attract, and I have seen long-term married couples where a high sex drive woman met, dated, and then married a low sex drive man, and I have seen these work, provided the wife is able to get her needs met from FBs on the side. I myself have had FBs who were these very women (they were in open marriages to low sex drive men). These marriages are rare, even among open marriages, but they do exist.

Be A Detective

Just like with the Disclosure Levels, certain women are angered in open relationships/marriages by certain things. One wife might be perfectly happy with you having sex with an FB on the side but might be absolutely furious if you have a threesome with two FBs. Another wife might be perfectly fine with you having all the threesomes you want but might get really angry if you have sex with an 18-year-old. Often these particular things that make your wife really upset won't make any sense. She doesn't like them for whatever internal reasons she has, most of which will probably be irrational.

Several years ago, I was discussing one of my FBs with Pink Firefly.

She was a young woman PF had no problem with me seeing. When I casually mentioned she had a roommate whom I also had sex with, PF immediately became very agitated. She had a huge problem with me having sex with two roommates.

Was there any logical reason for her not liking this? Nope. She just didn't like it.

Did I have any idea she wouldn't like me having sex with two roommates beforehand? Nope. If I had known that I probably would never have done it (though again, I'm allowed to; I just would have chosen not to in order to maintain Mutual Harmony since it's not something I felt strongly about).

Here's the main point. Was there any possible way I could have known that this very odd scenario would really make her upset in advance? No. The scenario was so specific and unusual that she would have never thought to tell me *and* I would have never thought to ask. Instead, the scenario had to actually occur, and I would have had to observe the reaction.

You won't know every little thing that upsets your wife about what might make her uncomfortable with you in your open marriage, since often *she* won't know it until it happens. Whenever something like this happens, make a note of it and keep track of these things. It may take as long as two or three years before you catalog an entire list of things she doesn't like, and this is normal. Hopefully, there won't be very many things that make her upset (and if there are, you probably married the wrong woman), but what few things that do make her upset, you should be aware of.

Chapter 15
SEX WITH YOUR WIFE

One of the core concepts of all non-monogamous relationships is that the better you make a woman feel during sex…

- The less drama she'll have with you.
- The less demanding she'll be with you.
- The less likely she is to leave you.
- The longer it will take to leave you if she does eventually leave.
- The more likely she is to come back to you after she leaves.

The reasons for this, beyond the obvious (it maintains Attraction), is that most men are terrible in bed and women are accustomed to this. Married women are also quite accustomed to the reality that their husbands will allow sex to start becoming routine and boring in short order. As I've already explained, *men* can be bored for long stretches, but women can't; women's tolerance for boredom is extremely low.

This means that you need to not only have sex with your wife on a regular basis, but you need to make her feel very good when you do.

Fuck Her Well

You need to fuck your wife <u>very well</u>. I go into great detail regarding sexual techniques in *The Ultimate Open Relationships Manual**, and they all apply to your marriage. Normal husbands, especially after a few years, get into the bad habit of defaulting into a wham-bam-thank-you-ma'am type of sex that might be satisfying for you (maybe) but is really boring to her, even if you take the extra time to make her orgasm.

Find out what your wife really likes during sex (you should already know) and do that. If it's something you don't like, you don't have to

*http://www.haveopenrelationships.com

do it every time you have sex, but you should still do it regularly. Make sure your wife feels really good. Make sure she orgasms every time you have sex *unless she specifically tells you she doesn't need it tonight* (which sometimes she will).

Make sure you do new things with your wife. Don't have sex with her the exact same way for years on end; again, that's boring. Here are a few examples of things you can try:

- Experiment with new positions

- Experiment with new sexual rhythms

- Use sex toys (or new sex toys)

- Role play

- Have sex in new, different, and/or interesting locations

- Integrate porn into your sex with her (make sure it's a type of porn she really likes; every woman is *very* different about this)

- Involve your FBs. This can range from threesomes with your wife, foursomes with your wife, you watching your wife have sex with your FBs, or your wife watch you have sex with one of your FBs. (Pink Firefly likes to watch me have sex with the side women I have she considers attractive. It turns her on, and obviously, I have a great time myself. Yeah, it's a rough life.)

- And so on; use your imagination

The point is not to get complacent with your wife sexually. Even men in OLTR Marriages are at risk for this since often they get their wilder sexual needs fulfilled from their side women and keep sex with their wives more vanilla. *Don't* fall into that trap.

What to Do If She Says No

The beauty of the OLTR Marriage for women is that your wife has every right to say no to having sex with you any time she wants without it ever threatening the marriage or ever becoming a major problem. This is very unlike the usual monogamous marriage, where if the wife says no to sex, it represents a serious problem in the relationship that is likely to lead to cheating, divorce, or even worse.

Women never really think this through and never really consider this a benefit to them until they realize they have this authority and can compare it to prior monogamous relationships they've had where it was a problem. Indeed, this is actually one of the selling points of an OLTR Marriage to a woman. "Sweetie, you have every right to say no to sex whenever you want, and it's never going to be a problem, and I'll never get upset." It really *is* a benefit to women since they don't have the near-constant pressure of feeling like they always need to put out for their horny husbands.

On the flip side, you need to respect this. This means that when you want to have sex with her and your wife says no, you can*not* get upset, you can*not* get frustrated, you can*not* argue with her, and you can*not* pressure her. Not only will this create drama, but it will also seriously damage Attraction since nothing is less attractive to a woman than a man who is begging to have sex with her and is clearly frustrated about it. Instead, if you act like it's no big deal at all, often she may turn around and ask *you* for sex once she realizes her "no" has no power over you (which, as a man in an OLTR Marriage, it doesn't).

Therefore, when your wife says no, here is the correct procedure. You need to practice it and follow it every time it happens.

1. If you are touching her sensually, immediately pull your hand away. *Do it slowly*, but do it as soon as she says no. If you are cuddling with her or hugging her, slowly detach from her. Don't maintain any physical contact with her once she says no to sex. This is very important.

2. Say, "Okay." Say it in a normal, calm, neutral tone of voice with a neutral expression on your face. *Do not show any frustration, disappointment, or anger of any kind.* If you feel any of these feelings, just remember how good it's going to feel when you have sex with your favorite FB tomorrow.

3. Once physically detached from her, continue having whatever conversation you were having with her before. Do not suddenly get up off the bed, couch, or leave the room. Finish out whatever you were talking about, and *then* leave the room in a happy or neutral way if you still want to.

Behaving this way when she says no to you will be very unlike anything else she's ever experienced with any other man she's had in past relationships where she's said no to sex. Very often, she may suddenly start touching *you*, and she may even have sex with you on the spot. Other times, she may wait an hour or two and then approach you for sex later in the evening. And still other times, she really meant it and she's not interested in sex that day (she's too tired, too stressed, or whatever) and you won't have sex with her that particular day or evening. That's fine since you always have your FBs to take up the slack.

Feel free to see your FBs more often if your wife starts saying no to you more often. If she has every right to say no to sex without any argument from you, you have every right to have sex with your FBs to make up for this without any argument from her. (It's called equality, which is exactly what women have been saying they want for decades.)

As your marriage ages, your wife will say no to sex more often, at least eventually, even if you do everything right. This is normal and natural. Plan on it, and don't be surprised when it happens. With rare exceptions, women have hard-wired biology that directs them to get more bored sexually with a long-term live-in male partner. It's nothing personal and likely has nothing to do with you (unless you are violating the guidelines I set out in Chapter 5 regarding maintaining Attraction; then it probably *does* have to do with you).

What if you *aren't* seeing your FBs? Well, that means you're violating all kinds of rules you've already read in this book, you're de facto monogamous, you're now screwed no matter what happens, and it's all your fault. *Remember the six-week minimum rule and always adhere to it. This is your insurance policy against your wife starting to say no to sex with you, which you can almost guarantee will eventually start to happen.*

Be Aware of Timing

As much as I hate to say this, sometimes you need to be a little strategic about when you approach your wife for sex. I'm a very high sex drive guy, and I *completely* understand being in a really horny mood at the same time as your sexy-as-hell wife is standing right in front of you. But if she's in the middle of angrily relaying to you what a horrible day she's had at work, or she's right in the middle of doing the dishes, or she's feeling nauseous, or she's clearly exhausted and is getting into bed to crash, then this is probably not the time to grab her ass and start ripping her clothes off, regardless of how horny you are in the moment. More than likely, she'll just say no and get a little angry to boot.

You need to be aware of the scenarios under which your wife has a tendency to say no to sex (if indeed she ever says no) and avoid going for sex during these times. While she has a right to say no, and while you shouldn't mind, her saying no to sex is still technically a negative event for both of you, so there's no need to create more of these situations than is necessary. Just keep reminding yourself that you can always go see your FB tomorrow or the next day.

The Two-Shot Rule

Nothing is less attractive to a wife than a husband who constantly begs her for sex when he gets repeated nos from her. If you keep repeatedly asking your wife for sex when she says no, it will not only frustrate you and her, but it will severely damage Attraction.

The cure for this is the Two-Shot Rule. This means that when your wife says no to sex, you may ask her one more time, either the same day or a subsequent day. If she says no a second time, *you never ask her for sex ever again.* Yes, you heard me right. You literally stop asking her for sex.

I didn't say you never *have* sex with her again. I said you just stop *asking*. If she wants to have sex with you at this point, *she* is going to have to approach *you* for sex. Otherwise, she doesn't get any sex from you, and you'll instead fulfill that need with your FBs. In other words, she has two opportunities (two "shots") to have sex with you before you stop asking.

Once your wife approaches you for sex, have sex with her like nothing bad happened. Then everything resets back to normal and now you can start approaching her for sex again... until she says no to sex twice in a row again. Then you do it all over again.

Adhering to this rule does several things, all of them good:

1. It prevents you from damaging Attraction by acting like the typical husband who is always pestering his wife for sex while she always (or often) says no.

2. It clearly shows your wife that she has zero control over your sexual destiny and can't use this to control you. If she says no twice, you'll never ask her for sex again and instead will just focus on your FBs for your sexual needs.

3. It sets up a punishment/reward system with your wife where she learns she'll get more sexual attention from you if she says yes to sex and less if she says no. This is the opposite of most marriages where the wife gets sexual attention from the husband regardless of if she says yes or no.

4. It completely eliminates all drama from your marriage regarding her saying no to sex. Most normal marriages experience regular arguments and other conflict when the husband wants to have sex and the wife says no. This will never be a problem in your marriage. If she says no once, you shrug and drop the subject. If she says no twice, you stop asking. Now the ball is in her court, and no drama is involved.

What If She *Never* Has Sex with You?

What if your wife gets to the point where she pretty much always says no to sex? What if she never has sex with you?

There some unusual OLTR Marriages where this situation exists, and I mentioned a few examples back in Chapter 2. The husband stays married to the wife because she's a nice person, or she's a good mother to their kids, or the husband needs the wife to keep up appearances due to work, family, or religious reasons, yet the husband and wife never have sex because they either aren't attracted or because one of them suffers some kind of debilitating medical issue. The husband hooks up with FBs on the side on a regular basis instead and gets 100% of his sex that way.

I have been asked if I would tolerate a marriage to Pink Firefly (or any other woman) if she and I literally never had any sex and *all* the sex I had was with side-FBs, either because PF would no longer be interested in having sex with me, or because PF becomes handicapped or gains 300 pounds and becomes too unattractive for me to get sexually aroused.

My answer is that I technically *could* be in a marriage like this, assuming everything else in the marriage was literally perfect (there was zero drama, we got along great, there were other very clear benefits to me being married to her, etc.) but it would not be ideal.

That's how I view this for me, and that's how I view this for you. Could you make an OLTR Marriage work where you never had sex with your own wife? Yes. I've seen marriages like this. Do I think they're the best marriage to have? No. As I mentioned earlier, I'd rather you be married to a woman you enjoy having sex with. But I admit marriages like this can work *only if everything else in the marriage is amazing.*

Chapter 16

ONEITIS MANAGEMENT

As I already talked about back in Chapter 4, Oneitis is something you simply can't have as part of your psychological makeup in regard to how you feel about your wife and your marriage. If you are terrified that she might divorce you if you take action on anything in this book (or anything else that would make you long-term happy), then true happiness won't be possible for you. Moreover, it's very likely you are actually risking the longevity of your marriage if you have Oneitis for the reasons I listed back in Chapter 5, namely because having Oneitis murders Attraction. *It is literally impossible to have Oneitis for your wife and maintain any degree of Attraction in your marriage.*

I have a detailed chapter regarding Oneitis management in *The Ultimate Open Relationships Manual**, and I *highly* recommend it since everything in that chapter applies directly to you as an OLTR husband. In this chapter, I will focus on those only aspects of Oneitis that specifically apply to you as a man living with a woman. These break down into three critical action steps

1. Always focus on your critically important non-marriage projects.

2. Keep your physical appearance optimal forever.

3. Never allow yourself to become de facto monogamous.

Always Focus on Your Critically Important Non-Marriage Projects

Men need projects to work on. Having no exciting or enjoyable projects in your life invites Oneitis for the married man.

Moreover, these projects need to be *critically important*. Working on the car or playing golf are certainly projects and they're perfectly fine things, but they aren't very important. An important project would be

*http://www.haveopenrelationships.com

something like building a business, perfecting your body, writing a book, traveling the world, hitting a big financial goal, and similar big-picture items. Critically important projects stem from important goals.

Whenever I see a married guy with Oneitis (and I see it all the damn time, including in non-monogamous marriages), it's almost always a guy with not a lot going on with his life outside of his wife and the basics. It's the typical husband living the typical life of going to work, coming home, performing the chores around the house, helping out with the kids, watching some Netflix, and then going to bed and repeating the same thing tomorrow. It's a guy with no big goals, no Mission, and no great drives in life.

One of the best ways to become Oneitis-proof is to have a few really exciting (at least to you) goals that have *nothing to do with your wife or your kids*. Set some goals like this, then put up visual representations of them (pictures, images, photos, etc.) where you'll see them every day. Remind yourself often of what your goals are and why you're excited about them. When you have some big goals in life *that have nothing to do with your wife or kids* that you're really pumped about, it makes it much harder for Oneitis to take hold of you. (It's not *impossible* to get Oneitis if you do this; it just makes it much harder.)

I'm not saying you shouldn't set goals regarding your marriage or your wife (or your kids, if you have any). I set goals regarding my relationship with Pink Firefly all the time. I'm saying these should not be your *only* goals or even your *primary* goals. Any goals you set for your marriage should be one of many goals in many different areas of your life.

The Unchained Man* goes into great detail about how to set goals and a personal Mission and formulate plans for their accomplishment. I strongly recommend you get a copy and start working on your goals as soon as possible if you don't have any yet.

Remember that I said these are not just goals, but goals you're excited about. You need to find something in your life with real meaning, beyond the day-to-day, "pay the bills" essentials. If the only goals you've got are things like "pay the bills," or "graduate college," or "be a good dad," then the odds of you getting Oneitis for your wife spikes upward, *especially* if you consider her to be very physically attractive as compared to other

*http://www.alphamalebook.com/

women you've had sex with in the past or present. You'll have no great focus or meaning in your life, so that's what your wife becomes.

I love Pink Firefly more than I ever thought I could love a woman. It's the most complete and wonderful feeling of love I've ever felt. At the same time, not only do I not have Oneitis for Pink Firefly or anyone else, but I haven't even experienced the emotion of Oneitis at all, for anyone, in about 20 years. There are many reasons for this, but the fact I have a deeply meaningful Mission and really exciting (to me) goals and projects is foremost.

Find a project and get to work on it.

Keep Your Physical Appearance Optimal Forever

Monogamous beta males (and Alpha Male 1.0s who get complacent and surrender to monogamy) can "afford" to be typical guys and start letting their looks go around their forties. The older most married men become, the uglier and less physically attractive they tend to get. You've seen it a thousand times. Their bodies get softer, weaker, and fatter. Their skin gets more wrinkly, loose, and loses its color. Their hair whitens and thins. Their teeth get more yellow and crooked. They start walking with a stoop, and their body language becomes more collapsed and beta. They stop giving a shit about how they present themselves, let their grooming go, and start dressing like dorks. A cool, decent-looking guy can get married at age 35, and by age 45 (assuming his marriage lasts that long), he can end up looking absolutely terrible. Again, I'm sure you've seen this happen a thousand times. I certainly have, that includes formerly bad-ass Alpha Males who formerly had real strength, drive, looks, and game.

As a man in an OLTR Marriage, and certainly if you've embraced the Alpha Male 2.0 lifestyle I endorse, *you do not have the option of letting your looks go as you age.* Here's why:

1. If you start to let your physical looks go, it will directly damage Attraction. You already know all of the serious problems this will cause in your marriage. You must maintain Attraction at all times throughout the entire length of your marriage, period. You're literally asking for problems if you don't.

2. If you maintain a high standard of physical appearance, it may motivate your wife to do the same. If you instead start letting them go, you increase the odds of letting *her* looks go. Of course, there's no guarantee your wife won't start gaining weight or letting her looks go eventually regardless of what you do, but keeping your looks optimized certainly puts the odds in your favor.

3. Unlike other married men, you will never be monogamous. This means you'll need to attract new women into your life *for the rest of your life*. If you let your looks go, this will be much harder for you. Most married men are under the mistaken impression that once they're married, they're "done" attracting new women and can now "relax" regarding their physical appearance. That's incorrect for you (since you'll need to semi-regularly add new FBs to your rotation), and it's also wrong for men in TMMs (because of the sky-high odds of divorce).

4. Maintaining a high degree of physical appearance throughout the rest of your life will keep your energy levels and self-esteem high. This will directly affect your ability to not only maintain your happy OLTR Marriage, but your other life areas as well (your sex life, your financial life, your social life, your family life, and so on).

One of your solid, forever goals should be to be as physically attractive as possible, for the rest of your life, within the constraints of your age and genetics. As I talk about in *The Ultimate Younger Woman Manual**, your goal should, in terms of physical appearance, always be in the top 15% of men your age and in your city.

In other words, if they randomly pulled 100 men from your city who are exactly your age and race, lined them up against a wall, then brought in 20 super attractive women in their early twenties, had them rate all of the men's looks, then re-order the men up in that order, you should be in the top 15 of those men. Moreover, you should never drop below the top 15 of those men *for the rest of your life*. Looking great when you're 37 and then looking like a pile of shit when you're 57 isn't going to cut it. When you're 57, you don't need to look like you're 37 nor look amazing compared to 37-year-old men, but compared to other 57-year-old men,

*http://www.older-men-younger-women.com

you need to look damn good.

The topics of skin care, fashion, grooming, health, anti-aging, posture, vitamins, testosterone, and physical energy are all critical to the OLTR husband, but they are beyond the scope of this book. I address all of them in my other books, blogs, and coaching programs. Refer to *calebjones.com** for more information on those topics. My point is that you must be as attractive as you possibly can be, limited only by your age and genetics, for the rest of your life if you want a high-quality OLTR Marriage (and even if you don't!).

As always, I walk the walk. I look *better* now as a married man than I did several years ago when Pink Firefly first moved in with me. Since then, I've lost weight, gained some muscle mass, improved my skin, and I dress a little better. And I'm still improving. I plan on being as physically attractive as I can, looking as young, healthy, and decent for the rest of my life, well into my eighties. You should have the same objective.

Never Allow Yourself to Become De Facto Monogamous

This is essentially a repeat of one of the Cardinal Rules I already stated back in Chapter 13.

Monogamy = Oneitis, almost always. Sexual monogamy creates a fertile breeding ground for Oneitis to blossom. It's very hard for a man to *not* get Oneitis for the only woman he's having sex with. The split second you stop having sex with your FBs, regardless of whatever bullshit justification you give yourself, is the split second Oneitis for your wife will start to grow in your psyche. If she's your only source of sex, you're going to start to get needier for her. Hello, Oneitis!

Don't ever let that happen. To repeat the six-week rule once again, *always have sex with at least one of your FBs once every six weeks for the rest of your life and never stop doing this.* The minute you stop is the minute you've set the failure of your OLTR Marriage into motion.

Chapter 17
JEALOUSY MANAGEMENT

Interestingly, the issue of jealousy in non-monogamous marriages isn't quite the challenge it is in non-monogamous non-live-in relationships. This is because either you and your wife have probably been non-monogamous for quite a while already and are both somewhat accustomed to it, or you and your wife have been married for so long already that the mutual familiarity and trust is such that neither of you is terrified that you'll fall in love with or run off with someone else just because some sexual activity occurs.

This is quite different from FB, MLTR, and non-live-in OLTR relationships where partners are often coming and going and the world of non-monogamy is often new to the man and almost always new to the woman. Jealousy is a much bigger problem in these scenarios, and I have an entire detailed chapter in *The Ultimate Open Relationships Manual*** that covers jealousy management techniques in great detail for people in those kinds of relationships. I recommend that chapter for anyone reading this book as well, but it's probably not as urgently needed for you as for those men in dating relationships who live alone. I briefly summarize some of these techniques below.

In addition, in the case of a live-in OLTR Marriage, it is usually the woman who will have more jealousy issues than the man. As I've already explained, over the entirety of your marriage, you are much more likely to be more sexually active with women on the side than your wife is to do the same with men on the side (though again, there are exceptions to this). This means that jealousy management is twofold; you need to manage *your* jealousy (if you have any), and you need to help manage *her* jealousy regarding what you're doing.

Managing Both of Your Jealousy Levels

The number one most important aspect of managing your jealousy

*http://www.haveopenrelationships.com

186 | *Jealousy Management*

actually applies to her jealousy levels as well. That is, to follow all the protocols in this book regarding the parameters of an OLTR Marriage. The OLTR Marriage model is specifically configured to keep the jealousy levels of both partners as low as possible. That's one of the advantages of the OLTR Marriage over many the other forms of non-monogamous marriages I described in back in Chapter 2.

In an OLTR Marriage, you are only allowed to have sex with FBs and one-night stands. No dating and no MLTRs or girlfriends on the side are allowed for you, ever. You are not allowed to date anyone else outside of your wife, nor spend any romantic time or context (like spending the night or long, intimate phone calls) with anyone other than your wife. Your wife knows this and knows that while you may be having occasional sex with some of your female friends, you're not actually dating anyone or getting feelings for anyone else other than her. If she is having any sex with any men (or women!) on the side, the same limitation applies to her, providing a level of protection for you as well.

In polyamorous, polygamous, Mediterranean, and open convenience marriages, this limitation either doesn't exist or barely exists in some loose way. Both husband and wife are "allowed" to have actual, romantic, emotional relationships with other people in addition to their spouse. That's what makes these kinds of marriages often troublesome and more difficult for most people. (Though as I said earlier, these kinds of marriages do work for some.)

It is your job, and the job of your wife if she's having any side-sex, to actually follow through on this limitation and never violate it. Outside of your wife, only have FBs and one-night stands, period, no exceptions for any reason. Treat your FBs like FBs, meaning like friends, not like women you're dating and certainly not like girlfriends or other wives. Keeping to these standards minimizes the odds of any severe jealousy.

We'll discuss how to manage your ongoing FB relationships in Part Five of this book.

Technique Summaries

Here are the briefly summarized versions of some of the anti-jealousy techniques I cover in *The Ultimate Open Relationships Manual** that will assist you in managing any jealousy you may have regarding the fact or possibility that your wife may get sexual with other men. Please refer to that book for more detailed descriptions and analysis.

1. *Remind yourself that your jealousy is fundamentally irrational.* It's a biological fact that *sexual* jealousy is an obsolete holdover of your caveman biology that is outdated by at least 100,000 years. In a modern world full of an abundance of women, condoms, birth control, and paternity tests, *sexual* jealousy is literally useless. (*Romantic* jealousy is still valid, but again, if you and your wife are following OLTR Marriage rules that should never be a problem.)

2. *Remember that while your wife is important, there are likely thousands, if not tens of thousands of women as hot, fun, smart, and wonderful as her within a two-hour driving radius of your home.* I'm sure you love your wife, and I'm sure you want to be married to her for the rest of your life as I do mine. At the same time, we need to acknowledge facts and reality. Your wife is not some kind of unique, special snowflake that can't ever be replaced. If she were to get hit by a bus tomorrow, would you wallow in sadness and celibacy for the rest of your life? No. Eventually, you'd feel better, have sex with other women, date other women, fall in love again, and eventually get married to someone else. (The same is true of your wife if you died tomorrow.) Never, ever, EVER get Oneitis!

3. *Remind yourself that monogamous couples have jealousy problems too.* I've noticed that some people who oppose non-monogamy seem to believe that monogamy is a cure for jealousy. That is the dumbest and most inaccurate thing I've ever heard. Monogamous people have plenty of jealousy problems too. In many cases, monogamous couples have more jealousy problems than non-monogamous ones.

4. *Remind yourself of all the massive positives you're getting by not being monogamous and being in an OLTR Marriage instead of in a TMM.* More sex, more freedom, more fun, less drama, more financial protection, on and on… remind yourself of everything you'd have to give up if you become monogamous like everyone else.

*http://www.haveopenrelationships.com

5. *Review and recommit to your goals and your Mission.* It's harder to be jealous when you're super excited about where your life is going.

6. *Visualize your wife having sex with another man who is better-looking and richer than you are, over and over again.* You probably won't like it the first time you do it, but eventually you'll stop giving a shit.

7. *If your wife is actually having sex with another man, objectively compare yourself to him.* Very likely, he's a needy beta male who is less intelligent, less confident, and less successful than you are. Focus on the areas in which you are superior to him, which will likely be many. He's no threat to you.

Is Jealousy Ever Valid?

Sexual jealousy is never valid if you're dealing with someone you trust with a long track record of responsible behavior. Hopefully, your wife is in that category (and if she isn't, I'm not sure why you married her). In that case, sexual jealousy is a purely emotional, irrational response based on false Societal Programming and Obsolete Biological Wiring, both of which I cover in great detail in *The Unchained Man**.

Romantic jealousy, on the other hand, can be valid under certain conditions. This is when you have romantic feelings for someone and they start having romantic feelings for someone else.

If Pink Firefly had meaningless, protected sex with another guy, I wouldn't give two fucks about it. I trust her, I know sexual jealousy is useless, I'm not threatened by other men, and most importantly, have much more important things to concern myself with, namely my goals and my Mission.

On the other hand, if she instead started *falling in love* with another guy, I would indeed start feeling romantically jealous and it would be a very serious problem in our marriage. I don't anticipate that particular scenario ever occurring (if she and I ever got divorced, it would likely be for drama reasons, not because there was someone else in the picture). I'm just illustrating the difference between *sexual* jealousy and *romantic* jealousy.

*http://www.alphamalebook.com

If you start getting romantic feelings for one of your side women, this is a serious problem. You need to eject her from your life immediately. Then you need to look in the mirror and ask yourself some very hard questions about why that happened, and more importantly, *why you let it happen*. Either you have a serious problem with controlling your emotions (which may require therapy or similar), or you really don't want to be married in this way and want to be more of an MLTR guy than an OLTR guy. Either way, you have some tough decisions to make.

If you discover your wife is getting romantic feelings for another man, you have several options, all of which are bad. Here they are with my subjective, personal opinions regarding each one in parenthesis.

1. Immediately but nicely end the marriage and move on. Remember that getting a divorce in an OLTR Marriage is relatively quick and painless. (This is probably what I would do.)

2. "Downgrade" the relationship with your wife from an OLTR Marriage to MLTR. You or she move out but you're both still dating, and now you can go date other people as full MLTRs if you wish, without living with her. (This something I might agree to, but it would be unlikely.)

3. Give her an ultimatum that she needs to eject this guy from her life immediately and forever or else you'll divorce her (and of course, she gets none of your money). Even if she agrees and dumps the guy, you still have a very serious problem in your relationship that you'll both need to work on with your marriage counselor. (I personally would never take this option.)

4. Immediately reconfigure the marriage from an OLTR Marriage to a polyamorous one where you are both allowed to fully date people on the side. (I personally would never take this option.)

I want to reiterate that *I have literally never seen a couple in a properly managed OLTR Marriage have the problem of one spouse falling getting feelings with someone on the side.* 100% of the time I've seen this problem occur were in open marriages, which were *not* OLTR Marriages and instead were polygamous, polyamorous, convenience, Mediterranean, or other marriage types. If you follow all the protocols in this book, you should never experience that problem (and if you do, it means you really didn't follow everything in this book, or you're a bizarre statistical anomaly).

Section Three
Legal and Financial Protection

Chapters 18

OLTR MARITAL LEGAL STRUCTURES

Sexual freedom isn't the only core aspect of the OLTR Marriage; legal and financial protection is just as critical. Protecting your hard-earned money, lifestyle, and children is just as important in the modern area as sexual freedom. More so, in fact.

Throughout this section of the book, I'm going to overview the various legal structures you need to have in place for your OLTR Marriage. It is important to understand that the content in this book is not legal advice, I am not an attorney, and I have no legal qualifications. More importantly, every city, country, state, and province in the world has radically different laws governing sex, marriage, cohabitation, property, children, child support, child custody, and divorce. Since it is impossible for me to cover all of those legal differences in this book, I am forced to generalize. Therefore, **you must retain a qualified family attorney in your local city to assist you with any legal aspects you read in this book**. Please do *not* attempt to do any of this yourself. You will either do it incorrectly (rendering it unenforceable if there is a problem down the road), or you will waste massive amounts of your time (or both!).

This chapter is written with the assumption that the reader is someone who is not married *yet* and is currently living alone but is planning on moving in with (and/or legally marrying) a woman in the near future. If that's you, just follow the instructions as stated.

If you already live with a woman or if you're already legally married, then you are going to have to modify some of the specifics of what you read but still take action on all the techniques as best you can. You have a lot of catching up to do in order to convert all the legal and financial aspects of your marriage to OLTR Marriage status. If you live in the Western world, *you are at great legal risk* by living with a woman (legally married or not doesn't matter) without having done all the things I will explain in the next few chapters. Read through them and make a to-do list to get all the things I explain that you haven't done yet. Some of the things I describe may need to be radically changed if you already live with a woman or if you are already legally married. A few of these techniques may not even be possible where you live, and if that's the case, you'll have some difficult decisions to make. Again, consult with an attorney on this, but get it done ASAP.

Speaking of an attorney...

Step 1: Find A Family Law or Divorce Attorney

This should be your very first to-do item. Go online and use whatever search functions you like (including looking up your local Bar Association if your country has those) and find at least three attorneys that focus either in divorce law or family law and have at least 15 years of experience (20+ is better). Interview all of them over the phone and pick the one you like the best.

Attorneys cost money. This is one of the many reasons why I tell men that they shouldn't even *think* about moving in with a woman until they are at least 35 years old and thus have the income that a properly structured marriage requires. You should plan on spending anywhere from $1000 to $3000 in total on various legal fees in order to get correctly OLTR married. If you can't afford this, you are *not* ready to be married or move in with a woman in my strong opinion, and you should instead just date your OLTR as a serious, non-live-in girlfriend for the time being while you get your income up.

Step 2: Understand the Terms

Here are the legal terms you need to understand before you embark on this process.

- **Communal property** means that everything you own and everything she owns, regardless of whose name is on it or who originally earned it, owned it, or purchased it, goes into a big pot, and if you break up, she gets 50% and you get 50%. That means if you have $500,000 and she has $20, if she moves out under a communal property arrangement, you have to give her $250,010 (50% of $500,020), or else you'll go to prison. Isn't that nice? That's what happens to guys in TMM when they get divorced. As you can see, it's a very fair and equitable system (yeah, right). There are possible exceptions to certain assets to which this applies; check with your attorney on this. In an OLTR Marriage, there is *no* communal property, and we'll discuss how to completely avoid communal property later in this chapter.

- **Alimony** or **spousal support** means you pay your ex-wife a monthly check for a certain number of years after you get divorced, even if you never had any children, or else you go to prison. It's because she was "accustomed" to living with your money while you were together, so she's "due" your money even after you're not together anymore. In some jurisdictions (like California) under some conditions, alimony can last *forever*. (Yeah. That means you pay her every month, *forever*.) Men in OLTR Marriages don't need to pay alimony post-divorce; I'll discuss that later in this chapter.

- **Palimony** is just like alimony, except it applies to ex-live-in girlfriends instead of wives. Yes, men who don't get legally married can still be forced to pay this if they don't structure an OLTR Marriage. This is because of…

- **Common-law marriage** or **"marriage-like relationship"** means that you move in with your girlfriend, don't legally marry her, but are still suddenly considered *legally married to her* after you live with her for several years. If she moves out after this, she may be due communal property and/or palimony from you. An OLTR Marriage avoids this; more on that later in this chapter.

- **Child support** means that if you have children with a woman, you may be forced to send her money every month to help her support those kids. Unlike with things like alimony or communal property, in the Western world, there is no way to legally pre-avoid child support unless you literally never have children or are unusually lucky, even if you have an OLTR Marriage, so we won't be covering the issue of child support in this book. I always recommend to any men who want kids that you should budget for monthly child support or similar child expense, per kid, for at least 18 years, regardless of if you stay together with their mother or not.

Step 3: Ascertain the Cohabitation Laws in Your City

Now that you have your attorney and you know the basic terms, the very first thing you need to understand before you move in with a woman is all the applicable laws in your city regarding when you live with someone in the same home.

The first question you need answered is: *Will the live-in relationship ever be considered a "common law marriage" or "marriage-like relationship" at a certain time down the road even if there is no legal marriage?"* You need to fully understand if these conditions exist in your city, and if they do, how many years it takes for them to activate. Otherwise, you may be forced to pay her palimony or communal property if she ever breaks up from you (or you from her).

Once you understand exactly how this works in your city, you then need to determine if there is any paperwork you and your OLTR can sign that prevents this from ever happening. In some cities, there isn't. If that's the case, you should probably refrain from moving in with a woman until you move to a city with more sane laws. Another weird option I've seen some men take is that they kick their OLTR wives out of the house right before the common law kicks in, then wait a few months, then move her back in, all with her understanding and consent beforehand. Sounds like a hassle to me, but I've seen it work.

In other cities, you can avoid common law marriage or "marriage-like relationship" status by signing something like a **cohabitation agreement** (though it may not be named exactly that in your jurisdiction). This legal document protects you from all alimony, palimony, and communal property when you live with a woman you're not legally married to, regardless of how long the relationship lasts (though again, this varies city by city, so check with your attorney!).

You *must* make sure the cohabitation agreement is actually enforceable! In many jurisdictions (such as Australia, the UK, California, etc.), attorneys will cheerfully sell you things like cohabitation agreements or prenuptial agreements, but they're actually worthless. If the woman actually challenges them in court later, the judge just lights them on fire, and you pay. Getting a cohab or prenup is one thing. Making sure it's actually enforceable is quite another. Always ask your attorney, *"If we break up down the road and she gets her own attorney and challenges this document in court, is the court going to uphold it with at least 95% certainty?"* If your attorney is at all wishy-washy about the answer, it may not be enforceable and may be a waste of your time. Time to either look for a second opinion or move to a different city.

If an *enforceable* cohabitation agreement is a viable option, have your attorney write it up (or get one online that your attorney approves), sign it with your OLTR before she moves in (ideally 30 to 60 days before she moves in) and get it notarized. *Always get everything the two of you sign notarized, or else it may not be enforceable in court if it is challenged later. Very important.*

The next thing you need to know is: *If the home is yours, are you able to quickly kick her out whenever you want?* In many jurisdictions, you are actually *not* allowed to kick your OLTR girlfriend out of your home whenever you like. In some places, you are actually required to give her 30 or even 60 days of "notice" before you can make her move out. In some other cities, you may actually need to wait *several months* before you can make her leave.

If you find you live in one of these jurisdictions, you've got some difficult decisions to make. Either refrain from moving in with her, or move to a different city with more sane cohabitation laws before you cohabit with a woman, or move in with her but make sure *she* is the one holding the lease or the mortgage and have an "escape plan" where you can move out really fast at and a moment's notice whenever you want.

You *must* have the ability to either quickly move out or quickly kick her out whenever you live with a female in a romantic context. I have heard way too many horror stories from men whose wives or live-in girlfriends turned into maniacs, and these men were stuck with them for *weeks* because they didn't check the local cohabitation laws first.

Step 4: Prevent All Communal Property from Ever Forming

Communal property is bad. That means she possibly gets legal ownership of half of everything you currently own or will own in the future. This means you can never establish any communal property in the first place. This is done by utilizing *individual* property instead of *communal* property. In a properly structured OLTR Marriage, 100% of the property you own is designated as individual property, meaning it belongs to you and only you, and she has no right to any of it in the case of a break-up or divorce. Slimily, everything she owns is 100% hers as well, and you can't take any of her stuff in a break-up either, so she's protected too.

The default setting for a live-in relationship in the Western world is communal property based. You switch this to an individual property basis by using *enforceable* prenuptial agreements, *enforceable* cohabitation agreements, keeping separate finances at all times, and asset protection (all of which we will discuss in this chapter).

If you are not legally marrying your OLTR wife, your *enforceable* cohabitation agreement should specify that everything in the relationship is individual property (hers or yours), and there is no communal property. It should also protect you against alimony or palimony (though it will not protect you against child support; no document is guaranteed to do that in the Western world).

If you are legally marrying your wife, then instead of (or perhaps in addition to) a cohabitation agreement, you'll need an *enforceable* prenuptial agreement (though it may be called something very different where you live). This is essentially the married version of a cohabitation agreement. Once again, you need to make sure it's actually enforceable, or else it's worthless. An enforceable prenup will specify that everything in your marriage is individual property (yours or hers) and nothing is communal so that if you get divorced, she can't take your stuff.

Step 5: Maintain 100% Separate Finances

The next critical step is to maintain 100% separate finances for the rest of the marriage, with no exceptions. Even if you sign an enforceable prenup or cohab, you can invalidate the entire thing if you start co-mingling finances with your wife. In many regions, even the most enforceable and rock-solid prenups can be instantly invalidated if your wife shows the divorce court that you both used a joint checking account, or you ever paid some of her bills from your account, or you own a home together, or any other co-mingling of finances takes place, even "small" things you probably think don't matter. They matter!

It is not enough to just get an enforceable prenuptial agreement or cohabitation agreement; you must also maintain absolute, 100% separate finances from your wife at all times, for the entire length of the marriage. As attorneys say, you must "live the agreement."

Separation of finance means the following things:

1. There are no co-owned debts, assets, accounts, or leases between you and your wife. Share everything with your wife but co-own nothing. This means every debt, asset, account, or lease in your marriage is either **in her name** or **in your name.** Absolutely *nothing* **has both of your names on it.**

Examples of things you can't have in an OLTR Marriage are (but are not limited to):

- Joint checking accounts
- Joint savings accounts
- Joint cell phone accounts
- Co-signed loans
- Joint car leases
- Joint ownership of a home or mortgage
- Joint apartment leases (in some regions, you might have to both be listed on the lease as living in the apartment; this is fine, but only one of you should be financially responsible for actual payments on the lease)

- Joint utility bills (only *one* of you is on *all* of the utility bills; the owner of the house or lease)
- Joint retirement accounts
- And so on

You get the idea. Every single item in your entire financial lives must be 100% yours or 100% hers, at least on paper. Nothing is co-owned by "both" of you. The split second you do something like set up a joint checking account, co-sign a car loan with her, or anything like that, you can instantly invalidate all the hard work and money you spent setting up your enforceable cohab or prenup.

Women tend to be mini-communists in their financial lives when living with a man. It's just how they're wired. When they move in with a man, and certainly when they marry a man, they will immediately look for ways to start combining finances wherever they can. If you resist doing this, they will fight back, using Societal Programming-based excuses such as "It's easier to have a joint checking account to buy groceries," or "It's safer/better for both of us to be on the lease since we can report both of our incomes."

Don't fall for it. Don't get lazy. Stay strong and say no. Always maintain separate finances throughout the entire length of the marriage.

Is having all this stuff separate a hassle? You might think so, but I've been married under this financial model for several years now and I can unequivocally say that it isn't. Sure, when you first get started with a marriage like this, it feels a little weird. The standard societal model is to combine everything you can with your wife "because it's easier" or "because that's what being married is all about." This stuff is all based on blazingly outdated Societal Programming from the 1950s when the divorce rate was 8% instead of 76%. Regardless, going against this grain might feel a little odd when you first start doing it. Your wife certainly won't like it either since all the women in her family and social circle are in TMMs to beta males who combine everything.

However, once you've been married under this model for about six months, I promise that you and your wife will get used to it and won't even think about it anymore. It will simply become a normal and natural habit in your marriage.

Here's just one simple example. If Pink Firefly and I ever go to the grocery store together (and usually we don't), we use the same shopping cart and just go around and fill it up with all the stuff we both need. When we go to the checkout counter, I'll let her go first, and I will help her unload all of her items onto the conveyer belt. She'll then pay for them with her own debit card, which comes out of a checking account that is 100% hers, that I have literally nothing to do with and have no access to. Then I will load my stuff on the conveyor belt and pay for *my* groceries with *my* debit card coming out of *my* checking account that she has nothing to do with and no access to. The grocery store staff then bags everything and puts both her stuff and my stuff back into the same shopping cart, and we leave together.

We've been doing this for years now and not once has anyone at the grocery store said anything or even looked at us funny. It's perfectly fine. We don't even think about it.

When you start getting serious with your OLTR (well before you move in with her), you need to inform her during The OLTR Talk (refer to *The Ultimate Open Relationships Manual** for what that is, how to do it, and when to do it) that if you two ever move in together, you will enforce this 100% separation of finances forever, *even* if you both get legally married. I made this very clear to Pink Firefly way back when we were dating, so when I actually did it once she moved in, it wasn't a surprise to her and there was no argument about it.

2. Payments made for one person's bills or expenses can *never* be paid from the other person's account. This means that if the cable bill is in *her* name, you can't ever pay it from *your* debit card or a check from any of *your* accounts. It must be made from one of *her* accounts. 100% of her bills and expenses must be paid from her accounts, and 100% of your bills/expenses must be paid from your accounts. There can never be an exception to this, no matter how small.

This also goes for your business accounts if you own your own business. Don't *ever* use your business accounts to pay your wife's personal

*http://www.haveopenrelationships.com

bills or expenses.

You need to think this through based on your scenario. For example, you follow the separate finances protocol and buy your own house that is 100% yours with a mortgage that is 100% yours, and then your wife moves in with you. So far, so good. However, if she ever makes a mortgage payment out of one of her accounts, you're in trouble. Even if she makes a partial payment, like you pay half and she pays the other half, again, you're in trouble. You must make 100% of all mortgage payments from your own checking account that is 100% in your name, period, always.

If your wife works full-time like you do and you want her to contribute to paying some of the bills of the household (which I think is a fantastic idea), that's fine. Just have her pay you a monthly amount of some kind, then you pay all the utilities and mortgage/rent payment. It's best if she actually hands you cash every month or deposits cash directly into your checking account. She could do some kind of bank transfer instead, but in some jurisdictions, that may violate the separation of finances. As always, check with your attorney.

By the way, the reverse is also true if your wife makes more money than you or if she owns the house/lease and you do not. If she demands you help pay the rent/mortgage, then pay her a hunk of cash every month (based on whatever you two agree), and then she pays mortgage/lease and all the utilities (which are all in her name only) out of her own checking account.

How Do You Financially Support Your Wife in An OLTR Marriage?

Some men would rather have a more traditional marriage where they work and pay all the bills and the wife stays home with little to no income, particularly if they want to have children. Can this be done under an OLTR Marriage model? The answer is: sort of.

Technically you can have your stay-at-home OLTR wife still maintain separate finances. You own the house 100% and pay all the bills 100%, and she has her own checking accounts that don't have your name on them. You hand her a wad of cash once a month that she can use for her own living expenses and purchase groceries and other items for the kids if you have any. I did exactly this during my first marriage. I handed my wife a flat amount once per month that she was allowed to use for all of her personal expenses plus all the expenses of our two kids (the kids' clothes, groceries, toys, sports, etc.). I took care of my own expenses myself.

There are still no joint accounts, assets, debts, or leases between the two of you. Everything is either in your name or her name, and *nothing* has both of your names on it. This means that even if you do something like buy her a car, it's *her* car, not *your* car, and that car is 100% in her name, which means she can take it with her if you two ever break-up/divorce. Remember that there is no communal property in an OLTR Marriage! (And yes, you could perhaps buy a car for you and let her "use" as if it's "her" car, but that gets a little messier and more complicated.)

Technically this will all work. There's just one problem. It is my understanding is that if your wife never has any income on her own and a divorce occurs, the prenuptial paperwork *may* become less enforceable. Rightly or wrongly, the court may view your stay-at-home housewife as less able to support herself post-divorce, and you run the risk of them invalidating some or all of the prenuptial paperwork. Yes, you may actually get penalized for being a quality husband who makes enough money so that his wife doesn't need to slog it out in the work world unless she wants to. (As is usual today, men are penalized for being better husbands. I wonder why fewer men are getting married these days?)

As usual, please check with your attorney regarding this. In some areas, having a housewife with no income might be perfectly fine for prenup enforceability. In other areas, it might be better to show that your wife has some regular, monthly income (that ideally has nothing to do with you) so that if a divorce occurs, it's "on the record" that your wife has the ability to work in the real world and pay her own bills. This is great for the enforceability of your prenuptial paperwork.

As of this writing, Pink Firefly works full time as a toddler teacher, and that's just the way I like it. I have a nice, solid paper trail of PF being able to earn her own money without any of my help. In addition, I *want* her to have her own career and money as a key part of Her Zone so she can feel a sense of accomplishment and ownership outside of me. It's great for our Mutual Harmony. In my first marriage, we had tons of problems and drama because my bored, unfulfilled, stay-at-home wife at the time always felt she had nothing that was truly her own. On top of that, because she was a housewife, I was forced to pay her a decent amount of alimony when we got divorced. During the divorce, my attorney basically told me that if she was a stay-at-home mom, I could virtually "count on" paying her alimony (in addition to communal property and child support, of course), and there was no literally way around it. Lesson learned!

One counterargument to this is that you really want to raise small kids, and thus, you don't want your wife to work at a full-time job so she can be home for the children. No problem! Help your stay-at-home wife build her own location-independent Alpha 2.0 business online, which she can run for just a few hours a day while the kids are sleeping, at school, or otherwise preoccupied. Just make sure it's 100% her business and not yours, but you're certainly able to assist her in her efforts all you want (Pink Firefly sells jewelry online and I help advise her all the time; not a problem). Go to *calebjones.com** for more resources on how to set up a company like this.

Step 6: Engage in Asset Protection

Sadly, just getting an enforceable prenup and keeping finances separate is not enough in the modern era and in the Western world. Decades ago, doing these things was all you needed to make sure you were covered in the case of a divorce. However, with every decade that passes, the Western world becomes more left-wing and more anti-male. That means that even if you do everything correctly in terms of your cohabitation agreements, enforceable prenups, and keeping all finances separate, you can still run afoul of some new law you weren't aware of, or your attorney making a mistake, or some angry feminist judge ruling against you. (There's a saying among attorneys that judge's rulings in civil cases are based mostly on whatever the judge ate for breakfast that morning. It's not too far from the truth.)

This means that you need one final layer of protection just in case none of the other stuff works. That is *asset protection*.

Asset protection is a component of financial planning that legally protects your assets from creditors, lawsuits, your government, and angry ex-wives. This is done using instruments like corporations, trusts, family members, creative investing, stateless assets, paperless assets, and offshoring your assets to distant countries far away from your wife's reach. It's going to be very difficult, if not impossible for your angry ex-OLTR wife or the divorce court to go after assets in a rock-solid, legal, international trust in some country on the other side of the planet that isn't even in your name.

Some people think this kind of thing is illegal. Wrong. Asset protection, when done properly and with the assistance of experts, is 100% legal and enforceable. It is perfectly within your legal rights to protect your assets this way.

Moreover, asset protection is not "hiding your assets." In some cases, you *may* still need to declare that these assets (or some of them) as a legal requirement (called "discovery" in legal terms). That's okay, since even if you declare them *your wife still can't touch them* in the case of a break-up or divorce (assuming they are properly structured).

Asset protection is a huge and complicated topic. It is far beyond the scope of this book. The main point is that you need to *do it*, particularly if your net worth is over about $250,000. Get on the internet and look up at least three asset protection attorneys or financial planning firms that specialize in asset protection, interview them, hire one of them, and get to work. Tell them that the specific reason you want to protect your assets is to retain them in the case of a break-up or divorce from your OLTR wife.

Too many men make the mistake of just getting a prenup, then getting married and comingling all of their assets and not engaging in any asset protection whatsoever. These same men are shocked when they get a divorce and the legal system just plows through their prenup like it wasn't even there. Once you've executed all six steps in this chapter, you can breathe easy that no matter what happens, you won't lose your hard-earned money if you and your wife part company.

It's a great feeling.

Chapter 19
Prenuptial Details

In this chapter, I'm going to cover various items that I have learned from divorce attorneys over many years that will help you ensure that your cohabitation agreement and/or prenuptial agreement is actually enforceable. Most men who utilize these documents usually handle them incorrectly, rendering them only partially enforceable or worse, completely useless. You don't want to be in that category.

I will repeat yet again that I am not an attorney and none of this is legal advice. Please run all these things past your divorce law or family law attorney in your city.

By Any Other Name

When I say "cohabitation agreement" or "prenuptial agreement," please remember that these documents are probably not going to be called these things where you live. Every country, state, province, and county uses different names for these things, like:

- premarital agreement
- antenuptial agreement
- property settlement arrangement
- marriage contract
- matrimonial property agreement
- qualifying nuptial agreement
- domestic partnership
- and so on

Just be aware that the names may vary. Work with your attorney so that you thoroughly understand what the agreement is called in your region and how they work.

It May Not Be Legally Binding Where You Live

Remember that just because your region may offer these documents and attorneys in your region may happily write them up for you does *not* mean they're enforceable or even useful where you live. A prenup in the state of California is almost useless if you get divorced after ten years. Cohabitation agreements in the UK aren't legally binding at all.

In some regions, these documents are useless. In other regions, they only work if you add in separate instruments like trust deeds and wills. In other regions, they are quite enforceable, but only if you structure them in very particular ways.

Once again, it's your job to understand what is enforceable and not enforceable in your region before you move in with any woman. Work with your attorney on this.

If you are unfortunate enough to live in a region where these documents aren't enforceable at all, you've got some difficult decisions to make. I would personally refrain from living with a woman at all in such a region, and I would move to another region where these things were either enforceable or irrelevant before I moved in with a woman. ("Irrelevant" means you move to some developing nation far outside of the Western world where there are no alimony or communal property laws. I realize most men reading this book aren't going to do that, but it's still an option.)

The One-Year Rule and 60-Day Rule

If you have your wife sign the prenuptial agreement too close to the wedding, or if you have your girlfriend sign the cohabitation agreement too soon (or after) to the move-in date, the paperwork becomes less enforceable. This is because she could challenge the docs in court, saying she was "under duress."

This is easily solved. Make sure that any cohabitation agreement is signed at least 60 days before she moves in and ensure any prenuptial agreement is signed one year before any wedding takes place. By doing this, it's officially on the record that in both cases she had plenty of time to "think about it" before the actual event.

Witness Representation

I mentioned in the prior chapter that anything you sign with your wife must be notarized and logged by a professional notary. When signing any of the "big" documents, meaning cohabitation agreements and prenups, one additional step is required.

This is "witnessing" the signing of the documents. This means that an attorney or judge actually goes through the entire document with your wife and explains everything to her. Once she gives a verbal agreement to the legal professional, this person signs the document along with you and your wife, all of which is notarized.

This is done because it's possible a woman can challenge the docs in court saying she "didn't understand what she was signing." If the document was witnessed and signed by a neutral judge or by your wife's own attorney, she can't use this as a defense, since it's on the record that everything was explained to her and she indicated understanding.

As usual, different regions handle this differently. In some regions, a judge handles this function. In other regions, your wife must get her own attorney *that you have absolutely nothing to do with* (more on that in a minute), and this attorney will satisfy this function. You, in turn, will have your own attorney do the same for you. This means that on the docs there will be four different signatures when it's finally signed and notarized: yours, your attorney's, your wife's, and her attorney's. Now that's a solid prenup!

If you need to use attorneys, you can't have *anything* to do with your wife's attorney. This means:

- You can*not* use your attorney to witness the docs for your wife. She must have her own.

- You can*not* find an attorney for your wife to use. She must do it completely on her own.

- You can*not* pay your wife's attorney. She must pay her completely on her own.

- There can*not* be any communication whatsoever between you and your wife's attorney. One email, one voice mail, one phone call, any of these things can and will invalidate enforceability of the documents if they are challenged later. Limited communication between your attorney and her attorney is allowed.

Various attorneys have told me of real-life cases where the guy went out, found an attorney for his wife, had this attorney witness the prenup, then got married, years later got divorced, and then the wife challenged the prenup in court *and won* when it was discovered the husband found and set up the "wife's" attorney for her. When your wife needs her own legal representation, you must let her do literally everything on her own. You can't be involved in any way whatsoever. Pink Firefly used her own attorney and I had *nothing* to do with any of it. I literally know nothing about the attorney other than her name (since it's on our paperwork).

Enforceability Tweaks

Keep bugging your attorney, over and over again, that you want the documentation enforceable if it's ever challenged in court. Constantly throw "what if" scenarios at him and make sure he provides good answers.

If he's a good attorney, he'll provide you various little tweaks you can place in the paperwork to make it more enforceable, even if they don't make any sense. For example, in some regions, if you help provide your wife health insurance, it strangely makes the prenup more enforceable (even though it technically violates the separation of finances; this would be an exception to that rule). There are even regions where cohabs and prenups are more enforceable if you legally marry your wife instead of just living with her(!). Weird, but true (in *some* regions). Again, press your attorney to squeeze out as many of these strange enforceability factors as you possibly can, and include them in the agreements.

Be Generous

False Societal Programming has caused many people to believe that "prenuptial agreement" equates to "woman gets nothing." In more extreme cases, people think that "prenuptial agreement" means "man makes off like a bandit and woman gets screwed."

This is not accurate. Prenups don't mean that 100% of everything goes to one person. Instead, the prenup (among other things) states exactly what will happen if/when a divorce occurs. Often it states that the woman does indeed get *something*, just not half of the guy's stuff.

I still remember reading an article way back in the early 1990s when Donald Trump divorced his first wife, Ivana Trump. They had signed a prenup together when they got married, yet Trump still paid Ivana $25 million during the divorce. I was confused. Didn't a prenup mean she was due *nothing* from him? No. The prenup stated that Ivana was to receive $25 million while Donald kept his $2 billion. Do you think Trump cared about $25 million when he had $2 billion? I'm quite sure he didn't, and you probably wouldn't either. I'm also quite sure that giving a woman $25 million instead of $1 billion (which would be half of his wealth) is a pretty good deal.

In many regions, perhaps most, prenups are more enforceable if the wife actually gets a little something in the case of a divorce. Even if it's a tiny fraction of your income or net worth, it still helps. In many cases, more enforceable prenups allow the wife to receive *something* if the marriage lasts a certain period of time before the divorce, like 5, 10, or 15 years. There are lots of variations. The rationale behind this is that you look more benevolent and less greedy if the prenup states that the wife gets something in the case of a divorce. If she gets literally nothing, her odds of successfully challenging it in court may go up a little. But if she clearly gets something, it makes *her* look like the greedy one if she tries to challenge it.

This is not the case in many regions, however. As always, check with your attorney on this.

Go Offshore

This goes hand-in-hand with the asset protection I spoke of in the prior chapter. Generally speaking, the more of your assets you have offshore, the safer they will be. Going offshore can be a little complicated, expensive, and time consuming, but if your net worth is high enough, all of that will be worth it. I have personally known men who protected themselves from financial ruin because they had assets offshore during a divorce. If 100% of their net worth was located in the countries in which they lived, they would have been screwed.

Once again, I am *not* recommending you illegally hide assets offshore. In today's age of big, powerful governments, digital banking, and interconnected internet-based finance, that's a time bomb just waiting to explode. Back in the 1980s, you could hide assets offshore and no one would ever find out. Today that just isn't true.

I'm not saying *hide* assets offshore. I'm saying *have* assets offshore. Comply with any disclosure laws your country has regarding marriage and divorce, but keep those assets offshore. They might just save your life.

The next level to this strategy is to *move* offshore. If and your wife move to a distant country, far from where you were married, this alone can help you greatly if a divorce occurs, especially if the marriage lasts a long time. I realize that you may not ever want to pursue that option (though I certainly am), but the option is still there.

Biennial Review

So you do everything in this book and get a rock-solid, enforceable prenup. Everything is perfect and you're set. You finally relax, knowing that your finances are protected no matter what happens in your OLTR Marriage.

Your marriage goes great for a long time. However, 16 years later, you and your wife encounter some irreconcilable problems and get divorced. It's not a fun day, but you know your money is protected, so you don't worry about it.

To your shock, a few weeks later, your attorney calls you and informs you that your wife has gone to court and is challenging the prenup she signed 16 years ago. Worse, she actually has a good chance of winning! You scream at him, "What? How the hell is that possible? We covered all the bases on that 16 years ago! It was rock-solid!" He sighs and replies, "Yes, we did, but that was a long time ago. Seven years ago, they changed some of the laws regarding prenups and invalidated some of the stuff we have in there."

Just because your prenup is rock-solid the year you create it doesn't mean it will remain that way forever. As I've said before, every year the Western world moves more to the political left, which unfortunately means more legal benefits for women and less for men. (I think the law should treat men and women equally in all scenarios and all respects, but that's not the world we live in. It never has been.)

This means that, for the length of your marriage, you need to do a biennial review. "Biennial" means every two years. Every two years, you need to sit down with your attorney and back through all the paperwork you and your wife signed and confirm that it is all still 100% enforceable based on any new laws that passed in the prior two years. If your attorney confirms that nothing has changed and everything is okay, great. See him again in two years to do it again.

If instead he says that indeed some new laws have been passed that may not make the documents quite as enforceable as they were, then you need to make addendums to the docs and have them witnessed, signed, and notarized with your wife (and possibly attorneys) all over again.

You must go through this process every two years or so. I suppose you could do this at longer intervals (like once every three or four years), but I think that's dangerous in this modern era, particularly if you live in the Western world.

Post-Nuptial Agreements

One odd variation on the prenuptial agreement concept is the *post-nuptial agreement*. This is when you get married the usual way (TMM) with no prenup or cohab then after being married for several years you go back and get a prenuptial agreement-like document with your wife even though you've already been married.

As always, check with your attorney on these things, but my understanding is that in most jurisdictions, post-nuptial agreements aren't very enforceable, mainly because your wife already married you and moved in with you before any such agreement was in place. This makes it much easier for her to challenge it in court during a divorce.

Another more serious problem is that you are in a terrible negotiating position when you work up a post-nuptial agreement as compared to being in a fantastic position to negotiate a prenup or cohab before she's living with you. With a post-nup, you're already married to her, so if she doesn't like any aspect of it, she can just threaten to divorce you (or stop having sex with you, or whatever). Therefore, you should never use post-nuptial agreements as a standard technique. They're more for men who discover this information after they're in a TMM and need them as a form of damage control.

That said, there are some strange jurisdictions out there (I believe some are in the UK) where prenuptial agreements aren't enforceable, but post-nuptial agreements are. Again, refer to your attorney regarding your local laws.

Chapter 20

HOW FINANCES TIE INTO THE REST OF THE MARRIAGE

Structuring separate finances in a marriage or live-in relationship is one thing, but deciding who actually pays for what is often a more complicated matter.

Some men are more traditional guys who want to work while their wife stays home without working at a job or a business (and thus has no income) while she raises the kids (or if there are no kids, just chills out and manages the household while the guy works). Other men (like me) are the exact opposite and want their wives to get their asses out into the real world and work just like the husband does. Some men have high incomes and/or net worths and marry women who are younger and or have lower incomes, meaning the man is going to pay for most or all of the lifestyle costs. There is also a steadily growing category of men who (sadly) make less money than their wives, making the wife the breadwinner of the family.

Technically speaking, all of these models can work within an OLTR Marriage. You just need to decide with your wife, before she moves in, who will pay for what. You can even pay for 100% of the bills if you wish, provided you've followed all the legal structures outlined in this book and are maintaining your Financial Barrier. This would mean that you give your wife cash and she would pay her own bills out of her own checking account; you could not actually pay one of her bills from your credit card or checking account.

Therefore, you really have three options:

1. You pay for most or all of the living expenses (by paying your own bills and then giving your wife cash to pay hers).

2. She pays for most or all of the living expenses (by her paying her

own bills and her giving you cash to pay yours)

3. You each pay your own bills through your own incomes. One of you is still going to pay a little more since the home will be in only one of your names; that person would be responsible for the rent/mortgage (though this person could charge the other person a monthly "rent" payment if desired).

The specifics of how you both operate under each of those three options are really up to the two of you, and there is no right or wrong way to do this. However, the dynamics of the marriage *must* change based on which of you is paying more of the household expenses. If you want to pay all of your wife's bills, that's perfectly fine, but you can't be the typical married beta male who hands over 100% of his paycheck to his wife while his low-Attraction wife bosses him around like a little dictator. Obviously, that's grossly unfair and doesn't make any sense. The reverse also doesn't make any sense: making sure your wife pays 100% of all of her own bills while you attempt to run her life Alpha Male 1.0 style.

I categorize the two main options as the "1950s option" or the "1970s option." I have often told the women in my dating, social, and work lives that, in terms of dating and relationships, they need to choose between the 1950s or the 1970s, but they can't have both. They're going to want both, but having both at the same time doesn't work in the real world, at least in the long term, as divorce rates clearly indicate. Let's look at both options.

The 1950s Woman

A woman in the 1950s (and prior) had her ass kissed during the dating/courting phase. Men would treat them like little queens, taking them out on the most expensive dates they could afford while dressing as nice as they were able. Men on these dates were ultra-polite, consummate gentlemen, pulling her chair out for her, laying their coats on puddles for her to walk on, and slathering her with compliments. 1950s women on dates received all kinds of gifts, including flowers, chocolates, jewelry, clothing, and often even more expensive items, as much as the guy could afford based on his socio-economic level.

Men on these dates never tried to have sex with her. That just wasn't done. At best, these men got a kiss on the cheek as they dropped her off, then quickly went home to masturbate.

In other words, during the dating phase, women were in the driver's seat, and men were the ass-kissing hopefuls.

Why in the world did men back then agree to all of this crap? It's very simple. If/when the woman actually married the man, *the entire scenario flipped*. He would take care of her financially for the rest of her life, but now *he was in charge*. 1950s wives cleaned the entire house, made all the meals, did at least 80% of the kid-raising work, and served their husbands like little slaves. She was expected to do all of this stuff, forever, and usually did.

Moreover, the 1950s (and prior) wife was expected to put out sexually for her husband and usually did. If he wanted sex, she obeyed and gave it to him, regardless of whether she was in the mood, or if she had a bad day, or if she was on her period, and so on. I'm generalizing, of course, and this didn't always happen with every marriage, but this kind of subservience was much more common in marriages back then than today. Go ask some really old guys in the retirement homes and they'll tell you all about it.

The historical stats also clearly show that married people back then were having much more sex than they do today, and this is a big reason why. Women in the 1950s, once married, did what they were ordered to do.

These women also virtually never got divorced and put up with all kinds of crap from their husbands, up to and including things like physical abuse and cheating. It was considered a wife's duty do to this, so they did it. (Obviously, I don't agree with physical abuse or cheating. I'm just reporting to you how things were back then.)

In other words, in a weird sort of way, it made sense for men to kiss women's asses during the dating phase because once the woman was married to them, these men had a virtual slave for the rest of their lives. The upside for the woman was that she was financially taken care of for the rest of her life, even after her husband's death (since divorce rates were so low and pensions were solid back then).

That was the 1950s woman. Now let's look at her 1970s sister, a very different gal...

The 1970s Woman

During the 1970s, second-wave, sex-positive feminism was a growing rage among unmarried women. Not all single women back then subscribed to this kind of thinking, but many did, especially in the USA.

This was *not* what passes for feminism today. Old-school, Gloria Steinem feminism of the 1970s was a strong desire for equal rights and sexual freedom. Since first and second-wave feminism achieved their primary goals years ago (women are now legally equal to men in every way and can have sex with whomever they like), today's feminism has nothing of substance to complain about, so they instead waste their time lashing out at men while screaming inaccurate slogans about wage gaps and "rape culture" (which makes no sense since there's been an 85% *decrease* in rape since the late 1970s.) 1970s feminism was much more independent, more sex-positive, and at least a little less angry.

When a man went out on a date with that 1970s feminist, it was an utterly different scenario than with the 1950s woman. The 1970s girl lectured him about how they would both pick a place together. When they went out, she would pay her half of the bill. She was an independent woman with her own income, so she didn't want a man to pay for her and thus have power over her like the 1950s woman, whom the 1970s woman viewed as a pathetic weakling.

If the guy tried to pay for the date, the 1970s woman actually got upset. "Excuse me? No, I'm going to pay for my own food. I don't need you! How dare you try to take that kind of power over me!"

I'm not kidding about this. These women back then would actually get offended if the guy tried to pay for a first date. I know that sounds alien to us today, but go ask some old 1970s feminists today and they'll tell you all about it.

If the two actually got into a relationship, she would poke a defiant finger in his chest and tell him that she was her own woman, that she didn't belong to him, and that she could do whatever the hell she wanted, including having sex with other men, which many of these women did. They were the original anti-monogamists (outside of historical polygamy). Usually, she would also boss the guy around, making him take out the trash and perform other beta male tasks.

The good news for the man was that he was not expected to support her financially. He could keep his money since she "didn't need his money" and could support herself (at least theoretically). Many of these women also avoided having children for similar reasons.

As you might expect, these 1970s women would often get into relationships with beta males upon whom they'd cheerfully crack the whip. They'd also have a lot of sex. This was before any big STD scare, so unmarried people in the 1970s got laid big time.

The 1970s woman was essentially the opposite of the 1950s woman. The 1970s woman didn't get her ass kissed at all during the dating phase but had massive freedom and control during the relationship. She didn't get the money, Disney, and gifts during the dating phase, but she was the boss, pretty much at all stages.

The 21st Century Woman

That covers 1950s women and 1970s women, but what, then, is today's woman? It's very simple. Starting around the 1990s, most women have taken the best parts of the 1950s woman and the best parts of the 1970s woman and have conveniently discarded the parts they don't like. Most of today's women – not all of them, but most – want and expect the money, financial support, Disney, and ass-kissing like the 1950s women *and* the "Don't tell me what to do – I'm in charge here!" power of the 1970s women. They want **both**.

Being a slave like the 1950s women? Nope, modern-day women certainly don't want that.

Paying for her own dinner on dates and paying her own bills forever like the 1970s woman? Nope, today's women don't want that either.

Again, they want the money *and* the power.

I have encountered (and I'm sure you have encountered) women who make decent incomes, can support themselves, and brag that they're independent who will still expect or even demand that you pay for dates and/or pay for most of the bills during a live-in relationship. I have also encountered women (and I'm sure you have too) who, while having their husbands or boyfriends pay for everything or almost everything, still run these guy's lives like little drill sergeants. It's a great deal – for the woman.

Unlike most people who discuss these topics, I actually blame *men* for this condition more than I do women since today's men go along with this insanity. Men and have become much more beta over the past few decades, but that gets into topics beyond the scope of this book.

The point is that the Alpha Male 2.0's expectation of a woman in a serious relationship (regardless of living together or not) is that he'll take either a 1950s submissive sweetheart or a 1970s independent bad ass, but he will *not* tolerate the ridiculous and grossly unfair 21st-century woman. I've told women they really need to pick one ('50s or '70s) and stick with it.

The Alpha Male 2.0 is a flexible guy. This attitude toward women in serious relationships is also flexible. You want to be submissive to me and I take care of you financially? Okay, I'll do that. Or, you want to do whatever you want, never have me tell you what to do, but I never have to give you any of my money? Cool, I'd be down for that too. But, as a third option, you want me to give you a bunch of money (either in the form of dinners, paid bills, financial support, cash, or whatever), *and* you want to be able to boss me around and tell me what to do? Sorry, not interested. (An interesting question to ask is if the roles were reversed, would a *woman* take that deal? Of course not.)

Therefore, your OLTR wife can be one of two types.

1. **1950s OLTR Wife.** You pay all or most of her bills and support her. If you have kids, she stays home and takes care of them. If you don't have kids, she doesn't work or perhaps only works part-time for a little extra income on the side. Finances are 100% separate, so you give her money (within the legal parameters we've discussed in prior

chapters; always check with your attorney), and then she pays her own bills. On the flip side, *you* are in charge of all financial matters, both for her and you. She gives up this freedom for the benefit of not having to worry about money. If she later decides she doesn't like this, she can either divorce you (and get nothing) or switch the relationship to a 1970s model, meaning she has to go get a full-time job and pay all of her own bills, but you can't tell her what to do with her money anymore.

2. **1970s OLTR Wife.** She pays her bills and expenses with no help from you. You pay your own bills and expenses with no help from her. She has her own income that has nothing to do with you that she uses to pay her own bills and expenses and spends how she pleases. She is 100% in charge of her own money and you can't tell her what to do with it, and the reverse is also true. She gets no money from you (other than things like gifts for her birthday and so on), but she has 100% freedom to do whatever she wants with her money. If she later decides she doesn't like this, she can either divorce you (and get nothing) or switch the relationship to a 1950s model, meaning she can "retire" (quit her job and be a stay-at-home wife or close to it), but you now control her finances.

What if you want to live off of *her* income? You stay home (or work part-time) and she pays all or most of *your* bills? I have seen marriages like this, and I admit they can work for certain personality types. However, I can't recommend these types of marriages because they do not fit into the Alpha Male 2.0 lifestyle I describe in my other books. The Alpha Male 2.0 has 100% control over his own finances, and if your wife pays all or most of your bills, this is not the case. Regardless, if you really want a non-Alpha 2.0 OLTR Marriage, you could pursue this option if you wish. It's your life.

Section Four
Family Matters

Chapter 21

RAISING CHILDREN IN A NON-MONOGAMOUS MARRIAGE

You are more than welcome to have children in an OLTR Marriage, and I personally know many open-married couples who have kids. Men and women in OLTR Marriages tend to be happier than those in TMMs, so they tend to make great parents. Unfortunately, there isn't much statistical data to back this up yet, since researchers don't focus much on non-monogamous marriages and those in non-monogamous marriages tend to keep that fact quiet. But based on my anecdotal experience with couples like this, I've seen a lot of success.

I have two children. Both of them are grown now and in their twenties. For half of their lives, I was in a TMM with their mother. Then we got divorced, and I've spent the last 13 years raising them part-time as a non-monogamous man, including when I was cohabiting full time or part time with other women. They are both intelligent and happy people today, and I'm very proud of both of them. Today, Pink Firefly and I have no kids by choice. I also know several men who live full-time with their OLTR wives while raising kids with them.

From all this experience and data, I can give you an overview of the best way to raise kids when you are in a non-monogamous marriage or similar serious non-mono relationship. Obviously, raising kids is a huge topic that could be the focus of several entire books, nor do I consider myself an expert on parenting. Therefore, what I'll present here is an *overview* directly related to the non-monogamous aspects of the marriage.

First, I *strongly* recommend you read the two chapters on how to be an Alpha Male 2.0 father in my book *The Unchained Man**. Those strongly relate to anything you'll do in an OLTR Marriage with your wife, even if your wife is not the biological mother of your kids. I consider those

http://www.alphamalebook.com/

two chapters as the foundation of parenting for the non-monogamous OLTR husband. I'll move on to other topics in this chapter, but and I can't recommend those chapters (and that book!) enough.

Access

The biggest issue for raising kids in an OLTR Marriage is how much access they have to the non-monogamous aspect of your relationship with your wife. How much do your kids know about this? Do they know anything about this already? What age, if any, is this knowledge appropriate?

Opinions vary on this, and I don't think there are any scientifically proven ideal answers, at least not yet. I will give you what I consider the best method on how to handle this based on my experience and the experiences of other men and women who live this lifestyle. Feel free to disagree, though I strongly feel that this is the best way (or least bad way?) to go about this.

When your kids are under the age of about 13, you should keep the non-monogamous aspect of your OLTR Marriage a secret. I don't like the concept of hiding things from children, but the reality is that the massive amount of Societal Programming your kids will learn from school, the internet, TV shows, friends, and other family members besides you is chock-full of "monogamy is how you do it" messaging. Kids this young aren't mentally or emotionally prepared to wade through the idea that you and your wife live radically different sex lives than what they are told is normal and appropriate. Trying to make sense of that, talking about that with other kids or adults they know, it's just too much work and pressure on them. Seriously, even children of an openly gay couple are going to encounter less pushback than children of a couple in a publicly open marriage.

Therefore, it is my recommendation that you keep this part of your life secret from your kids if they're under the age of about 13. At the same time, I don't think you should lie to your kids either and go out of your way to tell them that you're monogamous when you aren't. Just keep that part of your life to yourself for the time being and have your wife do the same. I kept the non-monogamous aspects of my life a secret from my kids until they were about 14.

Once your kids get into their teenage years, it *might* be okay to start letting some of this stuff "slip out" if you feel the need and if you feel your child could handle it well (or not care). Even then, it's perfectly fine to wait until they are older, even 18, before you talk about this stuff. Once they're past age 13 or so, it's really up to you.

Treat it as a case-by-case basis for each child. Some kids are more emotional, and some are less so. Some are more mature and others less so. Some are clingier to their parents, and others are less so. Boys and girls are also different. In my experience, teenage sons really don't give a shit about their parent's sex lives, but daughters are often pretty curious. All of that needs to be factored into your decision.

I strongly recommend that your kids have no access at all to any of your side women – ever. The risk of complications between your kids and your side women, your side women and you, and you and your wife are just too great. The only exception to this would be a full-on polyamorous marriage, but I don't recommend those for reasons I've already stated and can't advise you on those specifically. If your teenage children know you have a side-girl or two, that's all they need to know. They shouldn't meet these women nor spend time with them.

Once your kids are all grown up (i.e. well past age 18) and move out of your house for good, then there are no rules. Do whatever you want at that point. They're adults now and should be treated as such.

If you're curious about what I'm doing now, my grown kids obviously know Pink Firefly quite well and see her whenever they visit us or during family events. They are well aware I'm non-monogamous and have been for a very long time. They never meet any of my side women, nor do I want them to, nor have they ever asked or cared. When I was single before Pink Firefly and was dating FBs and MLTRs, my daughter (when she was over age 13) would occasionally meet a high-end MLTR or two and see pictures of the other women, but that was the extent of it.

Financial Aspects

Having children brings up an entirely new dimension to how you and your wife handle the finances. This can be a dicey topic, which is why it should be discussed during the OLTR Talk well before your wife gets serious with you or even moves in.

The best way to go about this to have one of you, ideally your wife, be "in charge" of all the financial expenses for the kids. For example, you have a 1950s OLTR Marriage where you work and your wife is a stay-at-home OLTR mom raising your two small children. You give her a flat allowance once per month that covers all (or your percentage of) the child expenses, including groceries, diapers, clothing, activities, toys, and health care for the kids. Once you hand your wife that money, it's 100% hers and she's free to spend it on the kids any way she wants with zero input from you because you trust her to do the right things. The alternative is that you're like most married couples and argue endlessly about exactly how to feed and clothe the children, which damages both Mutual Harmony and Attraction.

Caregiving

As I also talked about in *The Unchained Man**, if you want to live the Alpha Male 2.0 lifestyle, your wife needs to be the primary caregiver of the children. It's very difficult to live a free life if 50% of the time your baby cries in the middle of the night, it's "your turn" to get up at 2:00 a.m. to change diapers. Not only does it render true Freedom as near impossible, but it puts your Betaization Wall under constant bombardment. (There is absolutely nothing sexy or attractive about a dad changing poopy diapers under his wife's orders.)

Instead, before you ever get her pregnant, your wife or prospective wife needs to understand that if she wants kids with you, you'll help cover the costs (or all the costs if you wish), but she will be responsible for 90% of the child-rearing tasks, giving you time to live your life and work on your Mission. Note that I said 90% of the *child-rearing tasks*. I'm not saying you only spend 10% of your *time* with your kids. You can and should spend as much time with your children as you can. I'm only

*http://www.alphamalebook.com/

talking about the *work* involved in raising kids, like changing diapers, helping with their homework, driving them to soccer practice, and so on.

If she doesn't agree to this system, that's fine, but then you probably need to marry and have kids with someone more compatible with your life goals.

Parenting Plan/Custody

Before your wife gets pregnant, you need to both sign and notarize a parenting plan or custody agreement with your local government and file it at your local courthouse. These specify what kinds of visitation and custody each parent will have in case of a break-up or divorce. They will not protect you from paying child support (you'll pay that no matter what unless you're unusually lucky), but they can and often do protect you against the dreadful and expensive custody battles many divorced couples suffer through. Instead, you just get divorced and you both do what is in the already filed agreement.

Sometimes these parenting plans are legally enforceable and sometimes they are not, depending on the jurisdiction. These agreements are mostly a protective measure for you in case of a divorce, one your wife will know is in place regardless of its legal enforceability. However, they can also assist in Mutual Harmony during the marriage since your wife will always know in the back of her mind that the usual option of "taking the kids away from you" won't really be an option for her (or will at least be a more complicated option), giving her a little more motivation to work out disagreements with you regarding the children during the marriage instead of keeping a custody battle as a hidden weapon for her to use later.

Chapter 22
DEALING WITH FAMILY AND FRIENDS

One of the biggest reasons why OLTR Marriages are not more common in society is people's fears regarding what other people in their family and social circle will think of their unconventional marriage. I have seen (and written about at my blogs) numerous Alpha Male types in their thirties (and even forties) who make their marriages monogamous and with no prenup mostly to impress their mothers or grandmothers, even when these men are well aware these types of marriages are not going to work for them long-term (they know in advance they'll cheat and/or get divorced later).

Managing your family and friends as you establish and maintain your OLTR Marriage requires a combination of *discretion* and *confidence*. Simply put, you need to keep the open aspects of the marriage quiet to most people you know (co-workers, acquaintances, neighbors, more distant family members, etc.) and with the few people who you or your wife may feel need to know (parents, in-laws, close friends, etc.), you need to be 100% confident about what you're doing and not apologize for it.

If you do both of these things, you will not have any problems dealing with any strong negative reactions unless your situation is unusual. Most people won't know. The few that do either won't care or won't push you on it because they know they'll get nowhere.

I will give you my example, which is illustrative of what I'm talking about.

Throughout my entire relationship with Pink Firefly, including when she was an FB, MLTR, OLTR, and then an OLTR wife, absolutely no one knew anything about our open aspect with the exception of my very close family members, namely my kids and my parents. Only after Pink Firefly and I were married a while did I open up about this to my siblings, who didn't care, for the most part. Today, PF and I live a normal neighborhood filled with normal people and we look like a perfectly normal married couple. (Well, as normal as can be, that is. Pink Firefly looks like a skinny-but-buxom Playboy Playmate with platinum blonde hair down to her butt, and I'm a big, loud, outcome-independent barbarian, so we definitely turn heads, but you get what I mean.)

While PF and I were dating, her sister stumbled across one of my blogs, the Blackdragon Blog, where I bluntly talk about dating and non-monogamous relationships for men. As you might imagine, she freaked out and immediately told her mom. Her mom, a normal woman in her sixties, was horrified at my blog, just as much as my own mother was when she first read it.

PF's mom and I had already met a few times and we really hit it off, but when she saw my blogs, she panicked, horrified that her daughter was involved with some kind of weirdo or pervert who would crush her soul. She told her friends, her boss, anyone who would listen, and had a few nervous discussions with PF as well.

This is when I had to use a little confidence. I texted PF's mom and told her that she and I should go grab a coffee. She agreed. A few days later, we met at a Starbucks. She was polite but wary and cold. I smiled and proceeded to confidently and strongly (though nicely) explain to her the basics of the Alpha Male 2.0 lifestyle, how OLTRs work, and the failures of monogamy. I didn't do it in an effort to convince her of anything because I do not expect a woman in her sixties to radically change her mind on any of her strongly held views. I just wanted to let her know A) where *I* was coming from and B) that I was not a threat to her daughter. Indeed, I was a good thing for her daughter, which I am.

She asked me, "Okay, so it's non-monogamous for you, but is it also non-monogamous for *her* as well?" She was essentially asking me if PF was allowed to sleep with other men if I was allowed to sleep with other women. I answered, "Of course. If that's something she really wants to do, she's more than welcome to do it. Fair is fair."

Immediately I could see the anger and defensiveness drain out from her body as she visibly relaxed. I had scored a victory.

I went on to tell her about the separation of finances and other

OLTR aspects. I didn't get into any details and just kept the discussion at the overview level. Soon she was smiling, relaxed, and happy. She was even more excited when I informed her of my intention of marrying her daughter (under an OLTR Marriage, of course). Suddenly she was excitedly asking me about the engagement ring I was going to use, how I was going to propose, and other Disney stuff.

In less than 60 minutes, she had gone from cold and almost hostile to so happy and excited she was literally bouncing up and down as we left the Starbucks. She is now my mother-in-law, and we are still friends to this day.

Have balls. Be strong. It works. To the few people in your life who need to know this stuff, confidently state what you're doing and why you're doing it. Don't be an asshole, don't try to convert people (it won't work) but *don't back down*. Don't give too many specifics; that's none of their business. Just give an overview and do so with confidence and outcome independence. If you do this without being defensive or worrying about what they will think (outcome independence!), the odds are overwhelming that no one will give you any shit about this.

What if the odds don't work out and someone close to you indeed does lose their mind and give you all kinds of hell? If that happens, you may need to make some strong decisions about who you allow in your life. Your life belongs to *you*, not your mom, not your dad, not your brother, not your mother-in-law, not your best friend. If any of these people have a serious problem with what you're doing, that's their problem, not yours. If someone is actually giving you hell about this despite you standing strong, you may have to take a break from that person for a year or two. Yes, I would do this, even with my own parents, though thankfully I have not needed to. My dad had no big problem with what I was doing, but my mom did many years ago (before Pink Firefly), and I had to tell her to fuck off, literally. She never brought it up again, and today our relationship is great and she loves PF to death. Again, strength works.

I can't tell you how to live your personal life with your friends and family, but the bottom line is that you should never spend time with anyone you know in advance is going to give you a bunch of drama about how you choose to live your life. Refrain from seeing that person for a year, perhaps two, and circle back and try it again and see how it goes.

As always, stay strong with the people in your social circle and family. You'll be shocked at how well it works.

Section Five
Side Women

Chapter 23
MANAGING YOUR SIDE WOMEN

In the next few chapters, we'll discuss how to meet and manage your side women. "Side women" means all the women you're having sex with who are not your wife. Under an OLTR Marriage model, side women can only be FBs (friends with benefits) or one-night stands. In other words, they can be your friends, and you can have sex with them, but no dating, romance, romantic behaviors, or feelings beyond friendship are allowed.

This rule doesn't apply if you have a more polygamous or polygamous marriage, as I talked about back in Chapter 2. However, these types of marriages are outside of the OLTR Marriage model and are much more complicated. If you have the type of non-monogamous marriage where you are indeed allowed to have romantic feelings and interactions with your side women (or indeed have multiples wives or girlfriends), then feel free to ignore the FB limitations I refer to in the rest of this book. Just be aware that marriages like this take a lot more work and time to maintain and are prone to more conflict and drama. This is one of the many reasons why I prefer the OLTR Marriage model and find it the easiest non-monogamous marriage type for most men to establish and maintain harmoniously for the long term.

As always, this book assumes you're following the OLTR Marriage model, and that means that you can't date side women, just have sex with them. However, this doesn't mean you can't spend time with your side women in a fun, enjoyable, non-sexual context. You can certainly be friends with these people (the "F" in "FB" stands for *friend*). Having warm discussions with your FBs is perfectly fine and even enjoyable at times. This limitation simply means that your *romantic emotions and actions* only for your wife. This keeps jealousy and drama from your wife at a minimum, as well as maintains a high degree of trust from her as well. It's also a lot easier on you emotionally, logistically, and with respect to basic time management with your FBs (since FBs take very little time).

I describe FB management in great detail in *The Ultimate Open Relationships Manual**, so please refer to that book for the specific Cardinal Rules when dealing with FBs as well as the techniques they require for long-term, happy FB relationships. In this and subsequent chapters, I will simply discuss how to manage your side-FBs within the context of when you are married and/or living with your OLTR wife full-time.

One point of clarification. You are not allowed to go out on dates with your side-FBs since that's against the rules. However, the first *one or two* "dates" or "meets" where you meet a new woman from a dating site (for example) before you have sex with her *are* allowed. Obviously, your wife needs to understand that in most cases, you can't just hit up a cute girl on Tinder and tell her to come right over to your house to have sex. One or two quick meets at a Starbucks or bar to talk a little and get a perspective FB comfortable before you have sex with her is perfectly acceptable within an OLTR Marriage model. (For the exact process on how to best do this, get the book *Get To Sex Fast***.) Once you have sex with her, the FB rules kick in and no actual "dates" with her are allowed.

The Best Types of Women for Side-FBs

As you might imagine, some types of women are better than others when it comes to ideal side women. Ideal candidates for side women are women who:

1. Will keep things reasonably discreet.

2. Are reliable and trustworthy.

3. Are willing to cooperate with your unusual sexual logistics without complaint. (We will discuss sexual logistics with side-FBs while you're married in Chapter 25.)

4. Don't care that you are married, or at least not mind too much.

5. Are less likely to "catch feelings" for you.

6. Have their own reasons to maintain a discreet sexual relationship

*http://www.haveopenrelationships.com
**http://www.gettosexfast.com

with a married man, ideally above and beyond the fact they're physically attracted to you and/or enjoy having sex with you.

If all you want to have as side women are one-night stands (e.g. women you have sex with just once or twice and then never see again), then you can play with pretty much any type of woman you want. However, if you want any ongoing FB relationship (which I strongly recommend, since that's less work than constantly going out and getting new women all the time), then the above six items become very important. The more of those items a woman has, the more likely she is to be your FB a very long time and in a happy, low-drama way. The less of those items she has, the more likely you are to encounter problems with her.

Therefore, with those six things in mind, here are the best types (and worst types) of women to have as regular side-FBs, listed in order of best to worst.

1. Sugar Babies (i.e. Sugar Daddy Game)

Sugar babies are the woman you have sex with via sugar daddy game on sugar daddy dating sites, where you pay them a little for sex, or salt daddy game, where you *imply* you will pay them but may not actually do so.

Assuming you can afford them (and most older men can) sugar babies, particularly those under the age of about 28, are, hands down, the easiest and best side-FBs to have when you are married. They match at least four of the above six criteria (items three through six) and sometimes have all six. They don't care that you're married and many of them even prefer it. They're very attractive and have an extra incentive to please you and to keep things discreet so you'll keep seeing them and providing them with a source of side income. If you decide to pay them, you'll pay anywhere from $150 to $300 per visit, which is easily accessible by most men who want cute younger women a few times a month.

Sugar babies who have boyfriends are even better since they're getting their Disney desires satisfied by their beta male boyfriends, so you don't have any of that pressure. There is a growing trend of younger women doing the sugar daddy thing who have boyfriends but explain to these guys that they're going to hook up with older men whether the boyfriends like it or not (and the boyfriends, being young betas, usually agree).

I strongly recommend sugar babies to guys in OLTR Marriages who are either beginners at this stuff, or who are very busy and don't want to mess around with traditional dating, or men with higher incomes. It's the easiest category of woman to have as side-FBs, hands down.

I describe exactly how to do sugar daddy game and salt daddy game in great detail in *The Ultimate Younger Woman Manual**. I highly recommend that book if sugar/salt daddy game is where you want to focus.

2. Younger Women (e.g. women under the age of 28)

If you've read my blogs or books, you already know that generally speaking, the younger a woman is, the more likely she is to go along with your "program." Women between the ages of 18 and 27 or so are usually more flexible and less demanding than older women. They are also not on the hunt for husbands or serious boyfriends like most single women over the age of 33 are.

If you want normal (non-sugar baby) FBs as a married man, I strongly recommend that you stick with women under the age of about 28 and go as low as you're comfortable. (Obviously, stay within the age of consent laws in your city. Messing with underage women can easily land you in jail or branded as a sex offender these days.)

I'm not saying you can't make older women work. I certainly have as have many other men. I'm also not saying there aren't disadvantages with much younger women. They're certainly are (they tend to be much more flakey and disorganized). I'm just saying that generally speaking, younger women are far easier to manage when you're married.

3. Long Distance Women

If you don't travel much, then this won't apply to you. However, if you're the kind of guy who travels often, and certainly if you live an

*http://www.older-men-younger-women.com

international lifestyle like I do, long-distance women are fantastic. Having a few recurring FBs in various distant cities where you regularly (or semi-regularly) visit is extremely enjoyable. I have numerous sporadic FBs in various cities and countries all over the world. It's great!

Long-distance women are perhaps the "safest" FBs in that very little can go wrong because they're usually far away. You can also combine the other categories listed here (sugar babies, younger women, married women, and so on) with the long-distance category.

The only challenge with long-distance FBs is that they often get boyfriends quickly, forcing you to perhaps replace them on a regular basis. Regardless, that's their only downside.

4. Married Women (monogamous or open)

Some men in non-monogamous marriages (as well as men in normal marriages who cheat on their wives) focus mostly on other married women. Rumor has it, and I believe it, that Bill and Hillary Clinton have always had this arrangement in their marriage: Bill is able to sleep around as long as the other women are older and ideally married, who thus have something to lose if word gets out about the affair. In the late 1990s, when Bill violated this rule and had an affair with a young, naive intern in her early twenties (Monica Lewinsky), Hillary was furious, but she wasn't furious because he cheated. Bill's been a serial cheater his whole life. No, she was furious because he broke one of their open marriage rules.

The category of "married women" breaks out into two groups, one much better than the other. The first are women who have open marriages themselves. I have had several women as FBs in this category, and they were all wonderful. Women like this are, perhaps, the easiest and least amount of work you could have as a side-FB, even rivaling sugar babies (and married women are cheaper since they won't cost you any money like the sugar babies will). Obviously, open-marriage women are harder to find, but there are plenty of them out there. I've found many using normal dating sites, but there are various open or polyamorous websites and local groups available in most cities as well.

The other group are married monogamous women who are cheating on their husbands. While this is an option, I recommend either forgoing this option or using extreme caution. I've been with a few women in like this in my past, but that was before I was married. Today I stay away from women like this since I don't want any drama or fallout to affect my marriage.

If you decide to involve yourself with married-but-cheating women, I strongly recommend you adopt these three rules. These are the rules I used when I was doing this:

1. Do *not* "go after" monogamously married women. Consider this something you'll take if it's freely offered, not something you'll actively pursue.

2. Do *not* have sex with any monogamously married women when you personally know her husband, even if he's just a distant acquaintance. If you work with her husband, are friends with her husband, are related to her husband, or even if he's in one of your distant social circles, stay away. The potential for problems is too great.

3. Do *not* have sex with any monogamously married women when you could accidentally "run into" her husband sometime in the future, even if you've never met him. Examples would be when you have sex with a monogamous married woman you meet at work and then meet her husband at the office Christmas party, or if you hook up with a married woman in your neighborhood and then run into her husband while walking your dog one day. *Not knowing her husband is not enough.* If there is any chance you'll run into him at any point in the future, stay away. There are much safer women available.

I used those three rules as iron-clad back in the day when I was open to having sex with those women and I never had a problem. Violate those rules at your peril, or just skip monogamously married women altogether.

Men who prefer married women (monogamous or open) do so because these women don't need them to provide the Disney their husbands are already providing. These women will also go out of their way to be very discreet, something that is often not true with single women or much younger women.

This is also a good way for men who prefer older women to have older FBs since single older women are usually husband-hunting and have no interest in being in "second place" as the FB of a married man. (Though to be fair, there are exceptions to this.)

Now for the types of women who are problematic to have as side-FBs. They are listed in order of least-bad to most-bad.

5. Single Women Over the Age of 33

The vast majority of single women over the age of 33 would never have sex with a married man, regardless of if the man was cheating on his wife or in an honest, open marriage. There are definitely exceptions to this rule, though, such as more independent women, women going through a divorce, or older sugar babies. However, even then I don't often recommend these women as side-FBs. I've seen more than one married man have a sexual relationship on the side with women like this, and for a while, everything is fine. Eventually, though, many of these women start to get frustrated and demanding.

I've written about this in great detail in my other books (particularly *Get To Sex Fast*), but the reality is that being single is a very uncomfortable condition for most women over the age of 33 (barring rare exceptions). Women in their thirties and forties are uncomfortable having sex with a man that they perceive isn't leading to a relationship. Many of them are hardcore Provider Hunters actively looking for a husband (or second husband, as the case may be).

The only way to short-circuit this is to make sure that your over-33 side-FB already has a husband or a serious boyfriend. As I said above, these women are fantastic, and I highly recommend them as side-FBs. However, if she is completely single, my recommendation is to stay away unless there are mitigating circumstances.

6. Overly Emotional Women

Regardless of her age or relationship status, if a woman is prone to drama, mood swings, life chaos, crying, outbursts, or tantrums, you need to run away fast. Unmarried guys can have sex with these women as FBs if they wish (I had several FBs like this back before I was married), but as a married man, the potential for problems from these women isn't worth it. These women are time bombs ready to go off at any moment. They can give you all kinds of problems, not only in your life but in your marriage.

This also goes for women who are drug addicts, alcoholics, or have depression problems or personality disorders. I'll admit that sometimes these women can be fun as FBs, but leave them for men who don't have wives. As a married man, you need to be a little more responsible.

7. Women You Work With

This is likely the worst category of them all. Nothing is more short-sighted than having sex with someone you work with every day. This should go without saying, but I'm amazed at how many people, married or otherwise, sleep with people they work with. I realize it seems easy since the women are already provided for you and have to spend time with you, but doing this is extremely dangerous on several levels, and rarely do things *not* end up badly.

Here are the risks you incur when you do this:

- You will have constant awkwardness (or even full-on drama) at work indefinitely when (not if, but *when*) you break up with this woman and stop having sex with her.

- You risk problems with the HR department. As a man, you're much more likely to encounter these kinds of problems than if you were a woman.

- You actually risk your job. You face a nonzero chance that you'll actually get fired.

- The odds of this woman causing drama and conflict in your marriage are much higher due to the nature of the work relationship than if she was a normal side-FB you didn't work with.

- You risk everyone you work with learning about your affair and/or your open marriage. (You might not care, but if you or your wife do, that would be a problem).

If you work with her, don't have sex with her. Period. I give the same advice to single men.

What you *can* do is get her personal contact info and if/when you or she leave that job, *then* contact her and attempt to start a sexual relationship at that time. I've done that many times myself in the past, and this technique works very well. Just don't have sex with her while you work with her.

Women Who Are Related to or Friends with Your Wife

This one is a grey area. It can be good or bad depending on various factors, namely the nature of your marriage, your wife's personality, and the nature of the relationship between your wife and these women.

I do *not* recommend you have sex with anyone in your wife's family, regardless of if these women are blood relatives or not. I have never seen this work out well. Even if your wife gives you permission to do this, the odds of problems and conflict are just too high.

I do *not* recommend you have sex with any of your wife's acquaintances. Women often don't mind (and perhaps even like it) if you have sex with their friends with their permission, but having sex with a woman's acquaintances often causes jealousy. (I realize that doesn't make sense in a logical man-world, but in the emotional world of women, that's how it works.)

If your wife gives you clear permission to have sex with a particular acquaintance of hers *and* your wife has a long track record of very low or zero jealousy, then feel free to proceed. Outside of this, don't do it.

Having sex with one of your wife's friends when your wife gives you permission to do so is okay, particularly if your wife is involved somehow (a threesome, or your wife watching, and so on). You may be surprised to find that your wife may actually *want* you to have sex with her friends. I have dated many women like this. However, do *not* have sex with one of your wife's friends *without her very clear permission*. Having sex with your wife's friends behind her back is a great way to jeopardize your entire marriage. Always discuss any friend-fucking with your wife first and get her clear permission and consent. If you get it, go for it.

Relationship Management with Your Side-FBs

If you're the kind of guy who only has one-night stands (or similar) for your sex outside of your marriage, then you don't need to worry about managing any relationships outside of your wife, which is the advantage of that kind of lifestyle. (The disadvantage is that you'll have to exert energy to constantly get new women all the time.)

That said, most men in OLTR Marriages (and other non-monogamous marriage types) will indeed have ongoing and long-term relationships with their side-FBs.

The FB relationship you can have with side women can be a little more flexible than a normal FB relationship where you are completely unmarried. This is because your side women will know that you're married. The expectations for things like romance, dating, and/or future boyfriend or husband status will be far less for you than it would be if they were dating a man who was unmarried and lived alone. There can be exceptions to this, however, where you may have an FB who "catches feelings" for you. Therefore, it is your job to provide the frame for the relationship where you two are just friends, even close friends, who have sex, but that's it.

This means you must follow all of the FB Cardinal Rules described in Chapter Four of *The Ultimate Open Relationships Manual** 100% of the time with no screw-ups or exceptions. If you don't, you risk sending out "dating vibes," and you will be in for some problems, all of which will be your fault.

It should go without saying that all of your FBs should be aware you are married and that you are emotionally exclusive to your wife. All of my FBs, both now and in the past, since I have been married, were and are well aware that I am married. I even have pictures of myself and Pink Firefly at my office, where I usually meet my FBs, so they know what she looks like even if they've never met her. (Pink Firefly is very hot, so this provides a little extra social proof on my part with my FBs as well.)

Feel free to talk about your wife and your relationship with her freely with your FBs. Don't feel like you shouldn't say certain positive things about your wife or your marriage, or that you shouldn't talk about

*http://www.haveopenrelationships.com/

your marriage "too much." That's the exact wrong frame. Instead, you should talk to your FBs just like they were one of your guy buddies. You'd mention your wife on at least a semi-regular basis to them, wouldn't you? Therefore, it should be the same with your side-FBs.

Length of Relationships with Side-FBs

The length of side-FB relationships varies wildly. My experience plus the data reported to me by many other open married men shows that relationships with side women can last anywhere from a few sexual visits all the way to three years or longer.

You also need to account for the LSNFTE, which stands for Long Soft Next for Temporary Exclusivity. This is when an FB gets a boyfriend and then leaves you temporarily because she's excited about her new guy and doesn't want to cheat on him. However, if you are good at managing these kinds of relationships, she will eventually return to you once she gets bored with him, cheats on him, or breaks up with him. My return rate for women who LSNFTE me is 94%. I discuss all of this in great detail in *The Ultimate Open Relationships Manual**. The point is that you'll have many relationships with your side-FBs that last a very long time (many years) but will be off-and-on. You'll see her for a year, she'll go away for a year, then come back for two years, then be gone again for six months, then return again, and so on.

This is why you'll need multiple FBs if you want to maintain the six-week rule we talked about back in Chapter 13. This is one of the reasons I prefer to always have two FBs going at all times. If one gets a boyfriend or moves away, I still have one more to hold me over while I go get a new one or "resurrect" one of my old ones.

By the way, as I mentioned earlier, as non-monogamy becomes more common (and as sugar daddy game becomes more common), more and more women, particularly young women, are getting boyfriends but continuing to hook up with older guys anyway. This means that as time goes on, you'll likely experience fewer LSNFTEs than men did in years past. That's certainly been the case with me.

The precise length of your side-FB relationships (whether consistent

*http://www.haveopenrelationships.com/

or off-and-on) depends on the following factors:

- Your level of non-monogamous relationship management skill (the better you are at this stuff, the longer your relationships tend to last and the more likely she is to return after an LSNFTE)

- Her age (the younger she is, the more likely she is to stick around longer because older women get married, old, or fat sooner than younger ones do; it's just statistics)

- Whether or not money is involved (if she has a financial incentive to see you, obviously she's more likely to stick around longer)

- Your overall level of attractiveness, both externally and internally (obviously the more attractive she finds you, the longer she'll stay with you and the more likely she is to return to you after an LSNFTE)

- Whether or not she already has a serious boyfriend or husband (if she does, the relationship is likely to last longer because she is much less likely to get a new boyfriend or husband if she already has one)

Never allow yourself to get strong feelings for, or complacent with, one of your side women. If you value your marriage, and I've written this book with the assumption that you do, you will avoid strong feelings for women on the side. This means that you will permanently eject any side women from your life that you think you may become attracted to on an emotional or romantic level. This is doubly important if you're a more emotional or romantic guy.

If you really *want* a more emotional MLTR-like relationship with a woman who is not your wife, then that means you shouldn't be in an OLTR Marriage and need to either get divorced immediately or establish one of those other more "complicated" marriage types I talked about back in Chapter 2.

What If Your Wife Has Side Men?

Your wife is allowed to have her own FBs on the side if she wants. The odds are around 50% she will *not* want this (higher if she's over the age of 33), and even if she does, she will not always want these men, as I've explained both in this book and in *The Unchained Man**. If she doesn't seek sex outside of your marriage, then obviously you don't need to concern yourself with this aspect. If she does, she will have to learn how to maintain her side-men FBs.

Just like it is your responsibility to ensure your relationships with your side women are low-drama, problem-free, and don't threaten your marriage, it is your wife's responsibility to ensure all the same things in her relationships with her side men. *She needs to understand this clearly.* People in MLTR or FB relationships can just go out into the world and date people as they chose without worrying about certain boundaries being crossed, but people in an OLTR Marriage don't have this luxury. Your wife needs to clearly understand the responsibly she's assuming if she chooses to do this (as do you).

I would strongly recommend that your wife read the FB sections (particularly regarding the Cardinal Rules) of *The Ultimate Open Relationships Manual** or that you at least explain these things to her in detail and get acknowledgment that she understands. She needs to practice these techniques with her side-FBs. If she fails to do so, that's a real problem that may threaten the marriage, and she needs to understand that as well.

I have personally seen open marriages (that were not OLTR Marriages, to be fair) encounter all kinds of serious problems when the wife starts having sex with men outside of the marriage and she doesn't adhere to the basic FB rules. These wives will date other men, have long, emotional, intimate phone or online conversations with other men, spend the night with other men, and so on. Drama and even divorce are usually the eventual result.

I will repeat that if either person in an OLTR Marriage, husband or wife, has a desire to actually *date* and/or get *romantic* or *emotional* with other people (beyond just friends having sex), then that person should not be an OLTR Marriage, and major life changes are called for.

If your wife is brand new to the concept of having sex with a side man and wants to try it, you'll need to coach her on exactly what to do and what not to do. The downside is that men tend to be much needier than

*http://www.alphamalebook.com/
**http://www.haveopenrelationships.com/

women (Oneitis!), so the odds are higher that her side men will catch feelings for your wife than your FBs will for you. Your wife needs to be ready for this and know what to do (and how to put the odds in her favor that this won't happen to begin with).

Chapter 24

GETTING NEW SIDE WOMEN

While the core aspects remain the same, there are differences in dating and attracting new women into your life when you are already married. How do you go on initial dates when dating isn't allowed? When do you reveal to new women you're married? How do you do it? In this chapter, I'll address all these issues plus others.

That said, this is not a book on how to date women or get laid. That procedure is covered in my other books, specifically *Get To Sex Fast** (how to properly execute first and second dates so you get to sex quickly and cheaply), the *Ultimate Online Dating Manual*** (how to fill your calendar with first dates using online dating sites and apps), and the *Ultimate Younger Woman Manual**** (how to attract much younger women both with normal dating and with sugar daddy game). Refer to those books on specific details and procedures on how to bring new women into your dating/sex life whenever you need them. In this chapter, I'm only going to cover those specific aspects that apply to a man in an OLTR Marriage.

Choose the Best Dating Method

This is old news to anyone familiar with dating, seduction, or pickup already, but there are essentially four types of game:

Night Game – Picking up women at clubs, bars, or parties, usually during the evening.

Daygame – Picking up women during the day at non-dating locales, like out on the street ("street game"), at the grocery store, at the mall, and so forth.

Online Dating – Meeting women by going on dates via online dating sites and apps. (Sugar daddy game and salt daddy game are subtypes of online dating.)

*http://www.gettosexfast.com/
**http://www.onlinedatingsuccessnow.com/
***http://www.older-men-younger-women.com/

Social Circle Game – Dating women you meet via your large and active social circle.

My standard advice is for men to pick one of those game styles, learn it, and get decent at it. Married men are no different. As a married man, night game, daygame, and online dating (especially sugar/salt daddy game) are the most viable. Social circle game is *technically* possible as a married guy (I've seen married men do it), but I usually don't recommend it unless you have *very* strong game, *very* strong social skills, and a *very* understanding wife. This is because there are a lot of things that can go wrong with social circle game when you are married.

Based on my own research, tracking, and interviews I've done with hundreds of men in non-monogamous marriages over the years, the overwhelming technique most married men use is online dating or sugar daddy game at roughly 65%. Some more extroverted, variety-seeking married guys use night game instead. Very few married men use daygame or social circle game, but there are some exceptions to this. In my opinion, the safest methods (in terms of discretion) for married men seeking new FBs actually goes in that order: online dating/sugar daddy game is the best, followed by night dame, then daygame, and then social circle game last on the list.

True, with online dating, there's a photo of you on a dating site, but you can make your profile non-searchable, have only private-but-shareable photos, and you can delete or disable your profile whenever you like. There are also no names involved until you are actually scheduling a date with someone.

Night game is preferred by married guys who are more extroverted or who travel often. They meet women in controlled, safe environments, especially places they know their wives or wives' friends don't frequent.

Daygame and social circle game are a little more public and thus a little riskier. Again, they can be done, but you'd better be extremely careful.

The Process

The overall dating process with new women is the same as I describe

http://www.gettosexfast.com/

in *Get To Sex Fast**. That is, to schedule a first meet with the new woman (via online or meeting her in real life) at a cool bar or coffee shop, having one quick first meet that lasts only an hour or so, then having a second meet at the location where you intend on having sex and having sex there. If that doesn't work, you try again for a third meet and again attempt to have sex.

With sugar daddy dating, you can skip the second and third meets and have sex on the first meet if you're comfortable with that. (This is usually not an option with salt daddy game, however.) Personally, I have learned to avoid sex on the first meet with sugar daddy game since sometimes the woman who shows up is older, uglier, or fatter than the one you saw in the pictures on her profile, but that aspect is really up to you.

For more details on the specific process and how it works, refer to *Get To Sex Fast**. The only two differences for us married men are:

1. The issue of when to reveal you're married
2. Where to have sex with her if you're not allowed to have sex with FBs in your home

We'll deal with #1 in the next section. Number 2 is a much bigger topic, so I've devoted an entire chapter to it (Chapter 25).

When to Reveal You're Married

One of the biggest worries and sticking points for open-marriage men is the issue of when and how to reveal the "marriage bomb" to women you're meeting.

When working on new side women to bring into your sex life, the issue of when to reveal your marital status must be something completely planned and mapped out in your mind *before* you start approaching women. If you are at all wishy-washy about when, or if, to reveal to women that you're actually married, your confidence will suffer, which means your results will suffer as well.

There are several different ways to do this. All of them work, though some I don't recommend. Your job is to use the one best suited to your

*http://www.gettosexfast.com/

personality, style, and particular situation in your marriage. All methods break down into five general categories:

1. Telling her (or publicly revealing this in your online dating profile) well in advance, right up front, before you even get her out on the first meet.

2. Waiting to tell her during the first meet, but not until then.

3. Waiting to tell her after you have sex with her the first time.

4. Waiting to tell her after you've had sex with her several times.

5. Never telling her.

As I talk about in *The Unchained Man**, I think lying to women is a beta male move. Truly confident, outcome-independent Alpha Male 2.0s don't need to lie to women about anything. I certainly never do. Lying to women is also an unintelligent thing to do since it will simply create drama from these women down the road once they find out you were lying to them (or at least lying by omission for a long time).

Therefore, while all five of the above methods can work, you're almost guaranteed massive drama and headache in your life from these women if you choose options #4 or #5 (unless all you do is one-night stands and literally nothing else.) Option #3 is also risky, although the argument can be made that any discomfort can be alleviated if you have a very strong frame and/or if the woman is very attracted to you.

Therefore, I strongly recommend you go for options #1 or #2, or at the very least set these as goals to get to as quickly as you can. I have used both of these options and never had any serious problems.

The upside of option #1 is that you never need to worry about a woman getting upset or shocked since you were honest up front. It's also a good screening tool since you know in advance that every woman who agrees to meet up with you on a date/meet is already cool with you being married, at least to some degree.

The downside of option #1 is that it absolutely murders your numbers. Your response rates with online dating will plummet (though they will

*http://www.alphamalebook.com/

not go to zero unless you're doing something else wrong) as will your close ratios with things like night game and daygame.

Option #2 is the exact opposite. Your numbers for first dates/meets don't suffer, but some women are going to be taken aback when you reveal that you're married on the first meet. However, your odds of success are a little higher since you've already established a decent amount of rapport first.

Here's a direct quote from an OLTR Married man I discussed this with in the past that I think says a lot:

Until a couple of years ago, I used to reveal it when I knew they were into me, but always before laying them (I consider it unethical to have sex with them without revealing). Now I reveal it right away - it is in my OKC profile. It is a lot better this way - I lose some I might have laid, but I do not have to deal with the drama later. Also, they respect me more – I get quite a few flattering comments for having the balls to tell them up front who am I and where they stand with me.

Choose #1 or #2 and try it out. You'll quickly learn which one you're more comfortable with. If you really aren't comfortable with either, you could try Option #3, but I don't recommend it unless you stick with very young women (under age 23) who are likely to care the least.

Revealing Based on the Type of Woman

If you follow my advice in Chapter 23 and limit yourself to the optimal women for side-FBs (younger women, sugar babies, women who are already married, etc.), then you will experience far less fallout, surprise, anger, and drama when you reveal you're married. A 20-year-old girl may not even give a shit when you tell her at the end of the first meet that you're married, but a 40-year-old woman will be horrified, and you might get a drink thrown in your face. At the other end of the scale, some sugar babies and married women will actually *prefer* that you're married, meaning you can tell them even before you meet, and it may actually increase your odds of success.

If you're curious about what I currently do, I limit my FBs to women under the age of about 25 or so (younger women make the best side-FBs and care the least that you're married) and do a mix of normal online dating and sugar daddy game. In both cases, I don't mention I'm married before the meet, but I *do* answer honestly if I am directly asked before then (which I am sometimes). Within the first 15 minutes of the first meet, I tell them everything, and I do it in a very kind and outcome-independent way.

I usually say something like, "So just so you know everything about me right up front, I'm married and I live with my wife, but I'm in an open marriage where I'm allowed to sleep with other women whenever I want. I don't hide anything from her, but I don't give her details either. I just wanted to let you know." Then I just continue with the conversation as if what I just said is no big deal. If the woman asks questions about my marriage (and they usually don't), I answer honestly.

Doing this gives me an almost 100% success rate with sugar daddy game, about a 75% success rate with women under age 23 and with salt daddy game, and about a 60-65% success rate with women age 23-25 using normal online dating. I don't ever try this with women over age 25 unless I know they are already married or are in some kind of open relationship.

How to Reveal You're Married

As always, the more confident and outcome independent you are when you reveal this, the higher your odds of success will be and the lower the odds become of a truly negative reaction. Be sure that if you are verbally stating it, your body language and tone of voice convey a strong but no-big-deal frame. You need to be unshakable, calm, and cool. Your attitude must be that of a man who says, "Of course I'm married, and that's completely normal," and smiles, and continues right on with the interaction and/or sexual escalation like nothing is wrong or unusual.

Once you confidently and calmly display to women that you are married and they can clearly see it's no big deal *to you*, 80% of the battle is won. If you hem and haw and hesitate, or if you get defensive, or if you start denying things, you lose.

We're about to cover a few techniques on how to push through this barrier, but let me reiterate that if you are not confident about answering this objection in a confident and relaxed way (or are at least successfully faking the confidence and coolness, which also works), *no* technique will work very well.

Here are some proven techniques to assist you with this.

1. If you're nervous about this, rehearse exactly what you're going to say and how you're going to stay it. Stand in front of a mirror and pretend you're out at a bar on first meet. "Tell" the woman you're married and watch yourself in the mirror as you do. Practice. Also, practice dealing with the responses. Practice as if the woman has just said, "What? You're married???" or "I can't date a married guy!" Then answer her, again while watching yourself in the mirror. Try several different answers. Pick the one you like the best, and not only memorize it, but rehearse it. Make sure you're smiling, relaxed, confident, and outcome independent. Even if you're not feeling these things, fake them. After successfully doing this a few times, this will become much easier.

2. Redirect after saying it. For example, instead of saying, "Yes, I'm married," and waiting for her response, say something like, "Yep, I'm married. Didn't you say you were divorced?" Quickly redirect back to her and get her talking about herself. If you do this in a very confident, outcome-independent way, many women will drop the subject, at least for a while.

3. Don't say it unless she specifically asks. Several open-married men I've spoken with have a policy of telling women they're married before X occurs (options #2, #3, or #4 above) *but* they don't actually bring it up until and unless the woman specifically asked about their marriage or dating status *first*, often based on something else the man said or did.

4. Always maintain a strong sexual frame. I talk about this in great detail in *Get To Sex Fast**. Keep up the sexual talk, kino (sexual touching), the bedroom eyes, low tone of voice, the teasing, and so forth. Keep all of these things going strong even if the marriage topic arises in the conversation. Always be moving forward toward your objective

*http://www.gettosexfast.com/

of sex.

5. Tell her your wife approves of what you're doing. One recurring thing I've heard from several open-married men is that if they ever receive any resistance from women, they confidently state that their wives are well aware of what was going on and allow it. They report to me that this is very effective in nullifying a lot of the "marriage objections" they receive, primarily because the women were often concerned that the guy was actually cheating on his wife. If the woman clearly sees (from the man's confident demeanor) that his wife is okay with everything, often it makes it easier for her to agree to sex.

This is why I clearly state up front to all new women that not only am I married but that I'm *in an open marriage* and that *my wife knows exactly what I'm up to*. This sometimes even leads to interested and curious questions from the woman about how I structured this kind of marriage with my wife. I get very few objections from women because I state all of these things confidently up front.

6. Don't take objections too seriously. When a woman objects to you because you're married and/or starts throwing shit tests at you, just relax and don't take them as literal attacks you must answer. Instead, you can, if it's congruent to your personality, just smile and be sort of a smart ass. For example,

Her: I can't date a guy who's married! What if we start getting serious?

You: <big smile> Oh no! Us getting serious? How horrible! I'm flattered you consider me someone of 'serious' quality.

Sometimes women will throw one objection after the next. If you bat them all away with your confident, it's-no-big-deal attitude, often that's all a woman needs. And, of course, if she is still uncomfortable with it, just tell her you completely understand, politely wrap up the meet, get out of there, and move on to the next woman on the list. No one has a 100% success rate with this process (outside of perhaps pay-for-it sugar daddy game).

How to State It in Your Online Profile

As we've already discussed, the most popular method of attracting side women men choose is online dating, and most open-marriage guys who do this state right in their profiles that they're married. I talk about how to set up a profile for maximum response in my online dating book *The Ultimate Online Dating Manual**, but here are some proven tips on exactly how to do this for maximum effect when you're married.

1. Present a picky vibe in your profile. Many women will assume that since you're married, you're going to want to have sex with anyone, and thus they won't be "anything special" if they choose to spend time with you. (Some women will even believe this if they are just looking for sex and nothing else.) If you make it clear that you're picky and have high standards about the quality of women you want to spend time with, this will help.

2. If you're not running any sort of sugar daddy or salt daddy game, remove all hints of providership from your profile. This means you have nothing in your profile about what you do for a living, what your education is, how much money you make, or anything related to those kinds of "quality boyfriend/husband" traits. Many men have reported this works. However, the opposite has worked for others (i.e. playing up the "responsible" factor).

There are many factors involved in this, including your age, the age of the women you're targeting, and the type of women you are attracted to most. I would suggest you test both methods with your profile and track the results, starting with zero-provider.

3. Clearly state your wife is okay with it in your profile. Again, a lot of women don't want to be a *secret* mistress on the side and will feel better about it if it's clear your wife has given you permission to play around.

4. Show that you have a fun, rich life. Do *not* show that you have some kind of boring, horrible marriage and are looking for fun elsewhere because of it. Instead, you live an exciting life, and you want her to come along with you… if she qualifies.

**http://www.onlinedatingsuccessnow.com*

5. Put the fact you're married at the bottom of your profile text. This means that you select "single" as your dating status on the site, but that you do state you're married in your profile text, toward the bottom. This will help boost response rates a little.

What About Your Wedding Ring?

In research and interviews I've done in the past, the vast majority of open-married men do not wear a wedding ring. At a bare minimum, they take it off when actively approaching women. Interestingly, this includes the majority of men who *do* reveal to women they are married before they have sex with them.

The main reason they give for this is that they want the "marriage topic" to arise in the conversation at *your* choosing, not *her* choosing. If you're wearing a wedding ring, she may start asking the marriage questions way before you have established comfort, rapport, and/or attraction with her.

I personally *always* wear my wedding ring 100% of the time, even when I'm doing social circle game or daygame-type activities when I travel. This is the most confident, outcome-independent way to do this, at least in my opinion. The only time a woman has ever pointed out that I'm wearing a wedding ring is when they are over the age of 33 (which is no surprise). Younger women often either don't even notice or notice but don't care.

If you're following the path of the Alpha Male 2.0 that I espouse, you should wear your wedding ring at all times with confidence and not give a shit about it. If you're not quite confident or outcome-independent enough to do that yet, then take the ring off during initial dating activities with new women but set a goal to be confident enough to leave it on all the time like I do.

As a humorous side note, there is one possible *advantage* to wearing your wedding ring while in the dating phase with new women. There is a sizeable contingent of women out there who are *attracted* to taken men. Some of these women don't want any strings attached. Others just get excited about being with a man who is already desired by another woman. I've known at least two men who were single, but actually wore fake wedding rings when they went out to meet women! They lie and say they're "married," but these guys *do* get laid. Not my style, of course, because I don't endorse lying, but it shows that some women out there will actually be *more* attracted to you if you're married, especially if you proceed with them while clearly demonstrating the fact that your marriage isn't a problem. This actually makes me wonder if one or two of the women I've had sex with in the past while wearing my wedding ring had sex with me *because* I was wearing it rather than *in spite of it*. Funny, but possible.

Chapter 25

WHERE TO HAVE SEX WITH SIDE WOMEN

While there are certainly many exceptions to this, it is usually the case in most non-monogamous marriages that the husband will not be allowed to have sex with side-FBs in his home, or at least not in his home whenever he wants. If that's the case with you, this means you'll need to determine logistics on how to quickly, easily, conveniently, and cheaply have sex with your side women outside of your home whenever you wish. That's what this chapter is all about.

Before we get into the specifics, I have to be clear that having sex in your own home is the best and least-complicated option by far. Because of this, you need to push for this aspect when you discuss the ground rules with your wife. If your wife agrees to have your side women over for sex at your house, it's going to make things a *lot* easier for you on multiple levels. I know several open-married men who are able to have sex in their own homes, and believe me, these guys have a much easier time with their sexual logistics than men who are never allowed to have sex with FBs within their homes.

If your wife absolutely won't go for this despite your best efforts, then your fallback position is to get her to allow FBs at your house sometimes, under certain conditions. For example, I've seen some marriages where the man is allowed to have FBs over at his house, but only in certain rooms. In one marriage I know of, the man can have FBs at his house, but only when his wife is out of town for work.

Other possibilities are being able to have your FBs over when your wife is involved, like for threesomes with your wife and so on. In my marriage, Pink Firefly doesn't like threesomes, but she really enjoys watching me have sex with other attractive women. (I know, I have a hard life.) Our agreement is that I can't have FBs over at our house *unless* those FBs are going to have sex with me while Pink Firefly watches or is otherwise involved. We've done this many times and it's a lot of fun.

However, when I want to have sex with FBs one-on-one, I need to make other arrangements (though there have been one or two odd exceptions to this where PF relented a little). I'll get into more specifics on exactly how I handle this in a minute.

The bottom line is that the more sex you can have in your own home, the more advantageous this entire process will be for you, so try hard for this. Obviously, this will be less likely if you have small children or other people living in your home besides you and your wife, but do the best you can based on your circumstances. If you absolutely can't do it, you'll have to choose one or more "side locations"; places outside of the home where you can have sex with your FBs.

Side Locations

Despite the logistical downsides, there are actually some advantages to having sex with FBs outside of your home.

The first is that it makes bringing new women into your life a little easier. Many women will actually be more uncomfortable going to your home for sex if she knows she's going to see pictures and other evidence of your wife all over the place.

The second advantage is that you have much more control and independence regarding the location (or at least can, depending on the option you choose). Sometimes it's just "nicer" to do these things far away from your wife's Zones.

Here is the master list of all the options you have as side locations so you can have sex on a regular basis outside of the home. Some of them cost money, some less, and some more. Some are complicated, others are simple. There are pros and cons to every item on this list, and some may not apply to your individual circumstances. Regardless, your job is to pick one (or more) of these items and establish them as regular locales for you and your FBs.   They are listed in no particular order, and after the list I will examine each option in detail.

- Hotels

- AirBnB (or similar)

- Boat
- Camper or RV
- Rent a small apartment
- Rent a small office
- Rent a small place with a friend or family member
- Friend's home
- Your second home
- Her place

Hotels

No surprise here, but hotels are the preferred method for most open-marriage men. They're easy. There's also sometimes a strong sexual thrill associated with having sex in a hotel, for men and women both. There is never a long-term commitment like there is with many of the other side location options.

The big downside with hotels is, of course, the cost, especially if you use them more than once a week. Having a hotel stay seven, eight, ten times a month really racks up the costs.

Do some research and locate three or four hotels in different areas of town that are as *inexpensive as you can find* <u>without them being too crappy</u>. If you try to this on the cheap and end up with crappy hotels, you will actually lose women. Early on in my dating adventures, I lost potential lays when I brought women to really cheap but really disgusting hotels.

An hour or so on the internet will produce some nice, clean, cheap hotels in your local area. Think places like Holiday Inn. Make sure you locate several of them in different parts of town. That way, no matter where you are with a side woman, one of your hotels will be available to you within easy travel distance for you and her.

If you're not doing sugar daddy game and/or if your FBs aren't very young, you could split the cost of the hotel with your FB, and should if she has her own money (like if she's married herself, for example).

A second downside of hotels is that if you secure a room and then an FB flakes on you, you're out the cost of the room for no reason. This happened to me once early on in my marriage (back when I used hotels), and I never forgot it. Never pay for a hotel room until the woman has actually arrived on the premises. I also do not recommend you go right to a hotel for the first meet, even if doing sugar daddy game. Instead, meet her at a coffee shop or similar right by the hotel, make sure she's there and real, then move to the hotel.

It's also important to have your FB hang back outside or in a different room while you pay for the hotel room in the lobby. Her standing there while you handle this business often makes women nervous.

AirBnB (or similar)

This is an option for FBs who you already know well and trust since these are more complicated to cancel than hotel rooms. The good news is that they are much more discreet than hotels since there is usually no lobby or check-in procedure with other human beings, so if discretion is a strong concern for you (or her), AirBnB rooms are superior to hotels. Other than that, the pros and cons are more or less the same.

Boat

If this is an option or an interest for you, having a boat with a bed inside works very well. They're fun and relaxing too. Obviously, I would *never* buy a boat just so you can have a place to have sex with your FBs because the cost of the boat, fuel, dock fees, and so on are pretty damn high (unless you are wealthy, but if that's the case there are other less unusual options to utilize). Regardless, if getting a boat is already something you've wanted to do, you now have an extra reason to do so. It solves a lot of problems.

Camper or RV

This is an extremely interesting option that I almost did myself. You can buy used camper or small RV for as little as $3,000 to $5,000. This is *far* less expensive than a boat, apartment, or a second home. If you buy one for $4,000 (for example) and use it for just three years, that's only a cost of $111 a month(!), not including basic upkeep. Not only do you now have a fun RV you can use for recreation and transportation but you also now have a place to have sex with your FBs whenever you want. You can even pick them up in your RV if your FBs don't drive or don't have a car. It's a fantastic idea.

The only logistical issues are where to store the camper if you're not allowed to have it on the street in front of your house or if you don't have room on your property to store it. There are surprisingly inexpensive RV storage facilities in most neighborhoods you can use. Do some Google searching in your local area to get pricing and availability.

I almost did this myself before I choose the office option (that I'll describe in a minute). I strongly recommend it regardless. For a lot of married men, a small, used camper or small RV is the ideal solution for minimal cost with a lot of upsides.

Rent A Small Apartment

If you can afford it and if your area isn't very expensive, you can rent a small studio apartment 10-20 minutes away from your home. (I would consider a 10-minute drive a minimum distance; don't have this apartment right down the street from your house; the possibility of problems is too great.) Throw a cheap bed and couch in there, and you're good to go. Obviously, if your income isn't high enough to do something like this, or if apartments in your city are extremely expensive, then this isn't an option. Yet, if you can pull it off, there are massive benefits to having a second place like this, far beyond just a place to have side-sex.

It is my strong recommendation that any man in an OLTR Marriage has a place to go whenever he wants outside of his home that is 100% His Zone. A place to escape from the wife if he ever needs to, or a place to be alone when he desires it, or worst case, a place to temporarily use as a base of operations in the case of a contentious separation or divorce (especially if the deed, mortgage, or rent is in her name, as we discussed back in Chapter 18).

This place could be an apartment, office, second house, boat with internal rooms, rented warehouse or workshop, or anything like that. (A camper would not qualify, nor would going to a friend's home.)

Just the fact your wife knows you have this place to go to whenever you want keeps Mutual Harmony and Attraction at higher levels because one of the many reasons for Betaization in TMM is that the wife always knows the man has "nowhere to go" and is "stuck with her" no matter how much drama she throws at him.

There's also a tremendous amount of inner peace experienced by the married man who knows that he has another "base" outside of his home, configured just the way he wants, in His Zone. I also recommend that your wife never goes there. Make it truly *your* place, separate from her.

Having this second location is not a mandatory technique, but I *highly* recommend it if you can afford to do such a thing (and only if you can afford it).

If you choose an apartment, make sure to get an apartment as small as you can (studio apartments are ideal) and make sure to turn off all the utilities whenever you leave to keep those costs low. I recommend having no more than a one-year lease on the unit when you first get it. Once you've been there for a year and you know the location works for you, then you can get a longer lease at that time.

Rent A Small Office

This is the option I use. It's definitely not for everyone, but it works for me. I realized I could rent an office for much less than an apartment would cost, especially considering the office could be small, in an older building, and be otherwise unappealing toward other people looking for a real office to conduct business. I could also use the office as a real office, which would be advantageous not only for my work but also for tax reasons. It could also serve as my second location if I configured it as a mini-apartment if needed.

I took a few weeks and looked around on the internet for various offices for rent and visited several of them. I kept my eye out for offices that had these characteristics:

- Did *not* have a reception area (no receptionist, no security guard, etc.)
- Did *not* require a visitor to see too many other people during their trip from the entrance of the building to the actual office (ideally seeing no one).
- Was as far away from other offices in the building as possible
- Was in a convenient location, meaning close to my house but not too close (10-20 minutes away)
- Had convenient parking
- Was relatively inexpensive

I looked at several locations before I finally found it. I located a small office located on a second floor, with no reception area, quick access to the building exit, in an older building, that was only $250 a month. The office was only adjacent to one other office; its other three walls were facing a hallway, another hallway, and the outside of the building. Perfect for having sex. The office was really cheap since it had no windows, meaning no one wanted to rent it, but for me having no windows was actually a nice extra feature.

The only problem was that it had a door to the adjacent office. That would be a problem due to sexual noises, as well as making visiting women nervous. However, that office was also vacant because it also had no windows. I negotiated with the landlord to rent that office as well for an additional $150 month. He was eager to do it since no one wanted a tiny office with no windows.

So for just $400 a month, tax deductible, I now have *two* discreet offices joined by a door that I can leave open for one "big" office. I turned one office into a living area with a cheap collapsible futon (which can be either a couch or a bed) and some chairs. In the second office, I have a desk (lent to me by the landlord) with an additional two chairs. I got a strong white noise machine from Amazon, which I have going during an FB visit. It makes a great office where I can work when I need to and have fun FB visits. All for just $400 a month with no utility bill. (I use my phone Wi-Fi hotspot connection for the internet when I work there.)

I also made sure that there was a nearby fitness center so that I could use their showers in a pinch by getting a day pass in case I ever needed to spend the night there. I have never needed to use them yet, but it's nice to know I have that option.

If you hunt hard enough, you can find hidden gems like this. The advantage we have is that we are looking for office aspects that most people looking for an office *don't want*. It's perfect.

Rent A Place with A Friend or Family Member

This is an option when you want a second place but can't quite afford one. You can rent an office or apartment with a trusted friend or family member, split the costs, and share the place them. You then maintain a schedule with this other person (or persons) to use this place on specific days or evenings. I've seen many guys do this and it works well. Here are a few examples I've seen:

- Three brothers rented a cool apartment downtown. They split the costs three ways. One brother lived in a different city but regularly visited; he used the apartment as a place to stay during his visits. Another brother used it for parties and meetings. The third brother used it to have sex with his FBs. They used Google Calendar to maintain the schedule between them.

- A friend of mine with an open marriage who lived in a more rural area sublet a small, furnished, two-bedroom house for $300 a month. He split the cost with his massage therapist, who would occasionally use the house during the day for her clients.

- A guy I know with live-in OLTR girlfriend rented a cheap studio apartment with a friend who needed to store a lot of sensitive equipment he didn't want in a traditional storage unit. He was able to store his equipment in a safe location and the other guy had a convenient place to have sex with FBs.

Deals like this are not difficult to come up with if you network with people you know. Reach out to trusted friends and family and see if you can put something like this together. Ideally, you should find a cheap location first so you can use that as part of your sales pitch.

Friend's Home

This is a cheap or even free option. Some guys have set up specific or casual arrangements with single men they know where they can crash at their friend's houses for an evening. That doesn't mean they actually spend the night there, but they have that option if they want it and if they schedule it in advance.

One example of this I've seen a few times is a guy will have several single guy buddies downtown. The guy will hit the bars and clubs downtown to pick up women, then wrap the evening up by hitting one of his friend's conveniently located downtown places to have sex.

Other examples are where a guy will set up very specific nights with his buddy where the buddy's apartment will be free. The open-marriage man then schedules his pickup and sexual activities around that.

I've even talked to two men who will actually *pay* their buddies a few bucks to have their apartments temporarily available for them. Their argument is that it's less expensive compensating their friends than using a hotel.

Her Place

Obviously, the cheapest and perhaps simplest option is to have sex at your FB's home. However, the reason this opportunity is listed last is that it's usually not an option. More often than not, your FBs will not live alone, nor will want you over at their house. Yet, if you can swing this, it is indeed a lot easier. Some open-married men even screen specifically for women who live alone so they know this will be an option. Many men will feel this out during the first/second meets with new women. If they find that her place is an option, they will put in more effort into her than with other women who don't live alone.

I have personally never had sex in an FB's home since being married. For me, it's always been hotels (early on), my office (today), or at my home (when PF is involved). Even before I was married, having sex with my FBs or MLTRs at their homes was a rare event. But that's just me; if you can make that option work, please do.

The Dual Home Marriage

All of those locations aside, the absolute best method for having sex with FBs away from where your wife lives is to not live with your wife in the first place.

Huh? Yep, you heard me right.

I call this the Dual Home Marriage. I've seen several couples do this, including monogamous ones. Usually, couples who have a Dual Home Marriage are older (as in over age 50) since most young or middle-age women won't agree to it. Regardless, having a Dual Home Marriage is the marital configuration that minimizes drama the most and keeps Attraction at the highest possible levels.

The Dual Home Marriage simply means that you're married to your OLTR wife, but you still maintain completely separate homes. She has her home, you have yours. Perhaps she spends the night and "lives" at your home three, four, five nights a week, or you spend those nights at her place. She certainly has stuff over at your home and/or you may have stuff at hers. You live just like a normal married couple except that you both maintain your own residences, 100% in each of your own names in keeping with the Financial Barrier.

The advantages of the Dual Home Marriage are numerous, including:

- The ability to have true alone time whenever you want.

- The ability to have sex with FBs whenever you like without having to leave your home.

- The ability to soft next your wife. Men who have Dual Home

Marriages can actually soft next their wives when needed, something men who live full-time with their wives can't do.

- The ability to have a much larger Zone with less compromise.

- The ability to end the marriage much easier if needed.

- Heightened Attraction from your wife because you won't be over in her house 100% of the time like a normal husband. Heightened attraction means more Mutual Harmony.

- More Freedom.

Of course, there are some downsides as well, including:

- It's potentially more expensive and usually is, since you can't share living expenses like you can when you live with someone.

- The odds of divorce may be higher. I don't think there are any scientific stats on this, but my strong guess is that since a Dual Home Marriage feels a little more like a girlfriend/boyfriend relationship than an actual marriage, the odds of a breakup or divorce are probably higher than if you lived alone because your wife (as well as you) are more likely to start *dating* other people.

- Less social acceptance (though if you're a true Alpha Male 2.0, you shouldn't care).

- And the biggest one of them all: the vast majority of women will never agree to a Dual Home Marriage since it doesn't "seem like a real marriage" to them. If you suggest such a thing, women will usually snort and just marry someone else under a TMM. This is why most women that I've seen in Dual Home Marriages tend to be older women past their physical prime who can't afford to be too choosey.

If you can pull off a Dual Home Marriage (and realistically, you probably won't; even I don't have one), then I strongly recommend it. The advantages are tremendous. The next best thing is to do what I said above and live full-time with your wife but have a separate place that is all your own (office, apartment, boat, etc.).social circle.

Chapter 26
OTHER SEXUAL LOGISTICS

In this chapter, I'll cover the other sexual aspects of your life that you'll need to pay regular attention to as an open-married man.

Managing Discretion

Even though your marriage is open and your wife has agreed to all of this, in terms of discretion, you ideally need to keep things quiet to other people outside of your home. You and your wife might be enlightened, but the fact remains that as liberal as today's culture has become, when it comes to sexual monogamy in marriages, the rest of society is still sadly stuck in a horribly outdated, puritanical 1950s paradigm. In your own home, you can do whatever you want, but outside in the real world, if you blab your open marriage aspects to the world, problems may occur, such as:

- It may embarrass your wife, who likely cares much more about what other people think than you do.
- It will likely confuse your friends and family.
- It may even *anger* some of your family (particularly the female ones, religious ones, and/or more traditional ones).
- It may create some problematic scenarios with your children, if you have any, as I discussed back in Chapter 21.
- It might result in drama for you and your wife (and even your kids).
- In some jurisdictions, it may even threaten the legal enforceability of your Financial Barrier.

Obviously, it's your life. If you don't mind incurring the potential for those above problems and want to be 100% public with the nature of your marriage, feel free to do so. If instead, you want to keep things more discreet, here are several things you should do.

1. Don't tell anyone about your open marriage status other than perhaps one or two very trusted inner-circle friends or family members. Over time, as certain people in your family get more accustomed to rumors about what you're doing and you get a better feel for their reactions, you can start telling more people. This is what I did. I started with just two people in my family and finally "spread it" to most of my other siblings (I'm one of six children) after several years.

2. Tell your wife to do the same with her family. Of course, you can't control what your wife does, nor should you try. Women are women, and the odds are overwhelming that your wife will eventually tell another woman who will blab it to others. You have no control over that. Just accept it as part of the deal.

Moreover, do not let your wife's lapses in discretion somehow "give you permission" to be indiscreet yourself. Be better than that. Maintain a high standard of discretion no matter what your wife does, unless you *decide of your own free will* that you want to go public with your marriage life.

3. We've already talked about this, but it bears repeating. Do not have sex with women who may tell shared friends or family members about your OLTR Marriage. That means you consciously avoid having sex with women who know your wife, or who know friends of your wife, or are overly emotional, and so on.

4. If you have sex with women at your own home, always be consciously aware of nosy or gossipy neighbors. This can be a real problem in some neighborhoods or apartment buildings. The same goes for people you know in your social circle or at your work. 80% of discretion is simply being aware of what you're doing at all times and paying attention to who may see you.

Although I wasn't married at the time, for many years, I lived on a wide-open cul-de-sac where it was really obvious to the neighbors who was coming and going from my house. My neighbors constantly gossiped about the non-stop parade of different women who were coming and going from my place. As an outcome-independent Alpha Male 2.0, I didn't give a shit (I actually found it amusing), but it would have been really difficult for my wife if I'd had one at the time.

5. Keep the nature of your marriage far away from social media.

6. Be *very* careful about what you post on social media. Way too many people these days get lackadaisical about what they post on social media and then regret what they post to their entire social circle only after it's too late. Women in particular do this often. Your wife should also be careful (but again, you can't control her; as an OLTR Wife, she's free to post whatever she wants).

7. Be careful regarding all written, texted, emailed, videoed, or recorded correspondence you with your side women. This includes voice mails, emails, texts, social media messaging, etc. Encrypted services like WhatsApp or delete-after-24-hours systems like Snapchat are usually safest if this is a concern for you.

STD Prevention

I have several detailed chapters on how to prevent getting STDs in *The Ultimate Open Relationships Manual**. I'm not going to repeat all of that here; refer to that book for more information. Instead, I'll just summarize the basics as it applies to open-married men.

1. Always use condoms on new women, young women, hookers, and sugar babies. The only time condoms should come off with side women is if you have a *long-term* side woman who has demonstrated (not *verbalized*, but actually *demonstrated*) a long track record of responsible behavior (getting lots of STD tests, not getting drunk, not having sex with too many other men, etc.).

2. Submit to regular STD testing at least twice a year. Get hardcopy results of your tests and show them to your wife for bragging rights. Make sure the STD tests you get are comprehensive; too many places just test for the "basic" STDs like HIV and Chlamydia. You need to test for at least the following diseases:

*http://www.haveopenrelationships.com/

- HIV
- Chlamydia
- Gonorrhea
- Herpes 2 (HSV-2)
- Syphilis
- Hepatitis B and C (Hepatitis A is optional)
- Trichomoniasis

3. If she's having sex with men on the side, your wife must also submit to these tests around twice a year just like you are. Be sure to review the results yourself. (As usual, you can't tell her what to do, but if she's having sex with other men and absolutely refuses to get regular STD tests like you are, this is a very serious problem in your marriage that warrants strong action.)

4. I personally mandate that all of my side women who are going to see me on a regular basis over a long term be on some kind of birth control, and ideally this is *not* birth control pills, which are not very reliable (what if she forgets to take one that day?). *Lots* of younger women these days have implants such as IUDs or Nexplanon, so this is a much easier issue today than it was just 10 or 20 years ago.

5. If your wife is having sex with other people, be aware if she starts making errors or if she has sex with any questionable men. If this is the case, you need to start asking some strong questions and assist her. You're not doing this out of jealousy; you're doing this to protect her health and well-being – and yours!

Section Six
Converting from A Monogamous Marriage to An Open One

Chapter 27
THE CONVERSION PROCESS

The odds are pretty good that you purchased this book because you are currently in a normal monogamous marriage (TMM), or you're living with a monogamous girlfriend and you want to convert your current relationship to a non-monogamous one.

No problem. In this section of the book I'm going to give you a step-by-step procedure for converting a monogamous marriage (or live-in relationship) to a non-monogamous one. I know for a fact that the procedure I'm going to lay out in the next few chapters works at least 70% of the time when men with normal marriages try it. I have worked with and spoken with numerous men who have made this process work. Yes, it's not 100% (nothing in life is 100%), but realize you're attempting a titanic change in your existing marriage, so 70% is really, *really* good considering all of this.

The procedure you're going to learn over the next few chapters looks like this:

1. You're going to establish the correct emotional framework to make this often-difficult change.

2. You're going to prepare for the worst-case scenarios in case they occur.

3. You're going to choose one of three conversion techniques to use. The first one is the best, the second one is a back-up technique in case the first one doesn't work, and the third one is the worst, but I present in this book since some men *have* technically made it work.

4. You're going to learn how to effectively address her objections and other possible problems that may arise.

5. You're going to set up a specific battle plan for the first three weeks of your newly converted marriage, which are very important (and

again, whenever I say "marriage" in this book I mean *you live with a woman full time in a romantic context;* I don't care if you aren't legally married; what's important is that you're living the lifestyle of a married man, and that's you if you live with your girlfriend).

The Required Emotional Backbone

Converting a monogamous marriage to a non-monogamous one is difficult. You are transforming one of the key traits that Societal Programming and Disney have told your wife her entire life is mandatory for a "real" marriage or serious relationship: absolute sexual monogamy at all times. When you attempt to change this, even if she's an intelligent and easygoing woman, all of her cultural conditioning, Societal Programming, Disney, need for conformity, need to impress her family, need for emotional security, and religion (if she has one) are going to rise up within her like Godzilla and attack with all the nuclear breath she can summon.

This means that you need to be 100% emotionally rock-solid about what you're doing. You *must* be strong, confident, and have balls. If you don't, if you're at all wishy-washy about this, this process is likely to fail regardless of the techniques you employ.

Therefore, you *must* have the following four mindsets ingrained in your brain before you attempt this:

Item One: Resolve that this is absolutely, positively what you want. Do or die.

If your view is that this is something that you "sort of" want or that "would be nice," then it's not going to work. You need to have a "must make it work" attitude, a "do or die" attitude. You must be 100% sure this is what you want and what you must have. 90% isn't going to cut it.

Item Two: You must be okay with the slight possibility of losing your wife.

"What? Lose my wife?!? Wait a minute...!"

I'm not saying you're going to lose your wife over this. Indeed, the *entire goal of this book* is to convert to and maintain an open marriage while *keeping* your wife.

Regardless, as you'll see in some of the upcoming chapters, depending on your marriage and your wife's personality, it's entirely possible she will at least *threaten* to leave you. You also run the risk of her *actually* leaving you. The odds of this are low (especially if you've been a good husband), but it's possible.

As I discussed at the beginning of this book, you can't have Oneitis. You must be okay with the *possibility* of losing this marriage. Before you freak out, let me walk you through why this attitude is critical to your success. If your attitude is "I can*not* lose my wife no matter what," then when you start modifying major aspects of your relationship to open up the marriage, all she has to do is threaten to leave you or divorce you, and then you'll back off because you "can't lose her." In other words, you will have wasted your time. What, then, was the point of this exercise? What was the point of going through all that? What was the point of buying and reading this book? Do you see my point?

When I do personal coaching with guys who want to open up their marriages, my very first question to them is, "Is it worth the *possibility* of getting a divorce?" If they say they would not like to get divorced but they're willing to entertain the *possibility* since the monogamy isn't working, then we proceed. If they instead say, "Oh gosh no, I can't lose my wife," then I either nicely refuse to work with them (or radically redirect their goals to something different within the realm of monogamy, which of course is not ideal). I do this because any time or effort spent in opening up the marriage will be in vain, and I don't want to waste anyone's time.

I'm not saying you will derive zero value from this book if you simply can't lose your wife, but I think you understand what I'm saying. If your wife can simply stamp her foot and make threats (which in all likelihood she will do; wives have been threatening their husbands with divorce for decades now, and they've become very good at it) and this immediately stops you in your tracks, there's a strong limit to what you can accomplish.

Item Three: You must be willing to make changes in your life you are not accustomed to and may seem odd at first.

I've talked to a lot of married guys who desire to make this change into the open marriage world. They truly want it. They are willing to accept the possibility of actually losing their wives. They're ready! But then I'll tell them to do things like stop wearing their stupid khaki pants, or shave the long hairs growing out of the side of their face, or pursue really attractive women less intelligent than they're used to, and then the resistance begins.

"I've been married for 17 years. I've never had to do any of that stuff."

"That sounds like a lot of trouble."

"Do I really have to do that?"

"My wife doesn't care if I dress like this."

"Oh, I could never have sex with a woman less intelligent than my wife."

"Women shouldn't care if my hair looks like this... my wife doesn't!"

"I can't have a 'fuck buddy.' I have to have a REAL RELATIONSHIP with any woman I have sex with."

"I'm too old for that."

And so on.

There's an old saying: *doing what got you here won't get you there.* What you've been doing up until this point will get you what you've got and no more: a monogamous wife and a sexually boring marriage. If you want to go from that to an open marriage, with a wife so attracted to you she's willing to put up with you having sex with other women, and with women on the side eager to sleep with you even when they know you're married, then I'm sorry, but you're going to have to make some serious changes in your life. Married men get *really* complacent and set in their ways; sadly, you don't have that option. You're going to have to start doing things you've never done before, or at least have not done since you were unmarried all those years ago.

Item Four: Fully realize that you are doing nothing wrong.

99% of society works 24/7 to program you (and your wife) with the concept that marriage must be monogamous, and if it isn't, you're somehow a bad person (or sick person, or immature person, or sinful person, or <insert the negative, false bullshit here> person). If you receive permission from your wife to sleep with other women and then sleep with other women, you are doing nothing wrong.

- You are doing nothing immoral, unethical, or sleazy.
- You are not violating any vows or trusts.
- You are not being immature.
- You are not a sex addict.
- You are not being selfish.
- You are not being unfair. (She can sleep with other people too, remember?)
- You are not being a bad husband/father/citizen/Christian/architect/<insert your favorite title here>.
- You are not taking advantage of your wife.

I could go on and on with all the false, societally programmed excuses you will run into with your own mind and other people who will throw excuses at you, but you get the point.

I'm going to now continue with the actual how-tos of how to make this conversion work, but before you actually attempt anything, make sure you're solid with the above four mindsets. Otherwise, your success here is going to be difficult (if not impossible) no matter what techniques you use.

Chapter 28
How to Convince Your Wife

The toughest part of the process is, of course, getting your monogamous wife to go along with all of this, ideally while keeping her as your wife.

I have vast experience in getting women who only know monogamy as a way of life to "convert" to agreeing to open relationships. Of course, when you actually live with a woman, the process is a little different and can be more intense since there's more at stake. However, the core frames and concepts are the same. What you're about to read has been real-life field-tested by many men, all over the world, to great effect. It is the best method I know of to make this conversion. There are also two other, less effective methods that describe in case this one doesn't work.

Make sure you thoroughly understand the procedure outlined in this chapter before you actually try it. Re-read it as many times as you need.

There are three ways to convert a monogamous marriage into an open one. They are:

1. The Primary Conversion Method (best)

2. The Hail Mary Method (not ideal, but sometimes necessary)

3. Conversion-By-Cheating Method (worst, not recommended)

Your goal is to get your wife to convert by using the Primary Conversion Method. If this fails, you may choose the Hail Mary Method as a back-up plan if you wish, though it's more difficult. I do *not* recommend using the Conversion-By-Cheating Method, but I will present it in the next chapter regardless since I have to admit there is a decent amount of open-married men who converted their wives this way.

For now, just focus on the Primary Conversion Method, which is likely to work and which we will cover here.

You Must Be A Decent Husband

One key point before we get started: *If you have been a crappy husband, these techniques are far less likely to work.*

For example, whenever a man complains to me that his wife never gives him sex when he asks, the first thing I do is look at him, not the wife. How he looks, how he treats his wife, how motivated and masculine he is, and so on. If you're a fat slob who treats your wife like crap or constantly ignores her, of course she's not going to want to sleep with you because you've murdered Attraction. The same goes for if you're an uber-beta and kiss your wife's ass, follow her around like a puppy dog, and do whatever she wants.

This conversion process assumes that you are at least a decent husband and have not been a complete pussy. You don't have to be perfect. None of us are. Rather, I'm assuming that you treat your wife decently well most of the time and take at least moderate care of your physical appearance and masculinity.

If you are indeed a horrible husband, or a horrible father to your kids, or have really let Attraction drop to low levels during your marriage, you may need to focus on those areas first before you attempt a conversion to an open marriage, even if that means you take 6-12 months to improve these things before you initiate this conversion process.

The Primary Conversion Method

When you're ready to do this, here are the steps you need to take.

Step One: Get completely prepared before you talk to her.

You're going to have a very important discussion with your wife, broken up into several parts. However, before you have these talks, you need to be emotionally and logistically prepared. This means you have ingrained the four mindsets I described in the last chapter. It means that you have some strong goals, projects, and/or a Mission in your life that has nothing to do with your wife. It also means you are emotionally ready for your wife to start screaming at you or crying (which may not happen but is possible).

Being logistically ready means you're prepared for the worst if it happens. This means you have someplace to go outside of the home if she really freaks out. It may even mean you have a separate PO box set up for mail in case you have to get divorced. The level of logistical preparedness is really up to you, based on your particular situation. I'm just saying you need to be prepared. Don't go into this conversation blind.

Step Two: Choose the ideal time.

You need to pick a day or evening to do this when:

1. You're in a good mood, not stressed, and have no other looming problems or big concerns.

2. She's in a good mood. Do *not* do this when she's upset or stressed about something.

3. Your kids, if you have them, are not home (or, as a second-best option, are fast asleep and on the other side of the house). This is a serious conversation, and you both need to be free to speak your minds and even get emotional without worrying about the kids.

4. You are both together, alone, and in private. Do not do this in a public place. Do not do this with anyone else present besides just you and her.

5. You have no major events coming up in either of your lives in the next few days. If it's Thursday and you're both going to a big family reunion or client dinner on Saturday, wait until well after that to have these conversations. The same goes if you (or she) have a major project to finish at work over the next few days, or a big vacation coming up with the kids, etc.

Assume that for the next several days after this conversation, you and she will not be operating at optimal levels. Once again, I'm not saying that will automatically happen. I'm saying you need to be prepared for the possibility.

6. It's not a Friday or Saturday. If you do this on Friday, you increase the odds of her carrying an argument over into the weekend and just prolonging the drama. It's actually better to do this on a day like

Tuesday, where the very next day you both need to get back to your lives. You can always reconvene on Wednesday evening if you need to.

Step Three: Assume a very loving frame.

Before you talk to her about this, think very hard about how much you love her, care for her, and want good things for her. Go over and give her a big hug and kiss if you need to. Cuddle up with her on the couch in front of a roaring fireplace. Really *love* her.

As always, that does not mean you get needy for her. You're willing to risk losing her, remember? Loving her deeply and not getting needy for her is not a contradiction. Strong, confident, non-needy Alpha Male 2.0s can love a woman just as strongly and deeply as the needy betas.

You're about to drop a bomb on her head, so you need to soften the blow as best you can. Assuming a loving, caring frame will help.

Step Four: Tell her you love her and want to be with her for the rest of your life.

This is how you start the conversation. Be honest about how much you love her, want to be with her, and that you have no intention of leaving her, all of which should be true. (At least I hope so! If you actually want to leave your wife, stop messing around this open marriage stuff and just get a divorce!)

If you have kids with her, reiterate your love for the children as well.

Step Five: Tell her clearly but lovingly that the current system isn't working.

Use your own words in describing that the current monogamous arrangement in the marriage is not working. Do not go into detail about this. Your wife likely knows this already. Simply state it as a fact, which it is.

Tell her clearly that if things keep going the way they're going, the marriage is at risk. This is not a threat, so don't state it as one. Again, it's just a fact. The vast majority of men and women under the age of sixty in the modern era do not stay together in bad marriages. If marriages do not satisfy the needs of both husband and wife, people eventually get divorced. It's how it is. Convey this to her, again, using your own words.

If you have tried to fix things in the past, go over those things now. "Honey, we did our best. We tried marriage counseling, we tried role-playing, we tried…" Make it known that you (and perhaps her) have tried to make things work, and these things may have helped, but they didn't fix the problem.

Step Six: Tell her what you are going to do.

Next, you're about to tell her that you're going to start sleeping with other women. It is extremely important for you to understand that *you're not going to ask her for permission*, nor are you asking "what she thinks about that." You're just going to tell her what you're going to do.

To be clear:

- You are *not* asking her for permission.

- You are *not* asking for her input or her thoughts on the matter. In other words, you're not saying something like, "I'm thinking about opening up the marriage where we can have sex with other people… what do you think about that?" No!

- You are *not* threatening her. You're going to do this regardless of her behavior, positive or negative.

- This is *not* a negotiation. This is *not* something you'll do unless she does something or stops doing something else. This is *not* conditional. This is something you are going to do, period, regardless of what she says or does or promises. Your decision is already made; your path is already set. What she says doesn't matter.

This is all crucial because I've seen lots of men screw this up. This is something you are going to do, period. You are not going to change your mind and refrain if she "shapes up" or starts having sex with you more often or loses weight or whatever. No! This is going to happen, period.

Simply tell her, in a calm loving manner, that you are going to start sleeping with other women. Then *immediately*, before she has a chance to respond, you need to quickly verbalize these five things:

1. You are not leaving her. You're going to stay right here as her loving and supportive husband.

2. You will use condoms on all side women and show her the results of regular STD tests.

3. You will keep it discreet. No one will know except you and her.

4. You will not date these women or have any emotional attachment to them. It's going to be just sex. You can even play this up, such as, "They'll just be young, dumb bimbos. Not any women I'll actually *like*. It will just be physical, and that's it. That's all I want anyway."

5. Lastly, state that you're not going to start doing it right now. Instead, you'll start doing this in exactly two weeks. Not "about" two weeks – actually give her the specific date when you will start doing this, which will be in about 14 days or so. Also, let her know that you haven't had sex with anyone else yet (if that's the truth).

It's extremely important that you verbalize those five items as fast as you can before she starts in with her objections. You want to preemptively neutralize the threat she's going to perceive. The five immediate threat areas a woman feels when her husband tells her this stuff is:

"He's going to leave me and the kids!"

"I'll get an STD!"

"Everyone will find out and I'll look bad!"

"He'll fall in love with someone else!"

"Oh no! He's going to have sex with another girl TOMORROW! I can't handle this!" or *"He's already having sex with someone!"*

The Ultimate Open Marriage Manual | 293

It's your job to soften or eliminate these threats as fast as possible before they start to fester in her feminine, emotional mind.

I'm not saying that just because you state those five things, she's not going to complain about them. Women are not logical creatures when it comes to relationships, so she certainly might. Regardless, the fact you've said it demonstrates to her that you've thought it through, you're not knee-jerk reacting, and most importantly, you care about her feelings in this matter.

Step Seven: Let her vent.

In all likelihood, she's now going to lose it. Depending on her personality, she's going to start complaining, screaming, threatening, withdrawing, crying, or a combination thereof.

If this happens, let it happen. Let her vent. Women need to verbalize their emotions. It's how they're wired. She may say some nasty things about you. She may try to get a rise out of you. She may say that you don't care about her or the children. She may call you immature, or a sex addict, or selfish, or evil. She may accuse you of things you've never done. And so on.

Just keep your mouth shut and let her say whatever she wants. Look at her lovingly with your eyes as she talks and keep a calm, accepting expression.

Do *not* get defensive. Do *not* get angry. Do *not* respond logically to her emotions or her accusations. Your masculine biology and psychology are going to want to do all of these things. Fight the urge. Just take a moment or two and let her unload on you.

No, it won't be fun. It won't be nice to see the woman you love get upset. Just realize this is a temporary but necessary part of the process. Other men who successfully converted their marriages went through the same thing.

Step Eight: If she remains somewhat rational, answer her objections. If she can't keep her cool, terminate the conversation immediately and continue it tomorrow.

This step is hard because you're going to have to objectively gauge how rational she's being, and with women we love, this is tough sometimes. We always want to give them the benefit of the doubt even when the situation doesn't warrant it.

Once she's done ranting, you need to judge if she's able to carry on a reasonably rational conversation. Perhaps she will, but more than likely she won't. It really depends on the woman, the marriage, and how she feels that day.

If she is clearly remaining somewhat calm and rational and can carry on a conversation without screaming, crying, threatening, or attacking you verbally, then proceed to step nine below.

If instead she's just angry or hysterical, which is likely, then say something like this: "I love you, and like I said, I'm not doing anything for two weeks, so we have time to talk about this some more, which I really want to do. I hate seeing you like this, and I'm a little worked up myself. So let's talk just about this tomorrow. I'm sorry I upset you."

Then **immediately terminate the conversation**. Of course, you know damn well that when you try this, she's going to say something like, "Ohhh no! We're going to settle this RIGHT NOW!" You need to be strong. Just keep repeating that you're done discussing it because you're both too worked up, but you really want to talk about it tomorrow when you're both calm.

Make sure you say you're "both" worked up, even if you aren't. This is a basic communication skill and it helps a lot. You don't want to look like you're attacking her, which you aren't. You also want to reiterate that you *do* want to talk about this, just not now while you're "both" upset.

Keep repeating yourself, be strong, and soon she'll get the point. Once you've repeated yourself three or four times, just quietly get up off the couch, give her a hug (unless she doesn't want you to touch her right now), and then calmly leave the room.

It's possible she may take a few deep breaths, have a drink of water, and then calm back down. If she does this and still wants to talk, and you can objectively see that she's ready to be somewhat rational, then proceed. Otherwise, call it a night and continue on to step nine tomorrow or the next day once she's calmed down.

Step Nine: Address her objections.

This is when the conversation really begins. Once she's exploded and gotten over the initial atom bomb, during this part of the conversation (or second conversation if you had to wait a day or two), she's going to start pelting you with objections, questions, and veiled threats.

This is when you need to be on your game. Since at this point you will have already read this book and have already figured out exactly what you want and the parameters you will agree to, answering her questions and objections should be no big deal.

Here are some general objections and examples of proper answers. You don't need to use these answers verbatim and probably shouldn't. Instead, they are indicative of the *frame* you should be having in this conversation as well as give you some good ideas.

Objection: I don't want an open marriage! That's not a marriage!

Answer: I understand. All I know is what we've been doing isn't working, and I want to make sure we stay together.

Objection: That's it! I'm getting a divorce!

Answer: I love you and I don't ever want you to go. If you divorce me, it will be horrible, but I will understand and let you go. But I hope you will stay with me forever because that's what I really want.

Objection: We're Christian! We can't be married like that!

Answer: You're absolutely right. But you know what? I thought about this… is getting a divorce Christian? I've thought a lot about this, and this is the best way. I'd rather have this than get divorced.

Objection: You have some kind of sexual problem! (or) You have some kind of mental issue! (or) You're a sex addict! (or) You need counseling!

Answer: I will be happy to go to counseling if you want, as long as you come with me. That's a good idea.

Objection: You're going to get an STD!

Answer: Like I said, I will always be wearing condoms when I do this, and I'll go in for regular STD tests and show you the results. We'll make this work.

Objection: You're going to fall in love with some other woman and leave me!

Answer: Baby, if that was going to happen, it would have happened already. I don't love anyone else but you. I don't want anyone else but you. All I'm talking about is slapping on a condom and having meaningless sex with some bimbo every once in a while.

Objection: I could never be married to a man who isn't committed to me!

Answer: I *am* committed to you, 100%. I love you and I don't ever want you to go. If you divorce me, it will be horrible, but I will understand and let you go. But I hope you will stay with me forever because that's what I really want.

Objection: This is crazy! Do I get to have sex with other men then?!? (This is a fun objection because women will always assume your answer will be "no" and then be ready to pounce on that.)

Answer: If that's something you really want, then yes. I'll be jealous, but fair is fair. (Married women love the word "fair." Be sure to use it during this conversation as much as possible. By the way, do not get into Ground Rules at this point, just respond to her objections.)

Objection: We have children! You can't be out having sex with women while I'm here taking care of the children!

Answer: Oh my gosh, I would never leave you alone with the kids while I'm out doing that. I will schedule this so it doesn't interfere with our family life at all. I'll only do it during the day, or when you're at work, etc.

Objection: You don't love me!

Answer: I love you more than anything in the world. (Take her hand or hold her unless she doesn't want to be touched right now.) I love you more than I've ever loved anyone in my life, and I want to be with you forever. I'm talking about meaningless sex here, not love. I love *you*.

Objection: There's someone else, isn't there? There's some slut out there you like and you're just trying to find a way to get with her!

Answer: (If there are no other women you have your eye on, tell your wife that, and be emphatic about it. If there *is* another woman you have your eye on, that's fine as long as you are only attracted to this woman sexually, as an FB only. At this point in the conversation, you don't want to go over all of that. Just reiterate that there is no one else and use the answer to the "you don't love me" objection above.)

Objection: I should be enough!

Answer: You are enough.

Follow-up: Then why do you want to sleep with other women?

Answer: I'm talking about slapping on a condom and having meaningless sex with some bimbo every once and a while. You are my wife, and you are the woman I love, and nothing will change that, ever.

Objection: Okay, fine! I'll have sex with you more often, then! You don't need to fuck other women now!

Answer: We've tried that before. It's not about that. (Remember, this is not a threat that you'll only do if she does X, Y, or Z. You're going to do this no matter what. This is *not* a negotiation. Stay strong!)

Objection: If you won't be devoted to me like I deserve, I'll have to find a man who will!

Answer: I love you and I don't ever want you to go. If you divorce me, it will be horrible, but I will understand will let you go. But I hope you will stay with me forever because that's what I really want.

Objection: I can't believe you're treating me this way!

Answer: I love you. (Hug her or hold her hand unless she doesn't want to be touched right now.)

Your goal for this part of the conversation is to remain calm, don't get needy, don't "cave in" to her threats or demands, and answer her objections. You are not going to actually establish the open marriage during this conversation. That comes a little later. All you need to do is demonstrate that you've made your decision, that you've thought this through, and reassure her that you're not leaving her and want to continue to stay with her.

Don't let this conversation go past about 20-25 minutes. If you're not careful, she'll easily turn this into a two-hour slugfest, and that will only damage your frame and your marriage. 20-25 minutes is all you need to state your case, listen to her emotionally react, and (possibly) answer her objections. After around 20-25 minutes, just tell her, "Honey, I'm really beat talking about this, and I don't think I have the energy to keep going. Let's resume this conversation tomorrow night, okay?" Then bow out gracefully and take the blame. That raises the odds of you being able to somewhat gracefully end the conversation.

Step Ten: Leave her alone and let her process everything.

One thing I have discovered repeatedly through my open relationship experiences is that although many women initially react negatively to this news, once they think about it for a few days, they come back and are surprisingly okay with it, provided you're being 100% fair (i.e. she can sleep with other people too, you'll be discreet, etc.) and you're being strong (you're not caving in or backpedaling when she threatens to leave you). Most married men who have done this have discovered the exact same thing.

After your first initial conversation, you need to leave her alone and let her "process." Women often need time to mentally process things and (sadly) discuss it with one or two other women. It's a normal reaction.

For the next one to three days, you need to let your wife just get back to her life and think this stuff through. During this time, she will:

1. Think very hard on all the ramifications of an open arrangement. This is a good thing.

2. Consider the pros and cons of staying married to you. This is a good thing if you've been a good husband, a bad thing if you have not.

3. Think about how much she loves you. Again, a good thing if you've been a good husband.

4. Call one or two close female friends or relatives and get their opinions on the matter. This is usually a bad thing, but you have no control over it. The odds are at least 65% that any other woman she tells about this is going to react with shock and/or disgust. Remember that women have been incorrectly trained since childhood to believe that absolute sexual monogamy is the only "proper" way to be in a loving relationship. You just need to accept that this may happen and be prepared for the "My sister told me I should divorce you" speech.

That said, times are changing, and many times she will get a *neutral* or even *positive* response from her female friend/relative. They may say something like, "Well, at least it sounds like he loves you and wants to make it work, and he's being really honest with you. My friend so-and-so has a marriage like this and she does okay…"

The key here is to not talk about this again until she comes back to you. Likely she'll do this about two or three days later.

If for some reason she does not come back to you to resume your conversation about this within about four days, something is wrong, and you need to once again get the kids out of the house (or asleep) and start up the next phase of the conversation yourself.

Step Eleven: Have the confirmation conversation.

This is the second conversation (or perhaps third) you have a few days after the first one after she's had time to calm down and think through everything. The good news is usually this conversation is much easier than the first. Sometimes they're even enjoyable.

This is where she actually agrees to the new open arrangement in the marriage, albeit perhaps reluctantly and with some fear or hesitation (though some men have had wives happily embrace the new marriage once they thought about it).

Of course, the opposite is also possible. There's a small chance she will actually throw down an ultimatum about getting divorced or something similar. If that occurs, do your best to carry on with the conversation I outline below. Try to get the *reasons* she doesn't want to do this so you can address them. If she really wants a divorce (or says she does), I'll cover that in a minute. For now, I'm going to cover what usually happens in confirmation conversations, and that is reluctant agreement.

Confirmation conversations almost always start like this: your wife says something like, "Okay, I've thought about it, and I don't like it, but I'll agree to it *only* if you promise to do these things…" and then she will proceed to lay out her Ground Rules.

As soon as she says this, *you have won*. This is a victory! No matter how negatively it's stated, she just told you that she'll agree to let you have sex with other women. The hardest part is over. Now it's simply a matter of negotiating the Ground Rules.

I already covered Ground Rules in Chapter 13. Using that section and the below list as a guideline, your job now is to determine which of her Ground Rules you find reasonable and which you do not.

Some rules she gives you may be perfectly reasonable ("you must always wear a condom with other women"). Some rules may be irrational and ridiculous ("none of the women can ever be skinner than me"). Other rules might be fine for beta male husbands but would never work in an OLTR Marriage based in Freedom ("I must personally approve every woman before you sleep with her" or "you can only have sex with other women when I'm in the room"). Other rules will be in a grey area; for these, you'll have to make your own judgment call. Just make sure if you agree to it, you won't regret it several years from now.

Here is a list of rules you can expect your wife to bring up. It's not all-inclusive, of course, but will give you a good idea of what to expect. I've broken them down to reasonable rules you could agree too, ridiculous rules you should not agree too under an OLTR Marriage, and rules somewhere in-between that you'll have to decide for yourself.

Examples of Reasonable Rules

- You must always wear a condom.
- You can't have sex with my friends or family members.
- You can't sleep with our next-door neighbors/women in our immediate neighborhood.
- You must treat me like your wife, your number-one woman, always.
- You can't love these women.
- You can't date these women.
- You can't go on trips with these women.

(Notice that many of these are already within the Cardinal Rules, which you should agree to regardless.)

Examples of Unreasonable Rules

- They can't be prettier than me.
- They can't be younger than me.
- They can't have bigger boobs than me/longer hair than me/prettier eyes than me/etc.
- I must personally approve every woman before you have sex with her.
- I need to see a picture of her before you have sex with her.
- I need to see her on Facebook before you sleep with her.
- You can have sex with other women once a year (or twice a year, or once every ten years, or any other arbitrary time frame).

Grey-Area Rules (Use your own judgment)

- You can't ever be out at night while I'm home.
- It can't be anyone I know (without my prior permission).

- You can only have side-sex during the day, even if it's a workday.
- They can only be other married women.
- They can only be young, dumb women. No classy women "like me."
- You can't ever bring women home.
- You can bring women home, but only when I'm out of town.
- You can bring women home, but you can never use our bed.
- You must tell me everything about every woman you sleep with.
- You must end the sexual relationship with any woman I decide I don't like.
- Never add a woman you're sleeping with to your social media.

Regardless of what you agree to and what you do not, remember the core aspect of this that I covered back in Chapter 13, and this is to agree to *a minimum number of rules*. Two or three Ground Rules are fine. Five or seven or ten is not. Also, remind your wife you will be following all of the Cardinal Rules as well, which means there should be very little extra Ground Rules needed on top of all that, ideally zero. As I've said, the only Ground Rules Pink Firefly and I have is that I won't bring any women over to my house without her permission, and I will let her know in advance if I have sex with more than one FB per week. Literally *two* Ground Rules, that's it!

If your wife starts rattling off a litany of Ground Rules, then re-iterate all of the Cardinal Rules you'll agree to, then have your wife pick one or two Ground Rules she feels strongly about. She'll have to let the rest go. Be nice, but stay strong.

By the end of this conversation, you should have a very short list of rules you will both agree to. At a bare minimum, if one or both of you need time to think about the rules, give her a specific deadline by which you will both finalize your agreed-upon Ground Rules ("tomorrow at 6:00 p.m.").

Congratulations! You now have what most men in society only dream about! A wife who will let you have sex other with women.

If It Doesn't Work

The Primary Conversion Method will lead to one of three results:

- A successful conversion to an open marriage. (Most likely.)
- An adamant refusal from your wife. (Less likely.)
- Your wife seriously threatening divorce or actually divorcing you. (Least likely, but still possible.)

If you truly do everything in this chapter correctly and to the best of your ability and it just doesn't work (i.e. the result is a refusal or a divorce threat), then you have a tough decision to make. You have four options at that point, none of them very pleasant:

1. Use the Hail Mary Method (described in the next chapter).

2. Use the Conversion-By-Cheating Method (also described in the next chapter).

3. Forget this entire thing and just keep your marriage monogamous.

4. Get divorced, either now or at a planned date in the future.

Not a fun decision, since all four of those options are going to be difficult and/or painful, but you're not out of luck yet. My strong recommendation is to use the Hail Mary Method. If you don't want to do that for whatever reason, then I personally would get divorced, since I doubt you would have taken the time to purchase this book and read it this far if your marriage was working for you under its current monogamous conditions. I don't recommend you divorce your wife on the spot. Instead, set a date on the calendar (secretly) for when you will move out and/or file divorce papers, get all of your ducks in a row before you make the big move, and then execute. I did this myself many years ago, and as painful as it was, getting divorced was one of the best decisions of my life.

I do *not* like or recommend option #2 or #3, but it's your life, and you need to make your own decision regarding what's best for you.

Chapter 29
Other Conversion Methods

The Primary Conversion Method described in the last chapter is the best way to convert a monogamous marriage to a non-monogamous one. However, nothing in life works with a 100% success rate. There will indeed be some wives and marriage situations where the Primary Conversion Method isn't enough to work. Your wife could be unusually stubborn, or perhaps there was some history with her or with the two of you in your marriage that creates difficult roadblocks for a non-monogamous conversion today.

For whatever the reason is, if the Primary Conversion Method doesn't work for you, you have two other alternatives for marriage conversion that I know can work and have worked for some men in the past. The challenge is that these conversion methods are more difficult and emotionally painful in some cases. As always, it's up to you to decide if they are worth attempting in your particular situation.

Don't forget that divorce is also a viable option. If you are truly unhappy in your marriage and your wife clearly won't budge in regard to any positive changes despite your best and honest efforts, you may need to end the relationship. In coaching with men who wanted to convert their marriages, during the process, a few of these guys realized that they (the men) would be happier if they simply got divorced and started over with someone correctly rather than convert a marriage that was already problematic. To repeat what I said earlier, my divorce many years ago was something that honestly needed to happen, and it was one of the best decisions of my entire life.

It is my recommendation that if you would prefer to stay married, but the Primary Conversion Method did not work, you take a hard look at the Hail Mary Method below despite how scary it may sound. The choice is yours.

The Hail Mary Method

If you aren't familiar with the slang term "Hail Mary," it's a maneuver in American football where someone makes a last-ditch long-distance pass with low odds of success near the end of the game. Despite its name, the odds of success of the Hail Mary Method are not as low as it sounds, but it *is* risky. However, when Hail Mary works, it often works even *better* than the Primary Conversion Method described in the last chapter.

Some married men have allowed Betaization to completely dominate their wives' view of them to the point where Attraction is at or near zero. When a man like this tells his wife that he's going to open the marriage whether she wants to or not, she won't agree to it mostly because she can't believe it. She'll just laugh at him and give reactions like "You don't have the balls to do that!" or "Ha! No woman is going to have sex with you!"

Other times, the husband is so angry, or disgusted, or weary of his wife, just telling her he's opening up the marriage isn't enough for him. More drastic measures are called for.

In both of the above situations, and perhaps a few others, the Hail Mary Method may be called for, provided the man has the courage to do it. Many don't.

As I described in detail in *The Ultimate Open Relationships Manual**, the most powerful weapon in a man's relationship arsenal is the **soft next**. This is when you're dating a woman and she gives you drama, so you "next" her by temporarily leaving her life and cutting off all contact with her for two to seven days, ignoring all texts, emails, and phone calls from her. After the nexting period is over, you contact her again and resume the relationship like nothing happened.

Since women desire attention more than anything else in the world, nexting is extremely effective in maintaining a happy, drama-free relationship.

The problem for us married men is, as I mentioned before, when you live with a woman full-time in the same home, nexting becomes impossible. (Men with a Dual Home Marriage don't have this limitation.)

You can't just kick her out of the house for five days. You could leave

*http://www.haveopenrelationships.com/

and perhaps get a hotel for a few days, but that's a very disempowering move on your part. Plus, she knows you have to come back because you live in your shared home, so it loses a lot of power the soft next has (since in those scenarios, the woman honestly doesn't know if you'll be back or not; you don't live with her, so you don't have to return).

The Hail Mary Method is essentially a soft next on steroids. It's an actual separation. You literally pack *all* of your stuff, move out, and get your own place. There is no big discussion when you do this; you just do it. You simply state that you've done your best to fix the problems in the marriage, but they didn't work, and you're not pleased with the marriage, so it's time for you to leave.

The intention behind the Hail Mary Method is that at some point, you will reunite with your wife, but only after you moved out and been away from her for many months. During this time, you'll live your life like a man and an Alpha, on your own, and will be sleeping with other women.

During this time of separation, you are polite to your wife and you are still cooperative with her in terms of scheduling to see your kids, financial issues, and on. However, you are *not* spending any time with her, nor are you having long phone conversations about the relationship, marriage, or feelings. You're too busy living your life instead.

You do not initiate a divorce. If your legal jurisdiction requires paperwork to be filed regarding a separation, then this is acceptable, but the Hail Mary Method does not involve actually getting divorced. (Though you can certainly choose to get divorced if the Hail Mary doesn't work.)

After several months of this separation and focusing on becoming a better man, you will have (likely) regained a more Alpha status in her mind. At this time, you slowly start to "re-game" your wife. This time, things are a little different:

1. You're not the boring, submissive beta male she used to know. You're not the wimp who was scared to lose her and put up with her crap. When you come back to her months later, you're literally a new man, a strong, attractive Alpha male who takes charge of his life. This

results in a massive boost in Attraction.

2. You're now having sex with other women, hopefully younger and more attractive women, and your wife knows it. Your wife is now going to be one of several women in your life (and perhaps your favorite), but it's going to be an open relationship when you re-game your wife. She clearly knows that's your "deal" now.

3. Your wife is now 100% aware that *you don't need her*. You now have the balls and wherewithal to leave her whenever you feel the relationship isn't working. Again, yet another boost in Attraction.

If it all works, you re-acquire your wife under a completely different kind of marriage, one that's sexually open and on your terms. It took the separation for you to A) get your balls back and B) get your wife to understand how much she loved you, was attracted to you, and needed you all along.

Moreover, men who have successfully used the Hail Mary Method often have stronger, more passionate marriages once they return to their wives because now the wives' Attraction for the men is far beyond what it had ever been in the prior, monogamous, boring state of the marriage.

A Hail Mary is also not a "trial separation." Trial separations imply that both husband and wife want to "try" separating *for a while*. The Hail Mary differs from this in two ways:

1. The husband is leaving, and the *wife doesn't want him to go*. Which, by the way, is the exact opposite of most separations and divorces. Women initiate 82% of all divorces in the United States. The Hail Mary Method turns the tables on this.

You may have noticed that usually, the person with most of the power during a breakup or divorce situation is the one doing the leaving. The one being left is powerless to a large degree. In a Hail Mary, you are the one taking the initiative and taking that power.

2. The wife *has no idea if the husband is going to return*. It's left completely ambiguous. This brings in the power of the soft next.

Several men I have known, as well as many men I have interviewed for this book, have executed a Hail Mary successfully. In fact, some men say it was easier than the Primary Conversion Method. (Note: I'm not sure I agree with that in all cases. It really depends on the marriage and the personalities of the two people involved. Sometimes a Hail Mary may indeed be easier, though usually, the Primary Conversion Method will be.)

Obviously, there's a risk with the Hail Mary Method. Once you move out, your wife may use it as an impetus to simply get divorced herself or to start up a relationship with another man. You also need to be strong enough during the Hail Mary to A) not return to your wife too quickly (which will simply further damage the relationship and further beta you in her eyes), B) keep your distance from your wife during the separation, and C) actually have sex with new women during the separation. Separating from her and not having sex with any new women defeats the purpose of this entire exercise. Your wife needs to know you are a strong man who is attractive to other women

The Conversion-By-Cheating Method

This is a third way to convert a monogamous marriage to an open one. It's my least favorite, and I'm not a big fan of it, but I have to honestly report that it can work.

Many open-marriage men I've talked to and interviewed over the years have reported that the reason they now have an open marriage is that they simply started cheating on their wife behind her back, got caught, had a shitload of drama and arguments, were Alpha enough to entice the wife to stay married to them anyway, and eventually the wife just accepted the fact the husband was going to have sex with other women. In many ways, it's a three-part conversion from TMM to a Mediterranean Marriage to an open marriage.

As I said earlier, I am 100% against cheating on women. Cheating behind a woman's back and not telling her because you're afraid of losing her is what beta males do. A true Alpha Male, and certainly an Alpha Male 2.0 simply do as they please. If other people in their life don't like it, those people can leave. That's what outcome independence is all about.

Also, cheating creates drama, usually massive drama. No, you won't get any drama the first time you cheat because you'll be able to hide it from your wife. However, my experience clearly shows that when men cheat, they eventually get caught. Men just aren't very good at keeping sexual matters like this hidden. (Interesting fact: Women are much better at cheating on husbands than the reverse. Women are much more able to keep things discreet and hidden than us guys. This is logical when you think about it. Women are trained by society to be sexually discreet; men are trained to brag about it.)

The entire point of most of my relationship models is to show men how to create and manage open relationships where one or both partners are sleeping with other people with the full knowledge and permission (even if it's reluctant permission) of their partners without the need to hide anything or live a double life.

That all being said, a huge plurality of men I have known or interviewed who have open marriages got that way by cheating on their wives first.

Here's the bottom line regarding this. The reason people do it this way is simply because *they know of no other way to do it*. Once you've read this book, you're not in that category anymore. Both the Primary Conversion Method and the Hail Mary Method are superior to the Conversion-By-Cheating method for the numerous reasons I stated above.

Of course, if you're *already* cheating on your wife, this is all a moot point. However, you can still use the Primary Conversion Method or the Hail Mary Method to convert your marriage. There's no law that says you can't just because you've cheated.

What If *She's* Cheating?

This all brings up an interesting point. What if she has cheated on you? Or is still cheating? Or what if you have both cheated?

Generally speaking, this makes the Primary Conversion Method much easier since you now have precedent on your side, and she knows it. That doesn't mean she won't still attempt to use Disney or woman-logic on you when you tell her what you're going to do. You may get something like, "Well, okay, I know I screwed around, but I promise to stop now, and you need to promise too." We talked about how to deal with those kinds of objections back in Chapter 28.

Bottom line, if she's cheated, it's an absolute shoo-in for the Primary Conversion Method and raises the odds of its success. Go for it!

Chapter 30
Troubleshooting

The preceding chapters laid out the processes that usually occur with women most of the time. However, life being what it is, sometimes things don't go as planned and exceptions to the rule may occur. In this chapter, we'll cover the unlikely but possible problem areas you may encounter when you engage in a marriage conversion process.

All the challenges presented in this chapter are less than 50% likely to occur, especially if you've been a good husband and your wife has a strong bond with you. *Please don't read this chapter and get discouraged.* There are many variables that can determine success or failure in this, many I can't possibly know about and will be specific to your situation, but I can tell you that across the board, based on what I've seen, roughly 70% of the time, your wife will agree (even if reluctantly and with rules) to having an open marriage if you follow the techniques laid out this section of the book.

She Takes Action to Leave

Normally, when women make threats when you have the big talk with them, they don't actually mean it and are just venting. It's part of being a woman, especially a wife. As she screams and threatens, just stay strong. It will pass. We've discussed that already.

However, it's possible that she may actually take real action. Examples would be:

1. She runs into the bedroom and starts packing her clothes.

2. She goes to your kids and says, "We're leaving dad! Let's go!" and starts packing their clothes.

3. She calls her mom/sister/girlfriend and asks, "Can I come stay with you?"

4. She goes on social media and makes some ridiculous post, like, "Well, I guess I'm getting divorced!!!" (Of course, she'll make sure she does this so you can see it.)

And so on.

Doing things like this serve three purposes:

1. To vent her emotions.

2. To reassert her authority over you.

3. To test you (a "shit test" as they say in the seduction community) to see if you are actually resolved to do this.

I know I keep saying this, but this kind of threatening behavior is normal and natural for a lot of women. Your job is to stand strong, do not waver, and call her bluff. As we discussed before, don't get mad, don't get defensive, don't cave in, and don't fight back (i.e. don't say to her "Oh no you won't!")

Let her do whatever she's doing. If you need to, remove yourself from her presence. Go to another room, or if you really need to, leave the house and go see a movie while she does her thing. The odds are overwhelming she's just venting emotions, not really leaving you.

She Actually Leaves

Of course, we need to cover all possibilities here, so it is possible she really will actually pack her stuff and drive to her mother's house (or wherever). If this happens, it becomes one of those times you need to be congruent with the promise you made to yourself back in Chapter 27; that you are willing to lose this marriage rather than continue to be monogamous. You need to stand your ground and let her go.

To reiterate yet again, just because she drives away and spends a few nights with her mom/sister/girlfriend doesn't mean you're getting a divorce. You might be getting a divorce, but it's also just as likely she needs a temporary cooling-off period away from you so that both of you can regroup later.

I have seen, and I'm sure you have seen, many married couples go through this – huge argument, one of them leaves, and then they reunite a few days later (at the most).

She Gets Violent

As unlikely as it is, if she actually physically assaults you, now the game has changed, and you're going to have to make some tough decisions.

I personally know a little something about this. I divorced the woman I was married to years ago specifically because she got violent while we were discussing something. She didn't do anything major, but she did enough, and it was the second time she was violent after I had already warned her once. We weren't discussing an open marriage (we were arguing about our relationship in general), but it doesn't matter.

Less than 48 hours later, I moved out with zero hesitation. We eventually got divorced, I never looked back, and I never regretted it. Once again, it was one of the best decisions I've ever made in my life.

As a man, you can*not* tolerate violence from a woman in your life. It doesn't matter if this woman is your girlfriend or wife or mother of your children. The entire family court system, as well as the police, are hard-wired to take the woman's side any time there is a physical altercation. This means if she initiates violence against you, and you defend yourself, guess who's going to jail when the police arrive? I'll give you a hint: it won't be her.

Here's what you need to do if she actually gets violent:

1. Do *not* fight back. I know that sounds like odd advice, and I know it doesn't sound very manly or Alpha. Like I said, the law is on *her* side. If you fight back, the odds of you being blamed for the violence skyrocket. That means you may go to jail. It means you may lose your children in court when her attorney accuses you of violence against her.

The safest play is to resist the urge to defend yourself and just don't fight back. In my situation, this is exactly what I did. I didn't fight back; I just took it like a man for a minute. (Then once she left the room, I grabbed my cell phone and took some pictures of the scratches she left on my face and arm for the attorneys.)

If your reaction to this advice is "Screw that! No one's gonna hit me! If she hits me, I'm going to hit back," that's your choice. I promise you if you go down that road, you will have no allies, likely no marriage (open or otherwise), the entire legal system will be against you, and the situation will have suddenly become ten times worse.

2. If her violence persists, *leave the premises*. If she gets violent for a brief moment and then stops, fine. But if she keeps going, move past her as fast as you can, grab your keys, and get out of there. Don't stay and fight back. Don't try to calm her down. Just leave.

3. Take pictures of any physical marks she leaves on you or your clothing. You may need these photos later.

4. Begin divorce proceedings and move on with your life. I'm serious. Zero tolerance for violence, just as mentioned back in Chapter 9. I would *never* stay married to a woman who initiated physical violence against me, open marriage or not, and I hope you don't either.

If you seriously want to go back to a wife who physically assaults you when she gets angry, you've moved well past the scope of this book, and I can't help you. It's very likely you have codependency issues, and I would strongly recommend counseling or similar assistance.

She Gets Hysterical

In this scenario, she just loses her mind. This would include crazy things like if she threatens to kill herself, or starts screaming at your kids, or runs screaming down the street like a madwoman.

I'm not a marriage counselor, and there are many variations of this, so I can't advise you on the specifics. Regarding the "kill herself" threats, psychologists and professional therapists will tell you that if a woman has never actually tried to kill herself, any time she threatens suicide, she's likely bluffing, and you shouldn't take it seriously.

I'm going to repeat my core advice: stay strong, don't waver, don't fight. Let her rant. Don't get defensive, and don't respond to her irrational rants. Just let her vent, and when she's done, say, "We'll talk about this later," and then terminate the conversation.

Chapter 31
The All-Important First Three Weeks

So you've executed the Primary Conversion Method and it worked! You broke the news to your wife, navigated through her objections and her emotional reaction, and negotiated the rules you will have to follow in your new open marriage.

Or, perhaps you've now moved back in with your wife after a Hail Mary. Or worst case, you've "broken the news" to her about your cheating and she's angrily accepted the new parameters of the marriage.

Regardless of which conversion method you've chosen, the worst is over. She's agreed! Reluctantly perhaps, with rules perhaps, but you now have what millions of men all over the world desire more than anything else in the world, a wife who will let them have sex with other women and stay anyway.

Now what?

Although the *worst* part is over, the hardest part for you may have just begun. Now, you actually need to go out into the real world and have sex with new women.

Moreover, you need to do this *fast*. Once she's agreed to all of this, you need to strike while the iron is hot and actually go have sex with someone else.

I have known and worked with several men who got to this point and then fumbled the ball. They confronted their wives, took the drama, dealt with the objections and rules, finally got agreement from their wives that they could go have sex with other women... and then they did nothing. They didn't have sex with any other women.

Instead, they just thought about it. They fantasized about it. They flirted with a few women on the internet but never pulled the trigger. Some even bragged to their buddies that their wives will "let them do it now." Perhaps they even tried to meet some new women or go out on a few dates.

But they didn't have sex. They chickened out, or got lazy, or started feeling guilty because of ingrained Societal Programming (i.e. they didn't follow my advice from Chapter 27), and never closed the deal.

If you get your wife to agree to an open arrangement but then don't follow through on it with real action, it's actually worse than if you never brought any of this up in the first place. If you get agreement from your wife to do this, and then you don't actually go do it:

1. You damage your credibility with your wife.

2. You further betaize yourself in the relationship by clearly showing her you don't have the balls to do what you wanted.

3. You further betaize yourself by showing her through your actions that other women don't find you desirable or attractive (or, at a minimum, you're showing her that you believe that).

4. You and your wife went through all that arguing and freaking out for nothing.

5. You further her dominance in the marriage by her saying to herself, "Yep, I knew it."

Getting agreement and not acting on it is extremely destructive to your relationship on multiple levels. This is why it's so important to know for sure you're ready to do this before you proceed (as we discussed back in Chapter 27).

Move Swiftly!

Just as you told her during the Primary Conversion Method, ideally you should be having sex with a new woman *or at a bare minimum* going out on first dates/meets with new *women within two weeks of getting agreement from your wife.* If you're sure you can do that (or have already done that), like you're confident you can do sugar daddy game or you have a woman or two already waiting for you, then great.

On the other hand, if you're inexperienced with women or have been monogamous for a very long time and feel nervous or out of practice, you need to give this some thought first. Once you read through this book (and any other dating, seduction or relationship books), if you seriously believe that you will not be able to have sex or schedule some first meets with a new woman within two weeks (or so) of getting agreement from your wife, even if you were to use sugar daddy game, then I recommend you hold off on starting this process until you are more confident about this and get to the point where you are at least reasonably sure you can pull off at least one first date/meet with someone new.

To help you with that, I'm going to give you some tips on things you can do while you're monogamous to your wife to help build confidence in meeting (and later sleeping with) women. None of the below techniques require you to actually cheat on her; they're just primers to get you going before you attempt your marriage conversion. (If you're not a newbie when it comes to meeting women, feel free to skip this section if you wish.)

1. Start focusing on prolonged eye contact with women. Everywhere you go, the store, the street, the mall, wherever, when an attractive woman sees you, look her in the eye and practice not breaking her gaze until she does. When you first start doing this, it might feel strange. That's normal. Practice it. Get to the point where you can look into an attractive woman's eyes until she looks away.

Obviously, don't walk around staring women down like some kind of psycho. Just maintain normal eye contact as you move through your day, and don't look away until she does.

2. Start flirting with women often if you don't already. As women are well aware, flirting isn't cheating, so flirt away! Flirt with women at the office (flirt, don't touch!), flirt with the cute girl at the grocery store checkout counter, flirt with the girl waiting in line next to you at the coffee shop. Hell, flirt with ugly girls and old ladies too. It's all valid practice. Get comfortable talking in a flirtatious, semi-sexual context with women.

3. Start saying "hi" to female strangers. Make sure you smile when you say it. I don't care if they're cute or ugly or 20 years younger than you

or older than your grandmother. Just start saying hi to every woman that comes within five feet of you. Get to the point where doing this does not make you feel weird or uncomfortable.

4. Practice talking about sex with women. Pick a woman you know and talk about sex. You don't have to reveal sexual details about you and your wife if you don't want to, but talk about sex. Get comfortable talking about sex with women if you aren't already. Women *love* talking about sex, more so than men, and some women like talking about sex as much or more than actually having sex! So talk about it, and get used to doing so.

Feel free to use the above techniques or anything similar before you confront your wife if you feel that two weeks may not be enough time for you to get real results with new women. Get my books *The Ultimate Online Dating Manual**, *Get To Sex Fast***, and *The Ultimate Younger Woman Manual**** for the specific steps you need to take to make these things happen. Feel free to study up on this stuff and get comfortable with the basic concepts before making the big switch in your marriage.

*http://www.onlinedatingsuccessnow.com
**http://www.gettosexfast.com/
***http://www.older-men-younger-women.com/

Other Resources and Bibliography

Here are some other books and resources that can assist you in your OLTR Marriage.

My Other Books

I have several books on dating and relationships, most of which are under the author's name of Blackdragon, though my real name is Caleb Jones.

The Ultimate Open Relationships Manual

at *www.haveopenrelationships.com*

Almost required reading for anyone who has read this book on open marriages; how to maintain long-term non-monogamous relationships with "normal" women.

The Ultimate Online Dating Manual

at *www.onlinedatingsuccessnow.com*

How to schedule first dates and meets with new women using online dating sites and dating apps.

Get to Sex Fast

at *www.gettosexfast.com*

A specific, step-by-step system to get from zero to sex with new women in under 3-4 hours of face time with less than $27 spent using first and second dates (or meets).

The Ultimate Younger Woman Manual

at *www.older-men-younger-women.com*

How to date women much younger than you. Includes normal dating as well as sugar daddy game.

The Unchained Man

at *www.alphamalebook.com*

My core book on how to design a freedom-based lifestyle.

Other Books on Marriage That Will Assist You

I've read all of these books and I highly recommend them all.

The Seven Principles for Making Marriage Work

by John Gottman

Scientifically proven methods to help make your marriage work.

The Five Love Languages

By Gary Chapman

Men Are from Mars, Women Are from Venus

By John Gray

Although a little old and written by a beta male, there are a lot of good concepts and techniques in this book.

Love and Respect

By Emerson Eggerichs

The Passion Trap

By Dean Delis

More Direct Help

You can join my membership program in which I provide audio and video techniques unavailable anywhere else, as well as work with me personally in helping you through this process. Go to *www.joinsmic.com* for more details.

Glossary of Terms

Attraction: How much a wife genuinely likes and is sexually turned on by her husband.

Betaization: The natural process by which a woman turns a man she starts living with from an attractive Alpha Male to an unattractive but reliable beta male.

Betaization Scale: A 1 to 10 scale of how intensely a woman has betaized her husband.

Betaization Wall: A metaphorical wall you place to halt all Betaization from your wife beyond a certain point. This will irritate her but keep Attraction high.

Big Dumb Husband: How most women view their husbands after being married to them for more than about three years, a perhaps loveable but really stupid guy.

Cardinal Rules: An unbreakable set of rules every man in a non-monogamous relationship must follow to ensure maximum Attraction and Mutual Harmony. Every type of relationship (FB, OLTR, etc.) has a different set of Cardinal Rules. These are different than Ground Rules.

Conversion-By-Cheating Method: Cheating on your wife behind her back, getting caught, and then getting her to just accept that you're going to keep having sex with other women. Not a recommended way to convert your marriage to an open one but a method many men have successfully used nonetheless.

Disclosure Levels: Five levels of how much you verbalize to your wife about your side-FBs.

Drama Corrective Procedure: A specific procedure on how to minimize drama when your wife is upset.

Dual Home Marriage: When you live in separate homes from your wife.

FB: A woman who you're having sex with but with whom you don't date. Friend with benefits.

Financial Barrier: Your legal, logistical, financial, banking, and perhaps even international systems and legal paperwork in place to ensure that there is no co-mingling of finances between you and your wife and to ensure you don't lose any money in a possible divorce.

Freedom: Your ability to do whatever you want with your life without many rules or restrictions regardless of the fact you're married.

Great Paradox: The fact that you wish to strive to make your wife long-term, consistently happy when she doesn't have that ability.

Ground Rules: Rules that the husband and wife come up together and mutually agree upon. Every marriage has a unique set of Ground Rules. These differ from Cardinal Rules.

Guy Drama: When a man angrily "lays down the law" with a woman and places, enforces, or reinforces rules on her.

Home Zones: Physical Zones within the home that are either 100% Yours, 100% Hers, or Shared. Shared Zones should be minimized (or even non-existent).

Mail Mary Method: When a man in a monogamous marriage moves away from his wife for a few months, keeps his distance, has sex with other women, and then (hopefully) returns to his wife under a new open marriage.

Mediterranean Marriage: A high-drama, high-conflict marriage where the husband constantly cheats on his wife, his wife knows about it but doesn't leave and instead screams at him about it all the time. Not recommended.

MLTR: A woman you are dating and in a romantic relationship with but who is not your girlfriend or wife. One can have several MLTRs. MLTRs are not allowed in an OLTR Marriage.

Mutual Harmony: When both you and your wife are very pleased with the marriage and each other, ideally at least 90% of the time.

Negative Behaviors: Six really crappy behaviors common among married people, three for wives, three for husbands.

OLTR: A serious girlfriend where you can have sex with other women (FBs) but can't *date* other women (MLTRs).

OLTR Marriage: A non-monogamous marriage where both parties have 100% separate finances and can have sex with other people as long as they are only FBs. Highly recommended, and the easiest type of non-monogamous marriage for most men.

Oneitis: An overwhelming feeling of neediness where a man really wants one particular woman or goes out of his way to not lose one particular woman.

Open Convenience Marriage: When a man and woman are married, don't love each other, but stay married for reasons other than love, such as for the kids, religious reasons, cultural reasons, and so on. Cheating and even dating other people on the side is pretty common with these.

Polyamorous Marriage: When a man and woman are married but also carry on full girlfriend/boyfriend relationships with multiple other people. Not recommended unless both husband and wife already have extensive polyamorous experience.

Polyexclusive Marriage: An OLTR Marriage (or similar) where the husband (and/or wife) can only have sex with certain, small number of predesignated FBs who themselves have committed to only have sex with a very small number of specific people.

Polyfidelitous Marriage: Same as a Polyexclusive Marriage.

Polygamy: One man married to multiple wives. Prone to lots of jealousy and conflict. Not really feasible in the long term in the Western world and not recommended.

Primary Conversion Method: A specific procedure on how to convert a monogamous marriage to an open one.

Relationship Oneitis: The most common type of Oneitis, when a man is terrified his lover/girlfriend/wife might leave him.

Side-FBs: FBs a man in an OLTR Marriage has sex with on the side.

Side Women: Any woman a married man has who is not his wife.

Strategic Avoidance: When a man avoids his wife when he knows the odds of her starting drama is high (like when she's really angry about something or when she has a pounding headache, etc.).

Threesome Marriage: A marriage where the man is only allowed to have sex with other women if these women are in a threesome with his wife. Pretty much as bad as TMM and not recommended.

TMM: Traditional, monogamous marriage. The way most people get married, combining all finances (and risking them if a divorce occurs, which it probably will) while promising forever sexual monogamy to each other. A system that has not worked in several decades with extremely high failure rates.

Two-Shot Rule: Only asking your wife for sex twice, then never asking her ever again until *she* comes to *you* for sex.

Unicorn Marriage: An OLTR Marriage where one of your FBs actually lives with you and your wife. Risky and only recommended for very experienced and very strong Alpha Males.

Zones: A part of your life or a physical part of your home that is assigned to 100% your control (Your Zone), 100% your wife's control (Her Zone), or both of you (Shared Zones). Shared Zones should be minimized or even non-existent if Freedom and Mutual Harmony are to be maintained.

www.ingramcontent.com/pod-product-compliance
Lightning Source LLC
Chambersburg PA
CBHW030430010526
44118CB00011B/577